FINANCING
ECONOMIC
DEVELOPMENT

FINANCING
ECONOMIC
DEVELOPMENT

FINANCING
ECONOMIC
DEVELOPMENT

Fiscal Policy for Emerging Countries

ROBERT B. BANGS

THE UNIVERSITY OF CHICAGO PRESS

CHICAGO AND LONDON

Library of Congress Catalog Card Number: 68-27292

THE UNIVERSITY OF CHICAGO PRESS, CHICAGO 60637

The University of Chicago Press, Ltd., London W.C.1

To My Mother

Madge Babbitt Bangs

Preface

This book is about legalized seizure by government of money or property, or, by another name, taxation. So long as governments have existed, taxes have been extracted (forcibly when necessary) from citizens.[1] This taking of property is without direct compensation, although the indirect compensation may be substantial.

It is not, however, about the history of taxation, fascinating though it is, that I intend to write; but about fiscal policy, which is government policy concerning taxation and public expenditure. The term "fiscal" derives from the old Greek word for basket which symbolized the public purse. The Renaissance Italian word "fisc," meaning the Treasury or Exchequer, sounds sufficiently like the English word fist to connote the sometimes violent nature of the process of extracting taxes from a reluctant public. Incidentally, the Renaissance Italians were among the first of the modern writers on fiscal policy. One such writer was Niccolo Machiavelli.[2]

Although taxation in a fundamental sense is legalized seizure, in a more complete sense it involves the consent of those taxed. Thomas Jefferson, following John Locke, wrote that "governments are instituted among men with the consent of the governed."[3] Since governments cannot function for long in an exchange economy without some revenue, it follows that in consenting to be governed we also consent to pay taxes—making their collection, however forcible, legalized seizure rather than theft.

[1] In Middle English the word tax was practically identical with task, i.e., an obligation to perform services or to pay money to a sovereign.
[2] See *The Prince*, 1532, especially chapter 25. From Dacres' English translation, 1640; reprinted in *Three Renaissance Classics* (New York: Scribner, 1953).
[3] *The Declaration of Independence*, 1776. Attila the Hun and Ivan the Terrible had somewhat different methods of obtaining "consent of the governed" than Mr. Jefferson had in mind, but all three shared a common objective, namely obtaining that consent by available means.

Preface

Governments have always found taxation a necessity, and the governed have always found taxation inconvenient and have grumbled about it. Sometimes they have done more. Periodically, a body of citizens, outraged by what they considered unjust or excessive taxation, have asserted their natural right to bear arms. The American Revolution was one such episode; the Whiskey Insurrection another. Many examples from other countries could easily be cited.

The history of taxation is a story of violence and bloodshed; but also of social progress.[4] The more a government does, for or to its citizens, the more revenue it must have. Arguments about taxes are, at root, arguments about what governments ought or ought not to do.

The fact that in consenting to be governed we consent also to pay taxes raises the intriguing philosophic point whether an anarchist, who opposes all government, should be tax-exempt. Recently Edmund Wilson, a distinguished American writer, failed in his civic duty by not paying his income taxes. To make restitution, which he discovered he had to do unless he emigrated, he found an obvious method for one of his persuasion: he wrote a slender volume entitled *The Cold War and the Income Tax*.[5] In this book he pleads a case for nonpayment of taxes as a form of social protest that can somehow be effective in relieving, to a degree, the current cold war tension. Ironically, the book royalties will help Wilson to settle accounts with the Internal Revenue Service.

A massive unsolved problem in the world today is the undoubted poverty of the great bulk of the world's people. Of the roughly three billion population, at least two billion have incomes insufficient for the necessities of life. We in the United States, who live in what Galbraith has termed "the affluent society," often forget that citizens of other nations enjoy far less affluence than we.

Nineteenth-century British writers called economics "the dismal science." Its subject matter was and is overpopulation, underproduction, poverty, depression, inflation, and related calamitous conditions. Although dismal, its usefulness was to be found, then as now, in analyzing how and why nations and people move from poverty to affluence and how this movement may be accelerated.

This book is, in a fashion, in the classical tradition of economics. It is about the wealth of nations and how this wealth may gradually be

---

[4]The barons who gathered at Runnymede and in 1215 extracted Magna Carta from a reluctant King John were prompted by a money grievance. Cf. Sydney Buxton, *Finance and Politics*, 1783–1885 (London: John Murray, 1888), p. viii.

[5]New York: Farrar Straus, 1963.

increased. Today we call this process economic development. The process is accretive, slow—even glacial—and uncertain. The long road to affluence is strewn with the wreckage of good intentions joined with misguided economic policies. We do not know what the most efficient policies may be in many situations; nor would I presume to judge from a distance of space and culture what appropriate policies for particular countries may be at given times. All one can do is trace out what has happened when certain policies have been tried and then attempt to generalize from this experience.

In this book I hope to describe briefly a few of the many financial problems that accelerating a nation's growth rate involves, and some of the pitfalls that may be encountered in the process. If these difficulties are thoroughly appreciated, the real meaning of accepting accelerated growth as a national goal, and of the time required to reach that goal, may be better understood.

My interest in the subject of this study stems from a background of work in taxation and fiscal policy for the United States government and from firsthand experience over the past fifteen years as a foreign adviser to the central governments of five less developed countries: Egypt, Burma, Costa Rica, Iran, and Ethiopia. In each of these countries I have watched and participated in efforts at economic development and have learned personally how difficult the process can be; also what a key role fiscal policy can play in the outcome. I have also undertaken to study the available literature on the subject. Although extensive and growing rapidly, this literature is not yet very systematic.

This book was written in 1964-65 while I was a Federal Executive Fellow at Brookings Institution. I am grateful to the United States Department of Commerce for freeing my time, and to Brookings for providing a congenial atmosphere in which to work. I am also grateful to friends and colleagues who have given their advice and counsel, read portions of my manuscript, and helped me in other ways too numerous to mention. The debts I owe are too extensive to be acknowledged individually. The views expressed and the errors of judgment and of omission and commission are, of course, my own.

The following persons, each in some special way, have helped me: Lucretia Bangs, Eugene Birnbaum, Edward Denison, Richard Goode, Richard Holton, Grace Howell, Shireen Khazeni, Karl Lachmann, Alfred Landau, Krishna Naidu, Gilchrist Olympio, Joseph Poullier, and Norman Ture.

Bethesda, Maryland   ROBERT B. BANGS

Contents

1 CONCEPTS OF ECONOMIC GROWTH AND OF FISCAL POLICY   1

2 BUDGET STRUCTURE AND DEVELOPMENT PLANNING   28

3 AGGREGATE GOVERNMENT REVENUE AND EXPENDITURE   52

4 FOREIGN AID AND PRIVATE CAPITAL IMPORTS   76

5 INVESTMENT INCENTIVES IN THE PRIVATE SECTOR   97

6 TAX POLICY   119

7 FISCAL POLICY IN RELATION TO OTHER ECONOMIC
POLICIES   147

8 FISCAL ADVICE TO LESS DEVELOPED COUNTRIES   165

9 THE RELATION OF FISCAL POLICY TO THE
STAGES OF GROWTH   183

INDEX   205

1

Concepts of Economic Growth and of Fiscal Policy

Economic growth is today widely accepted as a major goal of national policy, both in the industrialized countries and in countries that are less fully developed. The advanced countries want more growth so that their expanding labor forces will be fully occupied and their living standards will continue to improve. The less developed countries want to begin closing the gap between their income levels and the more fortunate countries'; they want to enjoy more of the fruits of modern science and technology and to break the circle of poverty, low productivity, and stagnation within which too many of their people have been confined for generations. Individual aspirations for a better life have, to a considerable degree, coalesced into national aspirations for more rapid economic development.

NATURE OF ECONOMIC GROWTH

Economic growth is a complex process which, despite the intensive study given to it over the past two decades, is still none too thoroughly understood. In economics, discussion of policy questions has nearly always preceded the construction of formal techniques for analyzing these questions systematically. Only in the period since World War II has there been widespread concern for the problems of emerging countries. Moreover, the classical tradition in economics has concentrated more on the essentially static analysis of interrelationships within economic systems at given times (or on sequences within artificial time periods) than on actual historical processes over extended periods.[1]

---

[1] For a comment on the difference between logical and historical time in economic analysis, see Joan Robinson, *Essays in the Theory of Economic Growth* (London, Macmillan & Co., 1962), pp. 23–29. It is a curious paradox in the history of economic doctrines that the mercantilists, although taking an essentially static view of the world and its possibilities for growth, were intensely dynamic in their policy prescriptions for individual countries, whereas the classical economists, although greatly concerned about
continued overleaf

1

Although we economists who study it do not understand the process of economic growth fully, it is clear that stepping up a nation's growth rate significantly involves at least four kinds of changes in social attitudes and preferences. Accelerated growth requires more work and less leisure, more investment and relatively less consumption, more concern with the future relative to the present, and the replacement of traditional values and responses with greater inclination toward a spirit of experimentation and innovation. When the implications of these psychological costs of growth are fully taken into account, some societies may waiver a bit in their allegiance to accelerated growth as a dominant national goal.

Thus, while most societies appear to set growth or development as a national aspiration, not all people in these societies are prepared either to exert the effort or to accept the changes that a practical set of policies for accelerated growth may require. Many governments think development is easier to achieve than, in fact, it is. Many people in emerging countries do not fully comprehend either the time required or the sacrifices involved in a successful, sustained growth effort.

The less developed countries today quite generally regard development as a process to be planned and guided by the state. In the older industrial countries, although numerous special-purpose subsidies and incentives were in the past provided by the state to encourage particular aspects of development, it was not customary to have a comprehensive plan for the whole development process. To adopt and work within a comprehensive development plan does not mean that a nation must plan all economic activity on a totalitarian basis; but it does imply an intrusion of government into private decision making that would have seemed incongruous in the nineteenth century.

The mere fact that a nation attempts to plan its development does not insure that this development will actually proceed more rapidly than it would in the absence of a plan. Examples of poor development planning abound. Nevertheless, planned efforts at economic development have characterized the policies of many if not most nations since the end of World War II. Comprehensive planning has become the accepted technique in efforts to guide and hasten the development process in nearly all countries.

[1] *continued*
economic development, evolved an essentially static structure for analysis. For a fuller discussion of this somewhat arcane paradox see E. F. Heckscher, *Mercantilism*, trans. M. Shapiro (London: Allen & Unwin, 1934), vol. 2, chap. 1.

MEANING AND SCOPE OF FISCAL POLICY

Fiscal policy, within which I comprehend all aspects of the structure and magnitude of central government revenue and expenditure, is generally considered one of the more powerful weapons in the arsenal of government policies which the more advanced countries have at their disposal for dealing with short-run variations in the aggregate volume of economic activity, i.e., for offsetting cyclical disturbances. Although fiscal policy in the advanced countries during recent years has been primarily occupied with short-range or contracyclical objectives, economists and politicians have come increasingly to see that it has long-range implications as well; among these are possible effects upon a country's rate of economic growth, defined in the conventional sense as progress in per capita income measured in currency units of constant purchasing power.[2]

Fiscal policy, as I use the term in this work, refers to that segment of national economic policy which is primarily concerned with the receipts and expenditures of the central government; with the relation between these two flows; and with the economic effects of these receipts (primarily from taxation) and these expenditures, for all the functions in which governments today engage.[3]

Purpose of This Book

This study is primarily about fiscal policy and its relation to the level and trend of economic activity over fairly long periods of time. It will examine this relationship not for a single country, but for a range of

---

[2] Strictly speaking, growth should properly refer to the expanding capacity of an economy to produce greater output per head rather than to expanding actual product or income. However, since unambiguous capacity measurements are not generally available, per capita income, or value of output, is conventionally used instead. Growth which results from more complete utilization of capacity is easier to achieve and less fundamental than growth which involves actual expansion of an economy's capacity.

[3] A similarly broad view of fiscal policy has been expressed by a Mexican economist, Victor Urquidi, who writes as follows: "The sphere of fiscal policy may be taken to be the whole body of measures relating to the tax systems, public expenditures, contracting of internal and external debt by the State, and the operations and financial situation of the autonomous and semi-public agencies and bodies, through the medium of which the amount and distribution of investment and public consumption as components of national expenditure are determined, and the amount and composition of private investment and consumption influenced directly or indirectly." See his "Fiscal Policy in Latin America's Economic Development," mimeographed (Paper submitted to the Joint OAS/IDB/ECLA Conference on Fiscal Policy, Santiago, Chile, December, 1962), p. 3. See also his book *The Challenge of Development in Latin America* (New York: Praeger, 1964), *passim*.

3

countries in various stages of economic development, extending from stagnant or traditional societies to quite affluent ones. My main purpose is to inquire whether certain rules or maxims of fiscal policy which have come to be fairly generally accepted in the advanced countries are either adaptable or translatable into analagous rules more appropriate to the less developed economies, and how these rules may need modifying in this process of adaptation. My preconception, which should be stated at the outset, is that there are definite stages in appropriate fiscal policy just as there are distinct stages in the process of economic development. Not to recognize this fact when designing policies to promote growth is, I believe, to risk solecisms both in analysis and in prescription.

Recency of Modern Fiscal Theory

That fiscal policy can and should be employed to influence the level of economic activity is a fairly recent concept. Although hints at this idea can be found scattered through earlier economic literature, the systematic ground work for this view was laid only in the late 1930's;[4] in the United States, for example, it has been widely accepted by the general public only since World War II. Certain well-known congressmen and senators still do not accept it.[5]

Before World War II the conventional belief in this country was that the budget of the United States government should be balanced annually, regardless of varying economic conditions; for example, in the great depression of the early 1930's, efforts were made initially to raise income tax rates during a period of substantial unemployment. Few economists or public officials questioned the assumption that it was both necessary and desirable to protect the revenue and thus to compensate for the decline in tax intake that resulted from the great reduction in economic activity during the depression—in order to maintain a balanced budget.

The present-day view is that fiscal policy is a powerful tool which can and should be used primarily to influence to the volume of economic activity and to limit the rate of unemployment. When economic activity begins to decline and a recession threatens to develop, the modern view would hold that taxes should be reduced and government expenditures increased, thereby consciously planning for a deficit in the public

[4]Largely by Lord Keynes and his disciples.
[5]At this point let me hasten to deny accusing these eminent public gentlemen of cultural lag.

accounts, in order to expand the public sector contribution and thus arrest or offset the potential contraction of the national product. Conversely, in a period when the economy is operating at full capacity, with overemployment of its labor resources and undesirable inflationary pressure, the current view would hold that expenditures should be reduced and taxes increased, thereby developing a robust budget surplus that will serve to limit the boom in economic activity and to restrain the inflation. Budget balancing is something to be done over a full business cycle rather than annually. Another view holds that the Federal budget should be balanced only when a specific employment target, such as 96 per cent of the labor force, has been attained.[6]

Relation of Fiscal to Monetary Policy

Fiscal policy is obviously closely related to monetary policy—another big tool for influencing the general level of economic activity. Monetary policy does not operate directly on aggregate or macroeconomic categories (consumption, investment, etc.) that enter into the national accounts; rather, it influences these categories indirectly by changing the relative availability and cost of credit. In the United States, for example, when a restrictive monetary policy is in force—because it is judged by the monetary authorities (essentially the Open Market Committee of the Federal Reserve System) that the economy is in an inflationary condition—only limited reserves are supplied to commercial banks, resulting in a rise in interest rates and in lessened access to credit by business firms and consumers of all types. This credit scarcity helps to restrain economic expansion and to limit the rise in prices. Conversely, in a period of underemployment of resources and deflation, an abundant credit policy supplies reserves plentifully to the banking system, lessens the cost of credit, lowers interest rates, and makes borrowing somewhat easier because commercial banks have excess reserves they are anxious to put to work.

The less industrialized countries do not have as highly developed commercial and central banking systems as the United States; but their central banks (and even quite backward countries now have them) are characteristically assuming, over time, an increasing degree of responsibility for the general level of economic activity.

The point to be made at this juncture is the rather obvious one that fiscal and monetary policy must work in harmony if the national

---

[6] This view was pioneered largely by the Committee for Economic Development.

product, the volume of employment, and the structure of prices are to be influenced in the desired direction, with a minimum of lost motion. Later in this study I will inquire into the relations between fiscal and monetary policy, and the meaning of harmony between them, in a bit greater detail.

EFFECTS OF FISCAL ACTIONS

In addition to its aggregate, or, in economists' jargon, "macroeconomic" effect on the level of economic activity, fiscal policy has what may be called "structural," or "microeconomic," effects. These effects depend on the types of taxes imposed (and on the manner in which they are collected) and also on the varieties of government expenditures that are undertaken and on the repercussions which these expenditures have on different sectors of the private economy.

It is axiomatic that public finance involves transfers of command over resources from private to public use. In these transfers it is plain that the nature and degree of use of the resources change. When people are taxed for the support of government, obviously they have less income to spend or to save. In a particular government expenditure program, say unemployment compensation, these expenditures give certain people incomes they would not otherwise have, thus stimulating spending for certain items, especially food and clothing, that these individuals would not be able to buy in such quantities in the absence of the government program.

Obviously, a program of government expenditure for road building will have very different structural or redistributive effects on the economy than a program to pay unemployment insurance compensation. Structural effects of fiscal policy flow from both revenue and expenditure sides of the government accounts. These effects are quite different when revenue is raised, e.g., by a sales tax, than when it comes from a personal income tax.

In the system of value judgments within which fiscal policy is formulated, a particular form of taxation may be regarded by some observers as unusually repressive on business activity, whereas some other tax may be thought to be less so. Certain types of public expenditure, e.g., for military research and development, may be thought to cause undesirable competition for resources (e.g., scientists and engineers) with the private sector, while other types of expenditure are considered to raise this problem less acutely. Since in economics everything is related to everything else, the extent to which structural effects might

6

be traced through and weighed against one another is practically infinite. Different viewpoints on policy questions often derive from the different weights assigned to particular factors or to varying views about the linkages among economic variables.

If the degree of utilization of economic resources were precisely the same with and without taxes and public expenditure, we should be concerned chiefly with whether the shift of resources to the public sector involved their use in less significant or less efficient ways than if they had remained with the private sector. As already noted, however, the shift of economic resources from private to public use is not unrelated to the general level of economic activity or to the degree of employment of resources. Indeed, this relationship is a major preoccupation of fiscal policy in all industrially advanced countries, and to a lesser extent also in less developed economies.

BUDGET CONCEPTS

Government expenditures are proposed in budgets and authorized in appropriations legislation. To discuss fiscal policy intelligently one must examine budgets and the budgetary process in considerable detail. A government budget is simply a projection or plan of expenditures to be authorized and of revenues to be raised. The difference between revenue and expenditure is called the budget surplus or deficit. If a particular budget contemplates a deficit, it may encompass some plan for covering this deficit by borrowing; if it contemplates a surplus, the use to be made of this surplus—for example, debt retirement or expansion of government cash balances—may be indicated.

Most government budgets are taken up annually, although a tendency is becoming apparent in many countries to extend the budgetary process over longer periods, or at least to show in budget presentations the future expenditure consequences of long-range programs. For example, in the United States a five-year forecast of program cost is now required.

All budgets forecast the future because they must be made up well in advance of the period they cover. In the United States, for example, the federal budget is presented to Congress each January, covering the fiscal year to begin the following July 1. Fiscal years may correspond with or depart from calendar years, depending on custom in individual countries.

There are a number of different budget concepts in use; hence a budgetary surplus or deficit has meaning only with reference to the particular budget structure within which it is derived. In the United States there are three budget concepts in use at present. These differ in important respects.

Administrative Budget

The administrative or conventional budget is best known. It covers all the expenditures for which appropriations are requested and is arranged primarily by agency and object of expenditure (salaries, travel, equipment, etc.) rather than by program or function. This budget does not cover expenditures from trust funds, for which annual appropriations are not required, nor does it include those receipts from tax collections which are earmarked to go into trust funds. It is therefore incomplete on both the receipt and expenditure sides.

Tax revenues in this budget are allocated to the year in which they will be collected rather than to the year in which liability arises. Thus income taxes for 1966 are allocated to both 1966 and later years, since collection is only partially current.

Cash Budget

The consolidated cash budget is a complete projection of receipts to be obtained by the government from the public and of payments to be made to the public in other than public debt transactions. It includes receipts by trust funds, principally for the United States government, from social security, gasoline, and motor vehicle taxes, and also payments out of trust funds, e.g., social security benefit payments, payments for highway construction, pensions to retired civil servants, etc. A deficit in the cash budget is what actually must be financed by new borrowing.

The cash budget is more useful analytically for certain purposes, such as the formulation of monetary policy, than the administrative budget; the latter is significant primarily to the appropriation committees of the Congress.

National Accounts Budget

The national accounts budget is the federal government sector of the national accounts; it is geared conceptually to the conventions in use for social accounting. It drops from expenditures those outlays which are not drafts upon current output, such as land purchases; it also times expenditures to occur when goods or services are delivered to the government rather than when payment for them is made. In addition, it nets out certain intragovernmental transactions arising, for example, when appropriations are made to one agency but are reallocated to another for actual obligation.

On the receipts side the national accounts budget counts tax liabilities rather than cash collections. In this respect, because tax collections always lag somewhat behind liabilities, it is more nearly current than either the cash or conventional budgets. The national accounts budget is favored by economists, who regard it as somewhat more analytically significant than the other budgets.

Each of these budgets serves certain purposes best, and no one of them could easily be substituted for the others in all applications. The three will probably continue in simultaneous use for some time. Other countries will undoubtedly also come to use budget variants such as these more extensively.

Net and Gross Measures in Budgets

Budgets also differ in the extent to which they show receipts and expenditures on a gross or only on a net basis. The United States government budget shows only the net of postal receipts and outlay. Because the Post Office Department is not wholly self-supporting, this net figure is an item of expenditure.

An agency's operating results are typically shown net in budget schedules if it is authorized to keep and use its own receipts, as the Post Office is. If it must pay any receipts it gets over to the Treasury, its expenditures will probably appear gross in the budget.

Virtually all governments have some businesslike activities that sell services to the public, pay their own operating costs from the proceeds, and return any residual profit to the fisc. These activities may be included in the budget on a net basis or in many cases excluded from it altogether. In the United States, for example, we have credit agencies that make loans, insure bank deposits, and perform other services for charges or fees. Their results do not appear in the administrative budget since no appropriations have to be made for them; but they do appear in the consolidated cash budget.

In Costa Rica the manufacture and sale of alcoholic beverages made from local materials is a government monopoly. All proceeds from the sale of these beverages accrue to the national monopoly, while all expenses are met by the monopoly, operating essentially as a private business enterprise. The national budget simply includes the estimated net of receipts over expenditures as one item of receipts, along with tax collections.[7] The liquor monopoly profits are analagous to liquor tax receipts in the United States. Many other countries have government monopolities over certain products such as matches; usually in these cases only a net figure enters the budget.

It will be apparent from the foregoing remarks that the size of a government budget depends rather importantly on whether transactions appear on a gross or a net basis and whether the budget gives a complete or an incomplete accounting for government activities.

Extrabudgetary Items

A few more examples of varying budgetary practice may be cited to show how difficult international budgetary comparisons can be. In the United States, the Comptroller of the Currency gets the income to operate his office by assessing fees against the nationally chartered banks which he supervises. This income and outgo is extrabudgetary.

Likewise, the Federal Reserve System derives a large income from holding the required reserves of member commercial banks, on which it pays no interest, and from investing these funds primarily in United States government securities on which it receives interest at prevailing rates. At the end of October, 1967, the Federal Reserve portfolio of these securities was in excess of \$47 billion.

Interest on these securities is used first to meet administrative expenses of the System, second to build certain reserves required by legislation, and third to pay over to the Treasury any balance remaining as "franchise tax" on the privilege of note issue, which the Federal Reserve has as a monopoly right. Thus, both the receipts and the expenditures of the central bank are extrabudgetary.

This is common for the central banks of other countries also, even when these are wholly owned government institutions. The Federal Reserve is technically "owned" by the member commercial banks in

---

[7]The method used in Burma to collect tax on locally manufactured liquor is also interesting. The country is divided into more than eighty districts; an annual auction is held by the central government at which the exclusive right to manufacture and sell within each district is sold for the following year. The system is the acme of administrative simplicity so far as the central government is concerned because all problems of controlling bootlegging, etc., are thrown on the licensee. The system does not, however, insure equal pricing or taxing in the different districts. Moreover, collusive bidding for licenses has held the revenue well below what it could be and has thus distributed monopoly profits rather erratically among the successful bidders. Such a system attaches too much weight to administrative convenience, in my opinion.

the United States which subscribe to stock as a condition of membership.

Current and Capital Budgets

A number of countries divide their national budgets into current and capital sections. Usually this distinction applies more to expenditures or outlays than to receipts. Current expenditures are those which must be made every year for the continuing activities of government. Capital outlays are costs of special projects, often of an investment or non-repetitive nature, such as construction costs of public buildings. Although often tenuous at the margin, the distinction between current and capital outlay is useful in detailing the character of public expenditure.

The budget of the United States government does not classify expenditures in this way. In some countries particular revenues are reserved, by legislation or custom, for either the current or capital budgets. In Iran, for example, the major share of government revenue from petroleum exports is earmarked for the capital budget. Economic development projects fall mainly in this capital budget.

It should now be clear that budgetary concepts vary a great deal and should be used with some care. It is necessary to understand what they do and do not cover, which means appreciating how the entire budget structure is integrated.

Need for a Comprehensive Budget

As government functions expand there is a noticeable tendency to set more activities, especially those of a business nature, outside the regular budget process. Managerial control, financing by user charges, and the like are good reasons for so establishing some of these activities. It would appear, nevertheless, to be a sound principle of public administration that governments should, on some regular occasion, present for public scrutiny both conventional and comprehensive budgets—so that the full range of government activities and their operating results will be available for appraisal by the electorate.

In Burma, for example, with a socialist government engaging in all manner of businesslike activities, the extrabudgetary transactions far outweigh those in the regular budget that is presented for parliamentary review. Happily the Burmese government regularly presents both conventional and comprehensive budgets on the same occasion, namely the annual budget speech of the Finance Minister.

Many emerging countries do not have comprehensive budgets concerning all government activities. Construction of such an inclusive budget is a necessary preliminary step to proper development planning.

TAX CONCEPTS AND TYPES OF TAXES

Taxes are compulsory payments to government that are now imposed by legislation. They are commonly divided into direct, i.e., those imposed on persons or corporations; and indirect, i.e., those imposed on commodities, transactions, or services. Poll taxes, personal income taxes, and death taxes are direct; customs duties, sales taxes, and most property taxes are indirect. The line between direct and indirect taxes is often hazy and hard to draw; but the distinction is sanctioned by long established usage.

Progressive and Regressive Taxes

Taxes are also divided into proportional, progressive, and regressive —depending on the relation of the tax to the income of the individual, who is regarded as bearing the ultimate tax burden. A state income tax at a flat rate is considered roughly proportional because it takes about the same percentage of income from each recipient regardless of income size.[8] The United States federal income tax is progressive in that larger incomes pay higher average rates than smaller incomes. Mr. A., with twice the taxable income of Mr. B., pays more than twice as much tax. A sales tax on food is commonly regarded as regressive because it is believed to be largely shifted forward to consumers in the form of higher food prices and because a larger proportion of small than of larger incomes is spent for food.

Tax Shifting

Much of classical tax analysis was concerned with whether taxes were shifted and, if so, with how this shifting took place. A tax is shifted forward if the person or business on whom the tax is legally imposed is able to raise his selling prices by all or a part of the tax, thus passing it completely or partially to the purchaser. Most sales taxes are commonly believed to be largely shifted forward into prices of finished goods and services.

[8] Actually, if the flat-rate tax encompasses a personal or family exemption, the average effective rate will be mildly progressive. This is because there are really two rates, a zero rate (on the exemption) and a standard rate.

A tax is shifted backward if incomes derived from the point of imposition of the tax (or earlier in the production process) are reduced by virtue of the tax. For example, an excise tax on jewelry is partially shifted backward if incomes of jewelry workers are lower in the presence of the tax than they would be in its absence.

It is widely believed that indirect taxes are more easily shifted forward than are direct taxes. While this generalization may be roughly true, it is nevertheless quite an unreliable guide to specific problems of tax shifting; in actuality this shifting depends on the structure of product and factor markets, the imperfections of competition, substitution possibilities, mobility of factor inputs, and many other considerations.

Classical tax analysis referred to the eventual resting place of a tax as its incidence. If a tax on food was thought to be largely shifted forward into food prices, the incidence of the tax was said to be on consumers of food, who were believed to bear most of the final burden. The classical analysis of tax shifting and incidence concentrated primarily on the market forces specific to the object that was taxed and neglected the more remote, though not less important, results flowing from incorporation of the tax into prevailing economic arrangements. Today we are more concerned with the effects of taxation in a broad sense than with the partial equilibrium analysis of incidence.

According to classical tax analysis, income taxes were shifted little, if at all. Therefore, it was believed that the burden of a corporation income tax fell primarily on the stockholders. Today we are less certain of the accuracy of this view. To the extent that corporations sell their products in imperfectly competitive markets at administered prices they may succeed in shifting a substantial part of the tax forward into prices of finished products. To the extent that they buy or hire agents of production in imperfectly competitive markets they may be able to shift all or part of the tax backward into reduced wages, rents, and other factor incomes. The relative lack of resistance in the United States to high corporation income tax rates over the last several decades at least leads one to pause before accepting the classical position that these taxes are not shifted.[9]

[9]For an attempt to demonstrate that the corporation income tax in the United States is actually shifted, see M. Kozyzaniak and R. A. Musgrave, *The Shifting of the Corporation Income Tax* (Baltimore: Johns Hopkins Press, 1963).

Chapter 1

Tax Systems

The entire group of taxes to which individuals and businesses in a given country are subject is called the tax system or the tax structure. This system or structure may consist of taxes levied by several layers of government, namely local, state or provincial, and national. Fiscal policy in the sense used in this book refers primarily to national taxes, since normally only national governments undertake to influence significantly the total volume of economic activity.[10]

Traditionally, in the United States, local governments have relied most heavily on property taxes; state governments on property, sales, and business taxes; the national government on customs, excise, and (more recently) income taxes.

Different layers of government may use the same or similar taxes. The majority of American states as well as the federal government impose income taxes; virtually all states as well as the national government also tax wealth transfers at death.

Tax systems manifestly differ markedly from country to country because of differences in history, political systems, and attitudes toward government—among other reasons.

The Appropriate Tax Structure

Many writers have observed that the more developed economies characteristically have higher ratios of taxation to national product than do the less developed countries; these writers have noted also that the extent of reliance on direct taxation usually increases with greater economic development. While these associations may hold generally between the advanced and the less advanced countries, they are not very accurate as indicators within the group of developing countries, considered by themselves.

One such compilation of tax ratios for developing countries only is given in Table 1.

[10]National tax policy must nevertheless take account of the taxes levied by local government bodies and the effects of these taxes.

TABLE 1
TAX RATIOS IN DEVELOPING COUNTRIES

Country	Year	Tax Revenue of the Central Government as a Percentage of GNP	Income and Profits Taxes as a Percentage of Central Government Revenue
Israel	1960/61	21.4	28.5
Ceylon	1961/62	18.6	20.7
Iraq	1962/63	16.6	9.8
Dominican Republic	1962	16.4	12.7
Greece	1962	14.9	11.4
United Arab Republic	1963/64	14.8	13.7
Sudan	1963/64	14.1	5.9
Peru	1963	13.6	35.7
Chile	1963	13.1	12.2
Turkey	1963/64	13.0	31.6
Malagasy	1962	12.7	12.6
Thailand	1962	11.9	9.9
South Africa	1962/63	11.5	53.4
Ecuador	1963	11.2	11.1
Panama	1962	10.8	24.1
Nicaragua	1963/64	10.7	7.2
Tanzania	1961/62	9.3	31.6
Philippines	1961/62	9.2	21.5
Paraguay	1962	9.1	14.6
Korea	1963	8.9	32.8
Brazil	1961	8.0	22.2
Argentina	1962/63	7.5	9.1
Mexico	1963	7.0	34.3
India	1960/61	5.1	20.1

SOURCE: Compiled by J. Lotz of the International Monetary Fund from various sources and released in mimeograph March 4, 1966.

It will be apparent from this table that these tax ratios are not very consistent or conclusive indicia of the stage of the development, since Mexico and Brazil rank well below the Dominican Republic, Sudan, and Peru. Nevertheless, there is some loose association between the weight of taxation and the stage of development.

It would be erroneous, in my opinion, to conclude from these associations that less developed countries should move as quickly as they can toward higher and more direct taxation in order to encourage development. The tax changes are, in the main, effects rather than causes of economic progress.

Higher taxation will be necessary in a developing country chiefly because the strategy of development policy is to concentrate additional investment primarily in the public sector, and also because successful development always generates a demand for more public services. Greater reliance on direct taxation will be desirable only if the bulk of economic activity is already moving through market channels, since it is extremely difficult to apply direct taxes to the subsistence, or non-market-oriented, sector of an economy, i.e., to the peasant proprietor who grows and consumes his own food.[11] Direct taxation also requires a tradition of compliance and an attitude of cooperation with government that simply do not exist in many emerging countries.

Progressive Taxation and Inequality

Countries as a rule move toward direct taxation and progressive taxes only when it is thought politically desirable to diminish income inequality. Income inequality is often not considered to need corrective action until after a period of fairly rapid economic growth, in the course of which there has been considerable vertical mobility in the income scale. Less developed countries often tolerate greater relative income inequality than do more advanced countries. So long as this inequality remains traditional it may not encounter vigorous opposition. Even after development starts, a high degree of income inequality may be tolerated if a reasonable chance of moving up the income scale is thought to exist.

The effort to reduce income inequality too early in a nation's economic growth experience may, in the opinion of some observers, retard the social changes and blunt the responses to incentives that are deemed necessary to produce optimum economic progress. It is a well-recognized principle of lotteries that the size of the prizes is more important than the mathematical expectation of winning in encouraging participation. Economic development requires that large numbers of people work harder than before and that they change, often radically, their traditional ways of doing things. A country intent on development should be quite concerned about personal motivation and about strengthening incentives to change. A belief in the possibility of

[11] It has been estimated that in India, for example, up to one half of income originating in agriculture consists of output retained for own consumption. Cf. K. S. Knishnawasny, "The Evolution of Tax Structure in a Development Policy," mimeographed (Paper presented at the OECD conference on fiscal policy, Athens, Greece, December, 1963), p. 7.

advancing through one's own efforts is probably also essential to development.

Financial reward is only one among the many forces that motivate people, but it may be a powerful one; moreover, it is the one with which economists have traditionally been concerned. A country aspiring to develop faster ought, therefore, to think carefully before moving to reduce income inequality too severely or too promptly. When innovation is badly needed, permitting a few entrepreneurs to make and to keep large profits may attract other potential entrepreneurs more readily than a system in which modest rewards are more easily obtained and the average probability of some net reward is greater.

In the period of rapid United States growth and marked structural change from 1865 until World War I, we did not have an individual income tax designed to reduce inequality significantly. Inequality based on land ownership may be more inimical to growth than inequality based on entrepreneurial profits.

Progression and Net Income Taxation

While it is possible to build a considerable degree of progression into a tax system that consists mainly of indirect levies, emphasis on progression is usually associated with strong reliance on the individual income tax. Reliance on this tax requires a high degree of cooperation with the government by taxpayers, who must voluntarily assess themselves in compliance with the controlling law; it also requires the keeping by taxpayers of reasonably complete and accurate records, and some system of collection at source for at least certain types of income. Many less developed countries do not have either the personal attitudes on the part of taxpayers or the administrative capability in government that is necessary for a mass income tax to operate equitably. In fact, no tax structure can work well unless it is fairly generally understood and accepted as tolerably fair by the bulk of taxpayers.

An academic author expressed rather clearly the dependence of the personal income tax on appropriate institutional arrangements when he wrote as follows:

> One would not recommend the income tax for a major role in present day China where three quarters or more of the population are engaged in farming, much of it for subsistence rather than for the market.... Nor would one suggest the income tax for first choice in Soviet Russia, where the distribution of income is a matter of political control and where the maintenance of an adequate market for goods is clearly no problem. In an economy where the

government is the major entrepreneur, the tax problem is an entirely different species from the one we know. Price and tax policy are so intermingled as to be almost indistinguishable. Neither would the income tax have been recommended for an important role in this country in 1870.[12]

An appropriate tax system for a country anxious to step up its rate of economic growth and to progress toward the next stage of development is one that will raise the needed revenue without too greatly impairing incentives to work, invest, and innovate. The individual taxes that will make up such a system can and do vary a good deal from country to country—depending on the way business is organized and conducted, the attitude toward government, past tax history, and numerous other factors. The idea that any particular tax structure is uniquely suited to a particular stage of economic development is an illusion.

RELATION OF FISCAL POLICY TO ECONOMIC GROWTH

Perhaps the first thing to be said on this topic is that relatively little agreement exists among economists concerning the exact nature of this relationship. The orthodox contemporary view, in the United States at least, holds (1) that the primary aim of fiscal policy is to insure continuous high employment at stable prices, and (2) that pursuit of this aim will also maximize growth, since potential output grows most rapidly when constantly pressed by actual output. This point is made, in both negative and positive ways, in the January 1963 *Economic Report of the President* which opines that:

> . . . among the costs of prolonged slack is slow growth. An economy that fails to use its productive potential fully feels no need to increase it rapidly. The incentive to invest is bent beneath the weight of excess capacity. . . . When the economy breaks out of the lethargy of the past 5 or 6 years, the end to economic slack will by itself mean faster growth [p. xxiv].

This precept of maximizing growth by maximizing employment is applicable chiefly to the well-developed countries; moreover, it is significant only if a relatively short-run view of growth is taken. Such a precept is without much practical utility for the less developed countries—which are almost uniformly characterized by a substantial volume of structural unemployment, actual or disguised. Therefore, some other guiding principles for fiscal policies designed to encourage growth must be sought for these less developed countries.

---

[12]Harold M. Groves, *Trouble Spots in Taxation* (Princeton: Princeton University Press, 1948), pp. 51–52.

Alternative Paths to Growth

It has become trite to initiate discussions of economic development with the observation that this development requires an increase in the proportion of national product devoted to capital formation. Such an increase is, to be sure, one avenue to growth—so well marked that many national development plans have been directed down this route. Another avenue to growth is increased input of effort and skill by people. This greater personal input can, under many circumstances, contribute as much or more to growth than can increased capital formation.

Studies of United States economic growth experience over the past several decades seem to indicate that additions to the labor force, and qualitative improvements in that labor force attributable to better education and training, have contributed more to growth performance than has the provision of more capital equipment.[13] If this relationship holds for an advanced country already well supplied with skills, the possibilities for growth in less developed countries from upgrading work performance may well be equally or even more impressive.

Professor Smithies has described these alternative paths to development and has called the type of growth primarily dependent on capital accumulation Ricardian growth, and the type dependent primarily on more skilled effort Malthusian growth.[14] The terms derive from a difference of opinion between two famous British economists of the early nineteenth century.

Policy measures to promote growth obviously are quite different when the Ricardian path is followed than when primary reliance is placed on the Malthusian route. For example, Ricardian growth requires much more rigorous limitation of consumption than does Malthusian growth. This concept of alternative routes to development is an interesting one with rather important implications for fiscal policy.

That aspiration to improve the standard of living can be a factor raising the productivity of labor, a basic tenet of Malthusian growth, is an old idea going back at least to the eighteenth century. Sir James

---

[13]E.g., E. F. Denison, *The Sources of Economic Growth in the United States and the Alternatives before Us* (Washington, D.C.: Committee for Economic Development, 1962). See also his *Why Growth Rates Differ* (Washington, D.C.: Brookings Institution, 1967).

[14]Arthur Smithies, "Rising Expectations and Economic Development," *Economic Journal*, 71 (1961): 255–72.

Steuart, a mercantilist, expounded this idea at length in 1767.[15] According to him the size of the manufacturing sector depends on the agricultural sector's propensity to consume luxuries, which is itself a function of the level of aspiration for material goods.

It would appear that many of the less developed countries, in their development planning at least, hold an implicit Ricardian concept of growth—since they place such heavy emphasis on investment, especially in the public sector. This does not mean, however, that they accept wholeheartedly the other Ricardian prescriptions, e.g., about limiting consumption.

Accelerating Investment

When the Ricardian view lies at the root of growth policy, it becomes almost an article of faith with the planners that to achieve economic development requires increasing the portion of national product devoted to capital formation. This may be done either by providing appropriate incentives to the private sector, so that private investment will rise, or, more typically, by enlarging investment outlay in the public sector. Many policymakers in less developed countries have felt that only limited results were possible from the first course of action and so have concentrated on the second.

When, as a matter of government policy, public investment is increased, the question of investment priorities in the public sector becomes extremely important. The fixing of investment priorities is usually thought to lie within the realm of development planning. This realm therefore becomes a subsector of fiscal policy, in the broad sense in which the term is used here. For this reason the next chapter in this study will be devoted to the subject of development planning.

Why Tax Yields Must Grow

Fiscal policy in many underdeveloped countries reduces itself primarily to the search for ways and means of financing the accelerated programes of public investment considered to be the essence of efforts to start a cumulative growth process. Often this policy seems grounded on some implicit Keynesian assumptions.

The Keynesian theory of effective demand, which had its ascendency

[15]Sir James Steuart, *An Inquiry into the Principles of Political Economy*, 2 vols. (London: Miller & Cadill, 1767). The aspiration effect is treated in vol 1, pp. 1–523. See also R. V. Eagly, "Sir James Steuart and the Aspiration Effect," *Economica*, 28, no. 109 (February, 1961):53–61.

during the 1930's, taught that underemployment could be cured by a sufficient dose of public expenditure, which would prime the pump of private investment and consumer spending. It also taught that modern economies have a tendency toward excess saving, which does not realize itself in higher investment and more rapid growth but, rather, finds expression in unemployment and lower levels of aggregate income, in which actual saving falls short of planned or intended saving. The Keynesian world was also a world in which investment opportunities were diminishing and interest rates were too high to permit many of these opportunities to be effectively utilized.

The Keynesian prescriptions were developed primarily for the mature economies; they seemed to accord quite well with the prevailing economic climate of the 1930's. They have since been widely absorbed and imitated by the less developed countries, although their situations are very different. The fiscal policies of these countries have often taken on overtones of Keynesian dogma, particularly in the use of public expenditure as a mechanism to raise the level of aggregate demand within the economy. That Keynes's theories were never intended to apply to immature economies is not always realized.

Undoubtedly, public expenditure does have this expansive effect on aggregate demand, at least in its initial impact. Public expenditure employs men; it creates income; these incomes in turn are spent on consumption, creating a multiple effect on economic activity.

The size of this multiplier is commonly estimated to range between two and three; i.e., a given increment of public expenditure, say of $1 million, is believed to generate between $2 and $3 million of additional aggregate expenditure or increment to the national product. Out of this increment to the national product some additional taxable capacity is created; one result: given a properly flexible tax system, public revenues will rise by some fraction of the increment to the national product.

In some cases the fraction will be large enough nearly to compensate for the public expenditure which sets the process in motion; but this fortuitous chain of circumstances requires a system of marginally heavy and effective taxation that will divert to the public purse a really substantial portion of the increase in national product. Many less developed countries simply do not have an effective system of taxation.

Any country seeking to follow the Ricardian path to growth, primarily through public investment, must quickly face the need somehow to obtain a gross increase in tax revenue—if it aspires to escape the trap of domestic inflation, loss of foreign exchange reserves, and a progressively overvalued currency into which so many other emerging countries have fallen. Such a gross increase in tax revenue may be technically difficult to obtain, politically unpopular, and damaging to incentives; but these problems ought to be faced realistically.

The choice is not between a massive increase in taxation and no such increase, but between a planned increase in taxation and a haphazard but heavy "tax" resulting from inflation. It is curious that policymakers in some countries should be so alert to the need for planning public expenditure but so insensitive to the planning of means for financing that expenditure.

Not all less developed countries are unaware of their financial problems nor indifferent to them; these problems are often intractable. Underdeveloped countries frequently appear to lack the fiscal capacity needed to deal promptly with the emerging problems of economic development. Their leaders may recognize the need for an enlarged public revenue but may find this revenue difficult to obtain. Burdened as they often are with antiquated tax systems that lack yield flexibility, and encountering also the most determined political resistance to tax reform, they may resort to either outright or repressed inflation as simply the lesser of evils; in the long-run it may not prove to be so, but at least its effects are delayed while the effects of enlarged public investment are more quickly apparent.

The Special Burden on Agriculture

Since most less developed countries are primarily agricultural, the burden of an initial gross increase in taxation, if the need for this increase is faced squarely, will necessarily fall rather heavily upon the agricultural sector. This necessity to tax agriculture has often been noted by other writers who have examined the development process. One puts it as follows:

> The taxation of agriculture, by one means or another, has a critical role to play in the acceleration of economic development since it is only the imposition of compulsory levies on the agricultural sector itself which enlarges the supply of "savings" in the required sense for economic development. Countries as different in their social institutions or economic circumstances as Japan and Soviet Russia have been similar in their dependence on heavy agricultural taxation for financing their economic development.[16]

[16]Nicholas Kaldor, "The Role of Taxation in Economic Development," mimeographed (Paper presented at the Joint OAS/IDB/ECLA Conference on Fiscal Policy, Santiago, Chile, December, 1962), pp. 11–12.

Different countries have shown a wide variety of techniques and considerable ingenuity in devising systems of taxing agriculture.[17]

The effect of a marked increase in agricultural taxation on incentives to produce is complex; but on balance it may not be wholly undesirable. It has occasionally been suggested that—in some less developed countries, where incentives to work are not particularly strong and where labor input in well-established occupations tends to be limited to only slightly more than will secure a minimum of subsistence—an increase in taxation may provide an extra incentive to additional work and in this fashion contribute to economic growth. There may be some validity in this observation, provided that the taxation is generally recognized as tolerably equitable, and provided also that the extra taxes cannot practically be avoided by retreat from the market-oriented to the subsistence-oriented sectors.

Taxation is not, of course, the only technique for securing this extra input of effort; nor is it the preferred method in many instances; but it may work under the right conditions. To the extent it does this is a bonus effect of the main purpose of taxation, which is to mobilize funds for capital formation that would otherwise have gone primarily into consumption.

Inflation and Growth

Underdeveloped economies that follow a course of persistent public deficits, in an effort to accelerate their economic growth, are sooner or later faced with the problem of how to finance these deficits. It is important here to distinguish between a debt (or an increase in debt) that is internally held and one that is held externally, i.e., by individuals or banking institutions of some other country. An internal debt may often be handled somewhat more readily than one externally held. The latter requires for its service and repayment a transfer mechanism through the foreign exchanges. Many countries that have borrowed heavily abroad for development are now having to face up to debt service charges that will absorb a large share of their earnings from exports for some years. In Ghana, for example, creditor countries have had to extend repayment periods.

---

[17]Some of these techniques have been explored by George E. Lent of the IMF in a paper "The Taxation of Land Value," released in mimeograph in April, 1966.

Chapter 1

Inflation and the Balance of Payments

If a less developed country does operate on the basis of deficit finance for a number of years, in an effort to accelerate its economic development, this country will almost certainly be faced with a problem of imbalance in its international accounts; budget deficits are a portent of persistent deficits in international payments and consequent loss of foreign exchange reserves.

This is especially true when the development program involves industrialization or creating new manufacturing capacity in a country which has had little or none of this capacity previously. Most of the equipment and a good deal of the technical knowledge required to create new industries must be imported and paid for in foreign currency. This foreign currency can either be borrowed, earned by persistent efforts to increase exports, or conserved by diminishing ordinary imports for consumption.

At the same time, the economic development program will be creating new incomes by putting additional people into employment and raising wage levels. It will accordingly be increasing the demand for imported goods. Characteristically, people in a less developed country want more imported products as soon as their incomes rise above the critical point where they can cover necessary outlays for food and clothing. Thus a substantial increase in the demand for imported products occurs along with an economic development program and actually accompanies the increased import of capital goods which is necessary to implement that program. This double increase in import makes it vitally necessary to expand the normal sources of foreign-exchange earnings, either by additional exports, invisible earnings, or capital imports, particularly private foreign investment.

One difficulty with a fiscal policy of persistent budget deficits in a less developed economy is, therefore, that it worsens the balance-of-payments problem and makes the import of capital especially difficult; because capital does not as a rule flow to an economy which is undergoing an inflationary spiral. On the contrary, the mere existence of an inflationary state of affairs may be a powerful force driving domestic capital abroad, further worsening the balance-of-payments problem.

Inflation and Saving

Another difficulty with a fiscal policy that results in severe and protracted inflationary pressure is that it may be damaging to the volume of private saving within the inflating country. A persistent upward pressure on prices not only weakens the incentive to save but also causes accumulated savings to be diverted from productive investments into speculative outlets that promise a quick return, even though these investments may be inconsistent with sustainable growth for the longer run.

For all the above reasons, a fiscal policy that is compatible only with persistent inflation may well be damaging to the longer-term prospect for economic growth in a less developed economy.

Long- and Short-term Linkages between Inflation and Growth

To conclude that Keynesian economics has no application to the less developed countries, or that a dash of inflation can never help to start a development sequence, would be equally erroneous. Common sense and experience make it palpably plain that economic growth often appears to flourish, for a time at least, in the kind of inflationary situation where speculation is rife, where the prevailing expectations are that prices will rise, and where large profits can be made from organizing new combinations of resources. Growth seems also to flourish in a situation where population is increasing, new land is being opened up for settlement, and new inventions are making older products and processes rapidly obsolete. Where these conditions are present, a good deal of inflationary pressure can be dissipated by induced growth.

Manifestly we need, in the course of any study of the development process, to investigate whether the relationship between inflation and growth is a consistent one, i.e., whether a certain degree of inflation characteristically accompanies a certain growth rate, or whether the two are unrelated. It will be pointed out later that various countries exhibit many different combinations in degrees of growth and inflation, which suggests that the relation between the two is not actually very consistent.

Although the inception of inflation nearly always means a rapid shift to profit, which, generally speaking, is favorable to economic growth, speculative and unproductive profit opportunities may increase more rapidly than investment opportunities that would actually favor economic growth more over the longer run. Thus it would appear that, although a certain degree of inflation may be favorable to economic growth temporarily, an excess of inflation may be inimical to growth in the final analysis. This dividing line varies among developing countries.

Chapter 1

Inflationary Gaps in Development Planning

Some countries, in their development planning, have intentionally scheduled investment well in excess of the financial resources they could expect to have available. In establishing these inflationary gaps in their development plans, they have hoped either to fill them with foreign assistance, or in some other manner to suppress the inflation, often by resorting to price and other direct controls. Development plans obviously must be ambitious to accommodate national aspirations; but when they rely too much on inflationary finance one incidental result is the undermining of the factual basis on which the plan rests. Cost estimates become outdated, while patterns of resource use and expenditure are modified by the price spiral. The likelihood that output and employment targets will not be met, and the planning process thereby discredited, tends to increase. The fact that plan targets are unlikely to be reached is not, of course, the worst feature of a development plan with built-in inflation. This feature may be found in the lack of relation between contributions made to the growth process and rewards obtained from that process.

It is well known that development plans vary greatly from one country to another—in their realism, internal consistency, comprehensiveness, and financial feasibility. When less developed countries formulate more ambitious development programs than they can hope to finance with their own resources, these plans are apt to become mere shopping lists for foreign aid, which is solicited in order to complete the development plans and to maintain political alignments.[18] India has on several occasions used this technique to good advantage to get massive infusions of economic aid from the United States as well as from the Communist countries. Other Asian and Latin American nations have also used a similar technique.

Obviously a country can develop faster when it receives a substantial volume of aid from abroad on a loan or grant basis than when it must depend entirely on its own resources. Practically every country that is now well developed industrially was at one time a substantial capital

---

[18]One view of this technique has been expressed by American observers in the following vigorous language: "Nothing is more corrosive of the central purpose of our assistance programs than the knowledge on the part of recipients that, if they can only generate a sufficient sense of political or military crisis, they can blackmail us into supplying financial resources without their having to take the difficult, often painful steps required for the effective use of those resources." See *The Emerging Nations*, ed. M. F. Millikan and D. L. M. Blackmer (Boston: Little, Brown & Co., 1961), p. 120.

importer, although this capital import was primarily from private rather than public sources.

In the past, individual investment projects within a country attracted foreign capital if they promised to be self-liquidating and to earn the foreign exchange necessary to effect the loan repayment. Today there is much less tendency among lenders to look at the creditworthiness of individual projects—since attention has shifted from isolated investment projects to entire programs of economic development. Since it may be necessary for a country to import capital in order to finance economic development, a fiscal policy that will interfere with the ability to import this capital on favorable terms is likely to have an adverse effect on economic growth.

It would be possible to continue at length exploring the relations of fiscal policy to economic growth; but perhaps enough has been said to indicate that these relations are complex, ramifying, and only imperfectly understood. It will be the function of the balance of this study to explore a few of these relationships in depth and in a more systematic way, in order to draw together a few of the main strands of a new but rapidly growing literature.

My theme is the unifying nature of fiscal policy as a tool of economic management; also its relation to the time, place, and institutional setting in which it is applied. The essence of any general theory of economic prescription should be its relevance to different historical and environmental situations.

2

Budget Structure and Development Planning

Fiscal policy is carried out through a complex decision-making process of government in which the amount and distribution of public expenditure are determined, and the character and administrative contours of the tax system are fixed. This process naturally varies greatly in its details from country to country, depending on political institutions, past history, orientation of the administration in power, and numerous other factors. The policy formulation process should, however it is organized, involve a rational weighing of alternatives and an understanding of the probable effects of those courses of action that are actually selected.

My purpose in the present chapter is to develop some general principles of budget making and development planning and to compare these principles with actual practice in a few selected countries.

THE DEVELOPMENT PLANNING PROCESS

Economic development planning has become very popular; practically every country aspiring to develop now has its multi-year plan, by means of which it hopes either to initiate or to accelerate the growth process. These plans range from rather simple advance schedules of public expenditure to quite detailed blueprints of what is expected in investment and output in both the public and private sectors during the several years ahead.

Development Planning vs. *Central Planning*

As already noted, planning for economic development does not necessarily imply central planning of all economic activity. This sort of planning has been described by a number of writers as entailing an inevitable loss of freedom. For example, Professor Jewkes puts this point with some vigor when he writes that planning ultimately turns every individual into a cipher and every economic decision into blind fumbling, destroys the incentives through which economic progress arises, renders the economic system as unstable as the whims of the few who ultimately control it, and creates a system of wire pulling and privileges in which economic justice ceases to have any meaning.[1]

Despite strictures of this nature, leaders of most less developed countries are not chary of a pervasive planning process; indeed, nearly all of them probably believe that extensive planning accelerates economic development.

Authoritarian countries obviously plan economic activity in far greater detail than do democratic countries. The type of planning to be discussed here is not the completely authoritarian type, which is extensively treated in other literature. I shall assume, rather, that there is in the emerging country a significant private enterprise sector of economic activity, and that this sector responds to stimuli and incentives more than to central direction. The degree of direction given to the private sector obviously varies a good deal in different countries.

Structures for Development Planning

Let us look first at the governmental structure within which development plans are formulated and budgetary decisions made. The planning authority is typically a cabinet committee, smaller than the entire cabinet but including the highest and most influential policy and operating officials in the government. Typically, this planning authority functions primarily as a review body, appraising individual projects advanced by government departments and agencies and hopefully welding the parts into a coordinated and balanced scheme for expanding investment.

In a review of development planning experience in Pakistan, a member of the Economic Development Institute staff of the IBRD concluded as follows: "Pakistan's experience clearly indicates the importance of locating the Central planning agency at the highest level of government."[2]

The development planning process obviously will not work well unless it permeates most branches of government and unless many government agencies contribute to it. For this reason the planning

---

[1] John Jewkes, *Ordeal by Planning* (London: Macmillan & Co., 1948), p. 9.
[2] A. Waterston, *Planning in Pakistan* (Baltimore: Johns Hopkins Press, 1963), p. 133. For a similar view, not limited to Pakistan, see L. J. Walinsky, *Planning and Execution of Economic Development* (New York: McGraw-Hill, 1963), p. 16.

authority cannot be an agency apart but must lie at or near the very center of policy making and administrative control in the governmental structure. The planners themselves should be responsible political officials; they should be supported by adequate, expert staff, preferably drawn from existing ministries and other agencies so that varying viewpoints and different types of expert knowledge will be available. The planning authority should also use consultants extensively, drawing these from universities, business, organized labor, and other groups with varying interests in economic development. The authority should operate openly, i.e., should hold public hearings and discussions on the aims of economic development and on the techniques it proposes to use to see that its plans are properly integrated and carried out. The objective of all these activities should be the widest possible understanding of and support for the economic development efforts.

Role of Foreign Planning Advisers

The initial development plan for a given country may be put together with the help of foreign advisers or may be drawn without this help. International agencies such as the United Nations and the International Bank for Reconstruction and Development have strongly encouraged the formulation of comprehensive development plans, often requiring these as preconditions to extensive technical or financial assistance; these international agencies have also provided technical help in getting such plans outlined in the first instance. The United States government, in administering aid to friendly foreign countries, has also on numerous occasions pressed for comprehensive development plans. It has perhaps been less systematic in this respect than the international agencies.

A Latin-American economist takes another broad view of the planning process, similar to the one just outlined. He writes as follows:

> Taking into consideration the various forms assumed by planning in the Latin American countries, the machinery for adopting decisions will not be complete until it includes some means of submitting to the joint consideration of a body presided over by the Minister of Finance not only the manifold aspects of tax and expenditure policy at all governmental levels, but also the financing patterns of the semi-public agencies and enterprises (including social security services) together with the amounts involved, and the operations of the official banking system and of the agencies responsible for regulating supplies and prices. If no normal mechanism can be established for such purposes, the Minister of Finance, should at least have all the relevant information at his

disposal, punctually presented in systematic and well ordered fashion, so that the central government can make known, through the appropriate channels, the principles to be followed and exercise the necessary supervision.[3]

When a planning authority endeavors to formulate a comprehensive program of development for the first time, with or without outside technical assistance, it faces a bewildering number of ways in which capital might be invested. All these different investment possibilities will have their proponents, who will individually be sure that each suggested investment is of the highest importance to the development process. Not all the investments suggested can be made, since funds and other resources (skilled manpower and the like) are limited. The planning authority badly needs a rule or guiding principle that will enable the most productive investments to be selected. What should this rule be?

THE GUIDING RULE FOR INVESTMENT ALLOCATION

In theory the rule comes quickly to hand, namely that those investments are to be preferred which have the highest marginal social productivity. In practice, however, the measurement of marginal social product must be made by approximation. Indirect effects, such as the effects of better transport in making possible the broader marketing of agricultural products and in facilitating labor mobility, must be taken into account.

The Marginal Social Product Rule

The criterion of marginal social product is quite different from that of marginal private product by which private investment would be directed. For example, the social product of investments in education is high but the private product of such investments may be relatively low when education is financed by the employer because of uncertainty over whether the trained workers can be retained or may be lost to other employment or other countries through emigration. In an authoritarian economy, the disparity between the social and private marginal products of training would be minimal.

Although the rule for allocating a given quantity of public investment to obtain maximum social product is simple in principle, the difficulties in practice of obtaining accurate measures of the social productivity of different possible investments are formidable indeed.

[3] Victor Urquidi, "Fiscal Policy in Latin America's Economic Development" (Paper presented at the joint OAS/IDB/ECLA conference on fiscal policy, Santiago, Chile, December 1962), p. 12.

Care and tough-minded analysis must be applied skillfully if costly mistakes are to be avoided.[4]

Investment Allocation Often Casual

In any general survey of the development planning work that has been done in many underdeveloped countries over the past fifteen years, one cannot help being impressed by the seemingly casual manner in which investment priorities are often determined. In more formal economic language, one is struck by the lack of precise calculations of the expected marginal efficiencies of investment in the different spheres over which investment outlay is spread. Yet obviously, in any country where capital is extremely scarce, nothing is more important than that the socially most productive investments get made first while those which yield relatively less get deferred. When investment planning is done officially, however, priorities are often set on the basis of political considerations or national aspirations rather than by a hardheaded economic calculus.[5]

The result of politically dominated development planning is often misdirected investment, and consequently a good deal less sustainable growth in the long run than if priorities had been fixed more rationally. For example, monumental public buildings are far less significant as public investment in economic development than is training of skilled labor; even the roughest calculations of relative marginal social productivity should show this. Similarly, creating entire new industries that may or may not be able to compete in world markets (so-called inward-looking industrialization) is generally far more expensive and less efficient than improving existing industries that have

[4]H. B. Chenery suggests that alternative models of development sequences should be constructed so that policy makers may know more accurately the implications of alternatives. He stresses the importance of what he calls consistent alternatives, i.e., those that are comprehended within a given set of alternative models. Policies and programs that fall outside a particular model are not consistent with those within the model. This is a rather formal and narrow definition of consistency. Cf. his paper "A Model of Development Alternatives," *U.S. Papers for the U.N. Conference on the Application of Science and Technology for the Benefit of the Less Developed Areas*, vol. 8, pp. 81–92.

[5]In commenting on Mexican public investment, Raymond Vernon notes that one "still has to count upon the high probability that priorities will be heavily influenced by the timing of some national anniversary, by the need to show solicitude for some disgruntled section of the hinterland, by the desire to make public works large and visible, and by all the other diversions of politics which characteristically affect the public investment pattern of a nation." Cf. his *The Dilemma of Mexico's Development* (Cambridge, Mass.: Harvard University Press, 1963), p. 187.

already demonstrated a comparative advantage in the world economy. Very crude productivity calculations should also show this result.

Mistakes in Development Planning

Simply because countries in more advanced stages of development have relatively more of their employment in manufacturing, it is often rather naively assumed by officials in a poor country that manufacturing must be fostered, even though its chances of flourishing are slim. To manufacture successfully, even for home market consumption behind protective tariff barriers, takes raw materials, equipment, skill, organizing ability, and a functioning marketing structure. These preconditions take time to create and their elaboration uses resources that might often more profitably be employed in improving already established occupations and industries.

When mistakes are made in official investment plans they usually turn out to be big, costly mistakes, but they can be concealed for a long time behind uneconomic tariff barriers or covered up by subsidies. Mistakes in private investment may be made equally often, but they are generally smaller and more quickly corrected by outright commercial failure.

Too often development planners have allowed their preconceptions rather than objective calculations to govern investment priorities. India, for example, has given priority to heavy industry to the neglect of agriculture, and Burma to electrification of the entire country to the neglect of rice storage, shipment, and milling. Both these priorities involved heavy investment in capital-intensive fields with relatively limited employment-generating capabilities. Bauer and Yamey have suggested that "paradoxically, the best way for a government to foster industrialization may be for it to use more rather than less of its resources to encourage the enlargement of agricultural output and the improvement of agricultural techniques."[6] Kuznets takes a broadly similar point of view. He notes that the "underdeveloped countries are further behind the developed countries in product per worker in agriculture than they are in product per worker in the non-agricultural sectors."[7] He notes further that

[6]P. T. Bauer and B. S. Yamey, *The Economics of Underdeveloped Countries* (Chicago: University of Chicago Press, 1957), p. 236.
[7]Simon Kuznets, *Six Lectures on Economic Growth* (Glencoe, Ill.: Free Press, 1959), p. 54.

it is a pre-condition of industrialization as a world-wide phenomenon that productivity of labor in agriculture increases sufficiently to feed, at higher per capita levels, a larger proportion of the labor force than could be fed before . . . one may claim that an agricultural revolution—a marked rise in productivity per worker in agriculture—is a pre-condition of the industrial revolution for any sizeable region in the world.[8]

APPLYING THE MAXIMUM SOCIAL PRODUCT RULE

Investing in a manner that will maximize marginal social product is a well-established principle from welfare economics.

Economists have, almost without exception, accepted social marginal productivity as the proper criterion for investment in a less developed economy.[9] Given the difficulty of measuring social productivity accurately, they have suggested numerous pragmatic rules and techniques for approximating it.

In all development planning there is a clear need for basic economic data, often lacking in a less developed country. This need must be met if the planning process is to be realistic instead of degenerating into merely a statement of aspirations leading to eventual disillusionment.

Models for Planning

Colm and Geiger have given a good outline of the development planning process, stressing that it should proceed both from the top down and the bottom up, and that the broadest possible participation by both government and business groups should be obtained.[10] They believe, as does this writer, that use of complicated mathematical decision models for arriving at investment schedules should be avoided and that simple judgment models are more serviceable, given the data gaps and the limited formal training of many local officials who must direct

[8]*Ibid.*, pp. 59–60.

[9]See, for example, the Italian economist Gino Lombardini, "The Quantitative Analysis in the Determination of the Efficiency of Investment in Underdeveloped Areas," *International Economic Papers*, no. 9 (London: Macmillan & Co., 1959), pp. 125–45. Also P. N. Rosenstein-Rodan, "Problems of Industrialization of Eastern and South-Eastern Europe," *Economic Journal*, 53 (1943):202–11; A. R. Kahn, "Investment Criteria in Development Programs," *Quarterly Journal of Economics*, February, 1951; H. B. Chenery, "The Application of Investment Criteria," *Quarterly Journal of Economics*, February, 1953; Yuan-Li Wu, "A Note on the Post-War Industrialization of Backward Countries and Centralist Planning," *Economica*, August, 1945.

[10]Cf. Gerhard Colm and Theodore Geiger, "Country Programming as a Guide to Development," *Development of the Emerging Countries* (Washington, D.C.: Brookings Institution, 1962), pp. 45–70.

the planning process. They also stress continuous testing of a development plan, for internal consistency, and frequent revision as changes occur in basic economic conditions or as experience with new investments accumulates.

UNDERLYING ORIENTATION OF THE DEVELOPMENT PLAN

A development plan is basically an effort to specify and to control the paths along which economic growth will occur; the fundamental assumptions and preconceptions underlying such a plan are therefore of extreme importance. The plan may be oriented either toward export expansion or import substitution—a difference that will affect the whole character of the investment effort and many of the policies adopted to carry the plan out. Many countries seem instinctively to prefer import substitution, simply either because they feel that development should mean new industries or because they know how difficult it is to win new foreign markets.

Raising Agricultural Productivity

Because the less developed countries are primarily agricultural, schemes for raising agricultural productivity should occupy a prominent place in the planning process.[11] The capital requirements for such schemes are ordinarily quite modest; but the schemes often fail in practice because of inability to reach the peasant cultivators, owing to inadequate extension services or to the peasants' reluctance to modify traditional methods. Living close to the margin of subsistence does not breed an inclination to take risks on new crops or new methods which could result in total failure.

In the period of rapid economic development in Japan after 1878 an important factor in the process, according to competent students, was the marked rise in productivity in agriculture. This gain in productivity, once started, has continued ever since. For example, in the two decades before 1960, output per man in Japanese farming rose 76 per cent. According to one analyst this spectacular rise "can be credited largely to the introduction of new methods of rice cultivation, double

[11] J. P. Lewis, in his analysis of Indian development planning feels that a major mistake was made in underestimating the difficulty of meeting the food production goals set in the Second Plan. He finds in the Third Plan a "soberer appraisal of the obstacles that the farm production program must overcome." Cf. his *Quiet Crisis in India* (Washington: Brookings Institution, 1962), p. 46. Nevertheless, two years of crop failure have resulted in serious shortfalls in agricultural output below plan goals.

cropping, seed and fertilizer improvement, etc."[12] With a rapidly growing population and a limited agricultural land area, Japan has, of course, been under special pressure to increase farm output. This improvement in agriculture furnished both the labor surplus and much of the capital needed for expansion of the textile industry, the first large-scale manufacturing activity to emerge in Japan.

In more advanced countries, the growing availability of employment in factories as industrialization accelerated has, by steadily draining the agricultural labor force, forced resort to more capital-intensive methods to raise productivity in agriculture. In poorer countries, with their large surpluses of agricultural labor and their limited employment opportunities outside of agriculture, this spur to better methods is absent. Indeed, planners in developing countries may be reluctant to improve agricultural methods for fear it will worsen their already severe unemployment problem.

Despite a possible temporary increase in aggregate unemployment, agriculture may be the best investment opportunity in a country just embarking on an accelerated development effort. Objective calculations of social productivity should show this clearly. Indeed, the marginal social productivity of excess agricultural labor approaches zero.

Adding Value to Exports

A high priority in any development plan for a country that wants to keep oriented toward the world economy, not to lapse into autarchy, should be given to upgrading and processing more completely the traditional exports of the country. If these exports are minerals, they may be concentrated and perhaps refined near the mines rather than shipped in crude form, thus reducing transport costs. Materials of agricultural origin may be partially processed, e.g., jute woven and made into bags, rice milled more efficiently, sugar refined, and so on. Even if extensive processing is not done, better grading, sorting, warehousing, etc. will add value to the export materials. Foreign capital may be relatively easy to attract into limited processing operations where the supply of raw material is assured by past export performance. One problem that must be faced, however, is that import duties in customer countries are often higher on processed than on raw materials. Such tariff structures need reform.

[12]G. Ranis, "The Capital-Output Ratio in Japanese Economic Development," *Review of Economic Studies*, 26, no. 69 (October, 1958):27.

Many countries, however, show far less interest in export improvement as a field of investment than they do in import replacement, even though they may lack many of the essentials for success in this field. One reason for this view is that the international terms of trade in the past decade have moved generally against raw materials in favor of manufactured goods.[13] This is not necessarily a permanent trend, but it has colored the viewpoints of development planners in many emerging countries.

Because the guiding principle of investment allocation in development plans should be the prospective rate of return in the social product sense, it will be found, in applying this rule in most relatively little-developed economies, I believe, that the projects in which public investment ought to be made are generally those with a high labor intensity and fairly small capital requirements, since this represents the optimum combination of scarce and abundant resources. This finding, when confirmed by actual calculation, would give high priority to community improvement programs, construction of farm-to-market roads, and elementary education rather than to factory building or to monumental programs for port or power improvement.

Effects of a Limited Domestic Market

The principal obstacle to be overcome when building factories to replace imports is often the limited market for the manufactured goods that is available within the emerging country. Often a single minimum-sized efficient plant will more than satisfy total domestic demand for the product in question. If a foreign firm is to be persuaded to make the investment in a branch plant or a subsidiary, it may demand and obtain a monopoly position buttressed by tariff protection, tax concessions, and other special advantages. Proposals of this type often appear to be superficially but speciously attractive to the developing country. A more forward-looking solution might be to enlarge markets by entering into free trade arrangements with neighboring countries, to avoid creating duplicate manufacturing facilities within these free trade areas. This implies a higher degree of international consultation in development planning than has yet been realized.

---

[13]For example, between 1950 and 1961 world exports of primary commodities increased by 4.6 per cent per annum but those of the developing countries increased by only 1.9 per cent. Their share in world trade in primary commodities fell from 41 per cent to 29 per cent and the terms of trade between primary products and manufactures fell by 26 per cent. See the *Annual Report of the Secretary General for UNCTAD* (New York: United Nations, 1964), p. 18.

37

On the point of concessions to attract foreign investment and whether these are actually desirable, an example may be cited. In the 1950's, when Burma was first attempting to industrialize, government officials in that country were much taken with proposals for joint ventures then being offered by foreign business interests. Under these proposals virtually all the capital and the know-how necessary for a new plant would be supplied by the foreign interests; but the Burmese government would take a share in the profits. Actually, in so doing, it would merely be underwriting a preferred and monopolistic position for the foreign interest. This attitude toward joint ventures at that time was quite at variance with the treatment then being accorded established foreign interests such as banks, shipping companies, and trading concerns. These businesses were consistently being denied necessary foreign exchange for operating and profit remission purposes and were thus being prepared for "Burmanization."

How Many New Industries?

The balanced growth advocates, who constitute one group of economic development theorists, have contended that only simultaneous growth in a number of industries can enlarge markets for the products of all. In effect, the entire group of newly developed industries lives by taking in one another's washing. The unbalanced growth advocates, on the other hand, have contended that market expansion is less significant in getting a development sequence started than is the demonstration effect of better technology and more efficient organization applied to one or two selected industries in pulling static processes in other industries toward progress. Without taking exclusively either the balanced or unbalanced view of how best to get growth, it is plain that both market expansion and technological change are essential to getting the growth process started and keeping it moving. I shall examine in some detail the balanced and unbalanced concepts of the growth path to be preferred, in a subsequent chapter.

A program oriented toward export expansion has, in my opinion, some important advantages over an import-substitution program, for most developing countries, provided larger foreign markets can actually be obtained. These advantages include, first, the fact that it builds on a base of existing skill and entrepreneurship rather than requiring wholly new talents. In upgrading traditional exports something is already known about potential markets (which, being foreign, are less limited than domestic markets) and about processing technology.

The barriers to export expansion and improvement may lie in transportation, warehousing methods, or finance—as well as in the farm or mining methods used to obtain the export materials. Quality improvement in goods for export must go back to the original grower or extractor in order to be fully effective. In less advanced countries the assembler or shipper may be the chief agent for urging his suppliers to raise output or improve quality.

HOW MUCH SOCIAL OVERHEAD?

Assuming that the general thrust of a comprehensive development plan has been determined and accepted by a particular country, the problem what social overhead facilities are to be created and at what rate becomes important. These overhead investments are largely in public utility activities such as power, transport, and water supply—as well as in traditional government activities such as education and public health. The need for capital for overhead facilities is so large that the dangers to be faced are, on the one hand, spreading capital so thin that it is relatively ineffective, and, on the other hand, developing a few facilities out of proportion to the others, thus substituting new bottlenecks in intersectoral relations for old ones. There is also a time dimension to be considered. An integrated transportation network, for example, may yield large benefits but over a long period, while other investments may pay off more quickly but less permanently.

The Case for Concentration

In any overhead investment there is much to be said for concentration in as narrow an area geographically and structurally as possible. It may not be necessary to improve three or four ports all at once when one can be fixed now and the others later. Similarly, highway improvement, electrification, and waterway development can progress a little at a time over long periods. A new industry, on the other hand, requires a critical mass of investment before it can produce any output at all. Likewise, social investment in education must be offered to all citizens equitably and can hardly be reserved for a favored few.

Although concentrating overhead investment geographically will necessarily mean uneven development of different regions within the country, this is perhaps an inevitable feature of progress.[14] Not all

[14]T. Balogh has put the case for geographic concentration of investment as follows: "By concentrating at first on a few more privileged regions, a greater increase in income

continued overleaf

areas will be equally well prepared to accept the changes which development requires. Some may learn best from demonstrations in other locations.

Costs and Benefits

Although maximum social product from investment is wanted, getting good measurement of this product is, as we have already seen, no easy matter. The kind of program appraisal needed is one which will gather together and quantify all potential benefits and costs of different lines of investment and thus enable those with the most favorable benefit-cost ratios to be selected by responsible officials.[15] It is essential in benefit-cost calculations that future benefits be appropriately discounted at a realistic interest rate so that the comparison is actually between the present value of expected future benefits and the accumulated total costs.

This technique of benefit-cost analysis has been extensively used in advanced countries to appraise multipurpose river basin and other public works projects, and also in general budget analysis.[16] In principle it is not a difficult technique, although accurate calculation of indirect benefits is far from an easy process. What this approach does offer development planners in less advanced countries is an analytical technique they can learn to apply with their own knowledge and their own factual information in order to reach more systematic judgments concerning investment priorities. The essential feature of the technique is the need to reduce intangibles to quantitative measurements that are directly comparable one with another.

[14]*continued*

can be achieved for any given investment. Thus the time can be hastened at which cumulative growth can be attained. . . . Admittedly in the short run this would mean an increase in the inequality between the most favored and the backward areas." Cf. his article "Equity and Efficiency: The Problem of Optimal Investment in a Framework of Underdevelopment," *Oxford Economic Papers*, n.s., 14, no. 1 (February, 1962):31.

[15]P. G. Clark and E. E. Hagen make essentially the same point in these words: "To choose rationally among alternative proposed projects, a systematic procedure for comparing their prospective benefits and costs is needed." See their paper "Training and Assistance in Development Planning," in *International Cooperation and Problems of Transfer and Adaptation: Papers for the U.N. Conference on Science and Technology for the Benefit of the Less Developed Areas* (New York: United Nations, 1964), 10:16.

[16]In 1965 the President of the United States issued an instruction to all government agencies to install and employ henceforth a planning and budgeting system that would lend itself to quantitative appraisal of programs and to forward planning on a five-year basis.

The Choice of New Industries

Suppose that the development planners decide, after balancing all relevant considerations, that they wish to encourage new industry, to replace imports. They then have the option of leaving the selection of particular products to be manufactured largely to private initiative, or of building actual plants for public operation or perhaps for eventual sale to private interests. The former course has many advantages. An important one is that government can concern itself more with creating conditions favorable to the growth of manufacturing enterprises generally rather than with going directly into business as an operating authority.

The operating techniques of government and business are necessarily quite different. Government emphasizes deliberate procedure to make sure that all interests are properly considered, whereas business demands quick decisions and prompt adaptation to changing market conditions if profits are to be maximized. Moreover, aside from the fact that its normal procedures are inappropriate for business, government does not shed its traditional functions when it engages in business; it merely piles more demands on itself, with increased requirements for organization, skill, and administrative competence.

Where capital is the primary shortage inhibiting the growth of new business, governments can with good effect establish development banks to lend funds to local businessmen. Such institutions can also publish information about business opportunities, give technical help to new entrepreneurs, and discover new entrepreneurial talent with both the initiative and the drive to organize new ventures successfully. Such development banks are also often convenient vehicles for infusions of foreign aid, since they provide the mechanism for retail distribution of loan funds which are made available by international lending institutions or aid-supplying governments.[17]

The Case for Dispersion

In development planning, proper attention should be given to the geographical as well as to the industrial distribution of investment. Too

[17]For a good survey of the organization and functioning of development banks in different countries, see William Diamond, *Development Banks* (Baltimore: Johns Hopkins Press, 1957). Vincent Checchi has pointed out that by mid-1962 United States and international agencies had made 105 loans totalling $738 million to fifty such banks. See his article in *U.S. Papers for the U.N. Conference on Application of Science and Technology*, 8:137.

41

often, when programs are oriented toward import substitution, the investment is concentrated in or near major cities, with the countryside receiving little direct benefit. The social and technological changes that development requires may be slow to come if the average farmer can see little evidence of return from the investment for which he is being taxed. The widest geographical dispersion of investment, although in conflict with the principle of concentration mentioned earlier, may serve to advertise and dramatize the changes sought by the development program. This dispersion is especially important in education and welfare programs.

Anyone who has lived in an underdeveloped country has had experience with the local shortages and surpluses which lack of transport facilities makes inevitable. To overcome these, and to improve the distribution process quickly, any investment in road building ought perhaps to be spread as thinly as possible. It is far more socially productive to connect many centers of population with bad but passable roads than to build a few showoff highways, too good for the probable density of traffic that will move over them, between the major cities, which are already served by poor roads.

The case to be made here, then, is for a pioneering quality to investment: replacing nothing with something rather than merely something poor with something better. Development would be diffused throughout the country instead of merely creating isolated pockets of progress in a broad sea of backwardness. An excellent example of uneven geographical progress in economic development is Ethiopia, where transport links are very incomplete and costs of shipment extremely high. This problem of geographic balance or imbalance is somewhat analagous to the problem whether development should be industrially balanced or not.

Making Planning More Effective

Anyone who has observed the planning process at work in underdeveloped countries will be struck, I think, by the absence of detailed analyses of benefits and costs, as underpinnings, for most investment plans. Technical assistance can help to teach this method. Some students of the planning process are also of the opinion that input-output tables, if developed in sufficient detail, can help to test the internal consistency of the planning process by emphasizing the interindustry linkages. The difficulty lies both in the unfamiliarity of this technique to government officials in developing countries and in the lack of the data needed to construct such tables accurately. If these problems can be overcome, the technique may be helpful.[18]

PLANNING METHODS

If the planning process goes beyond the scheduling of public investment, broad participation by business, labor, and other groups is highly desirable. This is especially true when development plans fix targets or objectives for private investment. Businessmen must be convinced that the targets are both feasible and consistent with their own interests if their full cooperation is to be obtained.

Among the industrialized countries, France today makes quite extensive use of the investment planning process. This is done through use of a framework based on input-output tables, and through extensive meetings between government and private groups in which output targets are fixed by negotiation. The theory is that, through widespread knowledge of the desired pattern of economic growth, this desired result can more readily be obtained.[19]

Need for Detail

To be useful as a guide to current activity, an inclusive development plan must be disaggregated to a degree that will provide practical guidance to individual entrepreneurs. They need to know such details as what roads will be completed when, what the output of technical school graduates will be in particular years, and when power supplies will be available in particular areas and at what probable rates. Clearly the provision of this kind of detail calls not only for disaggregated planning but also for accurate reporting on plan implementation and actual movements toward planned goals. This prompt and detailed reporting is an indispensable tool to any government that seeks to direct activity in a comprehensive way by means of a development planning process.

[18]A. T. Peacock and D. Dosser, who have had experience in constructing an input-output table for Tanganyika, concluded that this technique is of limited usefulness because there is so little interdependence among sectors in a backward economy, and also because of the large expenditure of limited statistical resources necessary to construct such a table. Of the 316 individual cells in their matrix, only twenty three could be filled with quantities large enough to be significant. See their article "Input-Output. Analysis in an Underdeveloped Country: A Case Study," *Review of Economic Studies*, 25, no. 66 (October, 1957): 21-24.

[19]For a fuller discussion of the French system of planning see N. M. Hansen, "Indicative Planning in France: Model for the Future," *Quarterly Review of Economics and Business*, 60, no. 4 (Winter, 1964):17-18.

Coordination with the Budget Process

The kind of development planning described here requires for effectiveness an overhaul of the ordinary budget-making process of government, and full integration of budgeting with development planning. Technical advisers to countries just embarking on development plans have regularly noted defects in the budget processes in these countries and have recommended strengthening this activity of government. The most common criticism has been lack of effective control by the budget authority over certain semiautonomous activities of government, especially when these activities earn and retain their own income. A second criticism has been lack of a visible program structure by which different activities could be properly appraised one against the other.

To integrate development planning with the budgetary process may require some far-reaching changes in the form and structure of the budget itself. This document clearly needs, first of all, to be put on a program-and-performance basis, so that all costs of executing a given program are brought together and direct relations established between the performance to be expected and the costs of obtaining that performance. Only if the budget is cast in these program-and-performance terms can intelligent decisions be made about the necessary scale of government operations and the relative priority of different government programs.[20]

The program-and-performance budget is not new; on the contrary, it has been used successfully for some years in advanced countries such as the United States. Nor is it difficult to prepare from the details available to budget officers in particular ministries and departments. Preparing a program budget on a comprehensive basis does require, however, some analytical skill and both guidance and support from a strong and capable central budget authority or bureau, either located in the Ministry of Finance or at a higher level in the structure of government.

In the United States, for example, the Budget Bureau is a part of the Executive Office of the President and reports directly to the chief executive. It has primary responsibility for preparing the budget, which is forwarded to Congress as the president's own financial plan, and for seeing that all government agencies conform to the president's policies

---

[20]For a good general discussion of the budget reforms essential to economic development see the pamphlet *Modernizing Government Budget Administration*, prepared for AID by the Public Administration Service 1962.

in their own operations. The budget-making function, in a word, should be highly placed and should operate with such authority and efficiency that financial policies are, in fact, centrally directed.

With development planning in the hands of a cabinet committee, it may be desirable to take the budget authority out of the Finance Ministry and to have it report directly to the chief executive. If the finance minister controls the budget process he has, in fact, more authority over the development planning process than his other cabinet colleagues. The location of the budget authority in the government structure, however, is less important than the vigor and skill with which it functions. It must keep all government programs under continuous review, must suggest program curtailment and realignment when desirable, offer positive inducements to increase efficiency, and be on guard against waste of whatever kind. It must cooperate at every level with the planning authority if the two are not formally integrated.

Along with firm central control of financial policies should go decentralization of the detailed planning and budget-making processes. As already noted, planning should proceed both from the top down and from the bottom up. Projects for development should be put forward at the grass roots level and coordinated there to the maximum feasible extent. For example, planning for roads, schools, health centers, and the like should be done locally, subject to general guidelines laid down by the central planning authority. Likewise, the budget requests for local activities should be prepared locally, again subject to general direction and to final modification by the central ministry or department responsible for the specific activities.

Development planning should not centralize control over the economy by requiring preclearance of operating decisions that are within the agreed financial plan. Many of the wastes in Communist economic planning result from too much decision making at the top, with inadequate appreciation of the inconsistencies, delays, and other problems that make their appearance when a plan is disaggregated. Decision making ought to be decentralized as much as is feasible—so that those officials who must carry out a development plan will also have some responsible part in drawing it up.

Modifying a Development Plan

Effective integration of the planning and budget-making processes can occur only when the annual exercise of preparing the budget estimates is also the occasion for an annual review and modification of the whole development plan. In this annual review the priority of different projects may be shifted, geographical unevenness of development smoothed out, and changes in plan schedules made on the basis of actual experience and the developing financial situation.

The mere fact that a five-year development plan has been adopted does not mean that the planning process can stop for five years. There must be continual review and interim reporting on agreed projects, and annual modification of plan targets and plan strategy. The budget, if prepared and utilized in the proper way, is the major vehicle for this annual replanning exercise.

Personnel Requirements

Obviously, the personnel requirements for a successful development-planning authority are not easy to fill. Imagination is needed, but it must be tempered with mature judgment and dogged persistence in studying details and interrelationships. A systematic approach to problem solving is necessary, as is a willingness to reduce data designed for analysis of issues to quantitative measures. Exposure to advanced technology is desirable, but the real aim should always be the adaptation of technology to local conditions, rather than the mere copying of procedures from an environment where relative costs are quite different. Above all, the development planner needs to be open-minded, quick to learn from experience, and far-sighted in spotting future implications of current decisions before these implications have become major problems.

Feasibility

Development plans need to be tested for practicality as they are evolved, and continually modified as experience discloses their weak points. Very little good will come from building a factory unless the right sort of labor is trained to operate it, and unless materials supply, market outlet for its products, and proper maintenance services are assured.

In effect, a development program needs to be supported by a large number of budgets, not only financial but also statistical displays drawn in physical-quantity terms when these are most relevant. A manpower budget, a foreign exchange budget, and a consumption budget are all tools having important applications in the development-planning process. Perhaps budget is the wrong term to apply to these schedules of supply and requirements. Whatever one chooses to call them, they are useful in disaggregating development plans and in testing their feasibility. No technique that will throw light on critical areas where adjustment is required should be neglected by the development planner.

Judging the Results of Planning

Results of development planning are always very difficult to assess because it is impossible to measure achievement under the plan against conditions in the plan's absence. Thus a sudden upturn in the terms of foreign trade, while fortuitous, is not an event for which the development planners are entitled to take credit; neither are they to be blamed for an unfortunate twist of events, such as a sudden breach of peace in some other part of the world, that could not reasonably have been foreseen. In the face of inevitable uncertainty, however, planners should operate from conservative estimates of critical factors such as foreign exchange earnings; they should also make generous allowances for the time necessary to bring new enterprises to full productivity. Otherwise they risk overcommitting resources to plans that are too ambitious and that are likely to fail in execution unless rescued by emergency transfusions of foreign aid or in some other way. A development planner ought not to be a congenital optimist.

Development planning has so many dimensions—technical, financial, and cultural as well as economic—that the planner should always be looking for significant linkages or relationships that will help or hinder progress toward the agreed goals. He must search for organizing ability, management experience, originality in thinking, problem anticipation, and promptness in execution of agreed courses of action. When he finds these talents, he must see that they are placed where they can do the most good in the bureaucratic structure and that they are given enough freedom to obtain results. In summary, caution in conception but boldness in execution is the most valuable combination of qualities to seek in plan builders.

From the above discussion of qualities helpful to a development planner, it will be plain that officials charged with these responsibilities may often fall short of the ideal. This limitation in available human material should be weighed along with other factors in deciding how much development planning should be done.[21]

[21] For an interesting commentary on the mentality of planners see John Jewkes, *Ordeal by Planning* (London: Macmillan & Co., 1948), especially chap. 6. According to Jewkes, planners take an oversanguine view of the future; underestimate the complexity of
continued overleaf

THE CHOICE OF TECHNOLOGY

An important aspect of development planning is deciding on the complexity of the technology to be incorporated in the new or improved industries. There is a tendency in the less developed countries to feel that only the latest and best equipment and practice in advanced countries will do, and that investments in automation, electronic computers, and the like are necessary, even though the bulk of their existing industry is on an essentially handicraft basis. Actually these newer techniques are all designed to economize on labor, which is expensive in the advanced countries. In the poorer countries, where labor is cheap, these techniques may be quite out of place and uneconomic.[22] Particular skills may, of course, be extremely scarce and therefore expensive in less developed countries. Although to a certain extent computers may substitute for literacy, and machinery for craftsmanship, it is perhaps better in most developing countries to invest more in education than in labor-saving devices. Social productivity calculations, even quite crude ones, should show this.

Less developed countries do have an advantage in that a broad range of new technology is open to them, whereas many of the advanced countries had to develop these technologies themselves. Moreover, developing countries can sometimes skip stages in technology that more advanced countries had to work through slowly with no experience to guide them.

A difficult planning problem is always present in selecting the most appropriate technology for use in a less developed country.[23] This optimum technology is bound to differ from that which is most appropriate in more advanced countries, because of differences in relative factor cost. The most appropriate technology can rarely be prescribed from the outside; it must be evolved by local management on the basis of experience and good cost accounting. It is essential to have access to

[21] *continued*
economic arrangements; are suspicious of the price systems; and are distrustful of marketing, distribution, and other services. Jewkes's somewhat draconian criticisms refer primarily to the nationalized industries in Great Britain rather than to the less developed countries. He does not discuss directly planning for economic development.

[22] A similar point has been made by G. M. Meir and R. E. Baldwin in their paper "Technical Assistance," in *The United States and the Developing Economies*, ed. G. Ranis (New York: Norton, 1964), p. 121.

[23] For a discussion of this problem, see R. S. Echaus, "Technological Change in the Less Developed Areas," in *Development of the Emerging Countries* (Washington, D.C.: Brookings Institution, 1962), pp. 120–52.

information about various available technologies and their individual requirements for specific equipment, skills, and operating conditions.

Finding Business Talent

When a new industry is to be created entirely with local resources and without investment by foreigners, the key element is finding local entrepreneurs who can adapt available technology to local conditions. Merchants who have specialized in foreign trade and who consequently know foreign methods as well as foreign sources of supply are often in the best position to supply this talent.[24] Everett Hagen has contended that minority groups, often deprived of social prestige and traditional status, historically have furnished a disproportionate fraction of the supply of entrepreneurial talent.[25] Whatever the sources of organizational and pioneering talent may be, any country that is anxious to develop should allow all potential entrepreneurs access to available knowledge concerning business opportunities. Credit must naturally be rationed to those with the best chance of success, in the opinion of lenders. If new industries are to be publicly operated, it may be desirable to recruit management talent with business backgrounds rather than drawing from personnel already in the public sector.

Technology from Abroad

Foreign investment has been one of the chief methods of spreading industrial technology in the past; it still offers a good opportunity for an emerging country to learn new methods. Business firms investing in less developed countries now generally wish to use as many local employees as possible and to train these employees for supervisory and management responsibility as quickly as they demonstrate competence. Governments trying to attract foreign capital should consider the invisible import of technology a valuable offset to the profits which foreign firms remit. In this exchange they may be getting a good bargain from the standpoint of the national interest.

If foreign methods are to be emulated in a new industry, the appropriate methods may be those of an earlier era rather than those currently in use in the more advanced country. This is not to suggest that

---

[24]G. S. Papanek has shown that persons with a background in trade have constituted about half the successful industrial entrepreneurs in Pakistan since the partition in 1947. See his paper "The Development of Entrepreneurship," *American Economic Association, Papers and Proceedings*, December, 1961, pp. 51–54.

[25]*Development of the Emerging Countries*, pp. 21–24.

less developed countries should deliberately court obsolescence of equipment or methods by copying something short of the best practice. On the contrary, they should not copy at all but should adapt technology constructively to local conditions and local costs. There is no need to invest heavily in materials handling equipment when plenty of labor is available at low wages to carry material by hand. Every investment that is recommended needs to demonstrate a clear cost saving compared with alternative methods requiring less investment.

The cheapest and most efficient techniques in a less developed country may be quite different than in a more advanced country. Capital intensity of investment, for example, should be considerably lower in the less developed country. To discover the exact technology that will yield the lowest cost is an important task of entrepreneurial effort.

Planning and the Legislative Process

Development planning necessarily pervades all the other activities of government and bends these to its major purposes. The financial aspects of the development plan find expression in the budget, which controls the disposition of public funds among different programs and objects of expenditure. The budget should therefore be presented, for parliamentary debate and enactment, as part of a general report on the objectives, progress, and shortcomings in the movement toward development plan goals. Unless the budget is presented in this kind of context, it will be difficult to judge how well it suits the purpose at hand, whether development is actually being accelerated, and if so, whether this acceleration may be expected to continue.

Debates over the budget will thus become the occasion for broadly reviewing the country's major economic policies and its progress under these policies. While budgets may be cut and modified by a legislative process (and indeed this is an imperative of democratic procedure) to rewrite or restructure a development program by legislation is sometimes to court disaster. If the program is well drawn it fits together intricately. Changing a piece here and there may throw the entire mechanism out of alignment.

This does not mean that legislative judgment should not be brought to bear on development planning. It should be—since economic goals and policies can hardly be separated in practice from broader political objectives and aspirations. The floor of a legislature, however, is not the appropriate place to rewrite a development plan. This must be done slowly and carefully—with full attention paid to the interrelationships and the interdependence of parts of the plan.

Clearly, unless the budget is a comprehensive one, in the sense already discussed, it will not lend itself to proper examination within the framework of the development plan as a whole. If the budget is complete, and its relation to the program is made clear, the annual budget exercise can be an important vehicle for advancing public understanding of, and support for, the efforts which the development plan seeks to mobilize.

The right sort of development plan is not a rigid instrument designed to direct the economy down predetermined paths; it is, rather, a flexible, evolving instrument designed to mobilize and focus the constructive energies of a free people anxious to help themselves to a more abundant life.

3

Aggregate Government Revenue and Expenditure

It is obvious that any positive government program costs money and requires the raising of revenue. Promotion of economic development is no exception; indeed, short of war, it can be one of the most expensive activities in which governments today engage. The program for development followed by a particular country may be cheap or expensive, successful or unsuccessful. A development program will not necessarily succeed just because it is costly, nor fail because it is cheap. On the contrary, there are grounds for believing that almost the converse of these propositions is sometimes true. Nevertheless, a program must be sufficient in size if it is to achieve its growth objectives. This will normally mean a heavy volume of public investment.

This chapter will explore in some detail how the total volume of revenue and expenditure of a national government is related to the process of economic development, and how fiscal policy is concerned with internal relationships between government revenue and expenditure. Structural effects of taxation and expenditure will not be discussed in any detail in this chapter, although they are very important to the success of the growth process.

MEANING OF AGGREGATE REVENUE AND EXPENDITURE

The aggregate revenue and expenditure to be discussed in this chapter are the totals that would appear in a comprehensive, consolidated cash budget of the central government if such a compilation existed.[1]

[1] The rule of comprehensiveness, or universality, of the budget is an ancient one, honored, in principle at least, by virtually all advanced countries. As a French writer put it nearly seventy five years ago, "there is no unity of the budget if it is not possible to make all the revenues enter into one treasury and to make the money for all expenditures come out of the same one big common fund. There is no unity of the budget if it is not possible to handle all the appropriations . . . under the same conditions with regard to justification, annulment, and carrying forward." See M. L. Say in a letter written in 1891, quoted by Rene Stourm, *The Budget* (New York: Appleton, 1917), p. 166.

Very often, in less developed countries, it does not. Among the reasons for this gap are (1) that numerous activities of government are often treated as extrabudgetary; and (2) that certain sources of revenue are often earmarked for particular purposes, such as the repayment of foreign loans. More commonly, new sources of revenue are tapped and earmarked for the initial financing of newly established programs. As these programs age, their financing is not always promptly reviewed.

To have an intelligent basis for fiscal policy formulation it is manifestly necessary that a comprehensive budget be prepared and used properly in the decision-making process. Preparing such a budget involves not only drawing together all prospective outlays but also projecting receipts on the basis of reasonable assumptions concerning economic activity generally and the special factors that influence tax yields. It also means effective central control over expenditures so that estimates, once approved, cannot readily be exceeded. Without this kind of factual and administrative basis, no rational and consistent fiscal policy is possible.

A prime need in many less developed countries is to organize this kind of budgetary intelligence and reporting activity and to get it functioning properly. Technical assistance for this purpose is available from a number of governments in the free world, or through international agencies. More countries could benefit from this assistance than have already employed it.

To Balance or Not To Balance?

With the facts concerning expenditure plans and revenue prospects in hand, consideration can be given by the top financial officials of government to whether a balanced, a surplus, or a deficit budget should be put up for the year ahead. Let us assume that the country in question has already adopted a development plan which it is currently following, and that this plan contemplates a certain schedule of public investment to be made in specific projects. Let us assume also that the individual projects have been arrayed in a priority order, with those deemed most likely to contribute to generating or furthering a cumulative growth process given the highest ranking.

Let us assume also that a body of current intelligence on the state of the economy and on likely future economic trends is available. This intelligence need not be formalized in projections of national product, the labor force, and similar aggregates. It may consist, rather, of fragmentary data, impressions, straws in the wind, etc. which nevertheless reduce to a concensus concerning the existing economic situation and the outlook.

Although the development plan may be fairly rigid in its target objectives and in the group of projects that it encompasses, there is always room in a well-drawn plan for some flexibility in the timing of particular projects. Indeed, building in this year-to-year flexibility is an indispensable part of good development planning.

In any year after a development program has begun, there will inevitably be a number of uncompleted projects, on which decisions to go ahead have been taken in the past, which are still in process and therefore require new allocations of funds to finish or at least to keep progressing on schedule. Any savings made in carrying on public investment by slowing down projects arbitrarily is likely to be false economy, since the benefits from these projects will be delayed even more than their costs. A development program stalled in a morass of half-finished projects may be worse than no program at all.

Individual Projects As Building Blocks

Significant flexibility in timing of public investment will be attained if some of the smaller projects can be set in motion at variable times—depending on prevailing economic conditions. Current economic and financial indicators can and should be employed to reach final decisions on program content for the coming year.

It is essential that individual development projects, when integrated into a comprehensive plan, be costed not only in terms of the total outlay required for each project but also in terms of the foreign exchange component of each. This is desirable because available foreign exchange may become a limiting factor well before the overall budget position begins to pinch. Numerous developing countries have encountered this foreign exchange limit. Whether this will be the case or not obviously depends on the structure of the investment program (road building takes less foreign exchange than does factory building), on the magnitude of foreign exchange reserves available, and on the monetary or other constraints that restrict drawing down these reserves. Experience in a number of less developed countries has shown clearly that a foreign exchange budget may be at least as important as a comprehensive government budget in reaching proper decisions concerning public investment.[2]

[2]Burma in 1955–56 was one case in point; Egypt after Suez in 1956 was another.

Revenue Prospects

On the revenue side of the budget, realistic projections of tax yields should be based on past experience and on predictable relationships between tax intake and other economic magnitudes that are both forseeable and central to the general course that economic activity is expected to take.

One problem that may arise in budgeting for development is lack of proper yield flexibility in the tax system of a less developed country. The kind of relationship needed as development proceeds is one in which aggregate tax yields will increase more than proportionately to total personal income. This relationship in advanced countries comes partly from heavy reliance on personal income taxation at progressive rates, but even more from reliance on corporate profits taxation. These profits in the aggregate increase disproportionately during an expansion so that, even without being taxed at progressive rates, they contribute importantly to tax yield flexibility of the contracyclically correct sort. Many less developed countries have tax systems in which yields rise less than proportionately to advances in aggregate income. These systems need to be made more responsive.

Less developed countries often have a special problem because their tax revenues are heavily dependent on the foreign trade sector and are therefore subject to disturbances originating in the world economy which are largely outside their own control. Most less developed countries are exporters mainly of primary products, i.e., products of tropical agriculture and mining. World demand for these products tends to be somewhat inelastic with respect to price, so that relatively small variations in demand or supply are associated with fairly large price fluctuations. If export taxes are a significant revenue source, as they are in many emerging countries, or if customs duties on imports are also important sources of revenue, budget receipts may be closely tied to developments in external economic relations that cannot always be accurately foreseen.

Is a Budget Rule Desirable?

Assuming for the moment that no unusual developments from the foreign trade sector threaten to upset budget calculations, let us turn to the problem whether there exists a general rule that a less developed country should attempt to follow in deciding on the appropriate relationship between aggregate central government revenue and expenditure and, if so, how this general rule should be stated. Will this rule be the same regardless of the stage of development or should it vary with these stages and, if so, how?

A basic problem to be faced at the outset is whether a fiscal policy is wanted that will be active with respect to aggregate economic activity or merely neutral toward this aggregate. As already noted, in the United States today we prefer a fiscal policy that is active toward the volume of unemployment, i.e., one that is calculated to help reduce that total if it is considered to be too high, and conceivably to expand it if it is thought to be too low. An active policy in this sense requires a net contribution to national product from government, resulting from an excess of expenditures over receipts, when unemployment is excessive. A neutral policy, on the other hand, would be one that would not attempt by fiscal action significantly to influence unemployment.[3]

Less developed countries cannot, with realism, so readily orient their fiscal policies primarily to the volume of unemployment, much as they may desire to reduce this unemployment. Typically, they suffer at all times from substantial unemployment, especially widespread in the agricultural sector, which is not accurately measurable. It takes the form not so much of full-time unemployment of some of the potential workers as partial unemployment, often seasonal in nature, of the great bulk of these workers. It is persistent, traditional, structural, and not amenable to significant influence by marginal changes in government expenditure, unless this expenditure takes special forms directly beneficial to agriculture. Some other lodestar than unemployment must therefore be found for fiscal policy in these less developed countries.

Alternative Fiscal Policy Objectives

Growth itself is perhaps too amorphous a concept, and too incapable of precise measurement over short periods, to serve as an accurate guide for an active fiscal policy in a less developed country. The older objectives of stabilization policy, i.e., absence of general price level movements or avoidance of erratic variations in the money supply, may have somewhat more to offer as guidelines for fiscal policy in such countries.

The question should also be raised in this connection whether any

[3] The Swedish economist Bent Hansen defines a neutral fiscal policy rather differently, as one that will not react unfavorably on full employment or a stable value of money in spite of changes in other economic variables or policy parameters. In other words, his neutral fiscal policy is always active in precisely the right way. Cf. his *The Economic Theory of Fiscal Policy* (Cambridge: Harvard University Press, 1958), pp. 229-60.

kind of active fiscal policy can successfully be followed over a long period by a less developed country, or whether the aim should simply be neutrality in the sense of this policy's relation to employment and unemployment. A fiscal policy that is neutral in this macroeconomic sense may still have structural effects that are highly unneutral in the microeconomic sense. Such a policy can affect, e.g., the size distribution of income, the composition of total consumer expenditure, incentives to work and to invest, and numerous other variables that have great significance for actual growth performance.

The goals adopted for fiscal policy, and the amount of reliance placed on this policy, will clearly depend on the structure and force of the other controls and constraints to which the economy is subject. If economic activity is dominated by free-market principles, with only a minimum of government interference in business, the reliance on fiscal policy should logically be strong; if there are powerful direct economic controls in the form of rationing, foreign exchange allocations, and the like, the dependence on fiscal policy can be correspondingly weaker. It is necessary, when appraising any single economic policy instrument, to look at the entire policy complex by means of which government seeks to achieve its objectives.

This policy complex often does not reflect a unified underlying philosophy of government so much as it does an accumulation of diverse attitudes, rules, and administrative machinery for dealing with particular problems that have emerged in the past—in other words, an excrescence left from past compromises with political reality. Fiscal policy cannot be divorced practically from the total structure of economic policy, which, in turn, is merely a part of the larger cosmos of general policy within which any government administration operates.

The balance between fiscal and other economic policies must often be struck according to what is practical rather than according to what is ideal. Sometimes lack of elbow room in fiscal policy places unreasonable burdens on other policy measures. For example, although the administration in office in Costa Rica in 1961 clearly recognized the need for a more restrictive tax policy to cope with inflation, an unrealistic exchange rate, and lagging development, it felt politically unable to implement such a course of action; instead, this administration found it expedient to place an unreasonably heavy burden on monetary policy to repress the latent inflation which the country was then undergoing. Although in the main this course of action appeared to work, at least temporarily, it also imposed too much responsibility for investment direction—because of the technique of monetary policy used, i.e., credit ceilings on particular types of loans—on the central bank, which was relatively ill-equipped to deal with this responsibility. The bank was, by default, the development-planning agency, without a comprehensive investment plan.

Illustrations of such departures in policy composition from ideal or operationally most efficient mixes could easily be multiplied indefinitely. No country is free from these problems. Many people felt, for example, that the United States depended too heavily on monetary and too lightly on fiscal restraint in 1966, and that this imbalance produced some investment distortion.

Let us suppose, purely for the sake of illustration, that an approximately balanced cash budget seems to be the one best calculated to keep the planned growth process going, and that revenue estimates indicate this balance will be approximately the outcome, given the existing tax structure and the probable configuration of world trading relationships. In other words, the budget will be essentially neutral, although increases in employment may result from the investment projects that are included in public expenditures. The income effects of public investment should also induce some expansion in employment in the private sector.[4] The combined increments to public and private employment may, however, no more than offset the normal growth in the labor force, so that no real progress in reducing total unemployment is made. Under these circumstances such growth as is achieved will result primarily from the increasing productivity of the previously employed workers.

UNCONTROLLABLE FACTORS IN BUDGET IMBALANCE

Now suppose that a sudden favorable turn in the terms of trade occurs for our hypothetical country. Prices for its exports are rising, either because of poor crops in competing countries or because of a sudden surge in demand by consuming countries. Under these

---

[4]C. A. Hall writes that the argument for a balanced budget is basically political, although outlined in economic terms. He indicates that it is possible to promote stable growth with a balanced budget by utilizing other forms of policy to create the monetary impact otherwise generated by an unbalanced budget. See his *Fiscal Policy for Stable Growth* (New York: Holt, 1960), p. 262. R. A. Musgrave has also stated in some detail the conditions necessary for economic growth with a balanced budget. These include a growing rate of private investment and, in the case of less developed countries, transfers of resources to capital formation without inflation. See his *The Theory of Public Finance* (New York: McGraw-Hill, 1959), pp. 480–97.

circumstances, a budget surplus may occur fortuitously because tax yields from the export sector will surpass earlier performance. The question is whether, in these favorable circumstances, our model country should attempt to step up its scale of public investment; or should it remain content to run a budget surplus and to accumulate additional foreign exchange reserves?

Burma was in this fortunate position of having a heavy increase in export demand during the Korean war. Burma's exports consist primarily of rice; the profits from rising rice prices accrue primarily to government rather than to farmers or traders. Thus the rise in export demand automatically produced a large increase in government revenue.

Nonfinancial Barriers to Development

Finance may not be the most pressing limitation on a country's ability to carry a public investment program to successful completion. This limitation may be found in lack of organizational or operational skills, in the time it takes complementary development projects to mature, or in some other circumstances. Under such conditions the effort temporarily to accelerate investment, merely because finance is available, almost certainly will increase the risk of failure for the investment already made, as well as the likelihood of waste in the newly accelerated investment. A budget surplus under these circumstances may not be the worst of possible evils.

Burma during the early 1950's provided a good illustration of public investment's overreaching the administrative and organizational capabilities necessary to make this investment effective.[5] When Burma rather unexpectedly achieved its independence following World War II, virtually all political groups in the country favored a socialist pattern of organization as defining the preferred path to the economic goals they hoped to achieve. The Burmans identified capitalism rather closely with foreign imperialism and with past domination of business activity in their country by Indian, Chinese, and British nationals. Generally speaking, the Burmans felt they had not done too well under the prewar business system and that they would be more successful as politicians than as merchants or manufacturers.

With ambitious plans for state-owned industries, and with the means in hand to finance the initial phases of these plans, resulting in large part

[5] L. J. Walinsky reaches a similar conclusion. Cf. his *Economic Development in Burma, 1951–56* (New York: Twentieth Century Fund, 1962), chap. 33.

from the extraordinary boom in export earnings attending the war in Korea, Burma during the early 1950's invested heavily but rather erratically in development. Included in the country's public investment plans were expanded social services; a gradual substitution of state trading for private trade; progressive Burmanization of business, e.g., pushing out foreigners; and the creation from scratch of a number of new manufacturing activities.

By the mid-1950's, after a good sum of money had already been spent, but while most investment projects were still incomplete, it became progressively apparent that local managerial talent to operate the state industries efficiently was quite inadequate. This lack of managerial capability was a major factor contributing to the overthrow of the Nu government and its replacement by a military dictatorship which appeared to offer the promise of greater administrative efficiency.

The transition from civilian to military government brought no essential change in either prevailing economic philosophy or development objectives, and little initial slowdown in the pace of government investment outlay; rather, it was regarded merely as a change in the means of reaching agreed objectives—employing more-coercive methods, thought by some to be more efficient.

Budget Effects of Foreign Trade Changes

The improvement in export trade which has been posited as the prime mover in the sequence we are examining will, of course, be an expansive and potentially inflationary influence on the other sectors of the country's economy. As incomes in the export sector rise, they will create additional demand for consumer goods, especially imports, and also, to some fractional extent, additional private savings. We have assumed, however, a fairly high marginal tax rate on the sudden prosperity of the export sector, which will succeed in draining off into government receipts much of the income expansion. Progressive export taxes may be the vehicle to produce this result. In Burma the vehicle was state marketing board profits.[6]

[6]G. K. Helleiner has pointed out that from 1947 through 1954 Nigerian marketing board trading profits amounted to more than the total yield from import taxes and nearly twice as much as conventional export duties. In 1955–61 these profits declined to less than a quarter the amount realized during the earlier period. He concludes that, although marketing boards have worked fairly well as a fiscal device in Nigeria, they have unduly depressed export production and ought to be gradually replaced by a more normal tax structure. See his article "The Fiscal Role of the Marketing Boards in Nigerian Economic Development," *Economic Journal*, 74, no. 295 (September, 1964): 582–610.

Suppose, instead, that this yield flexibility has *not* been built into the revenue structure. In this situation the new prosperity in the export sector may produce no significant budget surplus and no unusual accumulation of foreign exchange reserves, since increases in import demand may offset practically all the upsurge in export earnings. Thus the question arises whether the government should undertake to obtain a budget surplus, to offset the expansion of foreign exchange earnings, either by increasing taxation on a discretionary basis or by reducing public expenditures.

Much will depend on how rapidly taxes can be increased, i.e., on the legislative process involved, and also on the consequences of expenditure reduction. A tax increase may be difficult to obtain, politically, because there has been no overt deterioration in the budget position but merely an increase in the income and expenditure of the export sector, which is in process of diffusing itself to the rest of the economy. The tax increase is needed primarily to stabilize the economy by combating inflation, rather than for the usual public finance reasons. Political pressure, however, is likely to be all for increasing rather than for reducing public outlay when the export sector is prosperous.

I conclude that opportunities to practice functional finance in a less developed country may be quite limited when the disturbances originate in the international accounts.[7] The difficulties are generally smaller, however, in coping with a surplus, than with a deficiency of income from foreign trade. Perhaps the best long-run policy is simply to build up a revenue structure incorporating adequate yield flexibility, so that the budget response to exogenous changes will be essentially automatic and will occur primarily on the revenue side.

Suppose now that the turn in the terms of trade becomes unfavorable to our hypothetical country. If the revenue structure of the central government is flexible, the decline in export incomes will create an unintended budget deficit along with the trade slackness and perhaps will also cause rising unemployment in the export sector. If the revenue structure is not flexible, the budget deficit will not develop or, if it does, will be of only minor proportions. In the latter event, should the government attempt contracyclical action by a discretionary reduction in

---

[7] A committee of United Nations experts meeting in 1951 similarly concluded that "it is not within the power of underdeveloped countries to control cyclical movements originating abroad and transmitted to them through the channels of foreign trade." See *Taxes and Fiscal Policy in Underdeveloped Countries* (New York: United Nations, 1954), p. 40.

revenues or by an increase in expenditures?[8]

To operate in this fashion means to cause the foreign-exchange position to deteriorate even faster than it would otherwise, and to risk orderly public investment in the future for the sake of an immediate and perhaps less orderly increase in this investment. Political pressure for an increase in home investment to offset part of the loss in external income may be strong, but it ought to be resisted.

A Possible Policy Conflict

Among other dilemmas in financing development, there is the conflict between what has come to be known as the discipline of the balance of payments and a contracyclical fiscal policy. The discipline, as it is conventionally understood, would normally require a country with declining export earnings to accept some unemployment, lower costs wherever possible, and retrench in all foreign exchange outlay, including that going into public investment. According to this view, a contracyclical fiscal policy merely delays the internal adjustments in costs and prices necessary to restore balance-of-payments equilibrium.

Clearly the discipline of the international accounts is a rather stoic doctrine, expressing the neoclassical notion that depression is attributable in some sense to the excesses of the preceding boom and is curable only by strong deflationary medicine. This spartan prescription is less fashionable today than it used to be and is also somewhat less acceptable than formerly to countries that are heavily dependent on international trade.

Many countries today look to exchange rate adjustment, antideflationary measures in the nonexport sectors, or other possible policies—instead of accepting without question the need for adjusting the rest of their economies to the vagaries in fortune of their export sectors. Each country must naturally decide for itself how best to resolve this policy dilemma; I suggest only that the will to accept balance-of-payments discipline is weakening as alternatives to this course of action multiply and become better known.

It remains true, nevertheless, that the more dependent a country is on international trade, the less freedom it has to pursue a contracyclical

[8]In its report on the economic development of Ceylon, the World Bank cautions against meeting an unexpected decline in export incomes with an effort to expand domestic demand by means of additional government expenditure. See *The Economic Development of Ceylon* (Baltimore: Johns Hopkins Press [for the IBRD] 1953), pp. 188–89.

fiscal policy. When foreign trade is small in relation to national product, constraints originating in the international accounts appear less quickly and carry less weight in broad policy determination. Very few of the less developed countries today enjoy the internal diversification of productive activity that is necessary if they are to be fairly independent of world trade. Markets for their primary products lie chiefly overseas, as do their main sources of manufactured goods. Their freedom to follow a fiscal policy aimed at short-run stabilization is accordingly limited both by their international position and by the practical difficulty of explaining and implementing such a contracyclical policy.

Problems of Correct Timing

The practical difficulties associated with a contracyclical policy are experienced by both advanced and less developed countries, despite the superior factual network of economic intelligence in the former group. In the United States, for example, forecasting of economic conditions is not a wholly accurate art; nor is instantaneous action on changing tax rates or expenditure programs possible. Under present conditions at least a year is normally required to get a tax bill of any breadth legislated, while discretionary changes in expenditure, although sometimes a little quicker to initiate, often take even longer to come into full effect.

The chief risk in discretionary fiscal policy is always one of poor timing. By the time tax and expenditure changes become fully effective, the phase of the cycle may have changed. Instead of suppressing the amplitude of cyclical swings, fiscal policy based primarily on short-term considerations may actually amplify these changes by inappropriate timing.

One remedy for this difficulty that has often been suggested is the substitution of what may be called formula flexibility for discretionary flexibility in fiscal policy. If enabling legislation could be secured, tax rates, for example, would automatically move when triggered by certain predetermined changes in other economic magnitudes. For example, legislation could provide, if the concept of formula flexibility were accepted, that when unemployment remained above 6 per cent of the labor force for three consecutive months, certain tax rate reductions would automatically become effective.

This or similar proposals have frequently been put forward in the United States but have always foundered on Congressional unwillingness to give up, even temporarily, its authority over tax rates. Aside from this purely political obstacle, there are those who would question the wisdom of substituting fixed rules for judgment in policymaking—in spite of the time saving in policy execution that such a course would make possible. Rules can grow obsolete and inappropriate also.

ALTERNATIVE FISCAL POLICY OBJECTIVES

Since it appears that the primary goal of fiscal policy in advanced countries, namely maintaining a high rate of employment in spite of cyclical variations, is not very practical as a guide in less developed countries, let us look at some other possible objectives that have been advanced.

Promotion of Saving

One suggestion is that the primary task of fiscal policy in less developed countries should be to raise the ratio of savings to national income.[9] This view stems from the common conception that, since successful development raises the ratio of investment (equal to saving) to the national income, operating directly to raise this ratio is a proper aim of development planning.

Taking the promotion of saving as a lodestar for fiscal policy defines, to my mind, a rather limited function for this policy; moreover, it is a function which is concerned primarily with the tax structure. Using this objective implies a tax structure that burdens consumer expenditure more than total income, and also implies making only limited efforts to advance greater income equality through taxation. On the expenditure side it emphasizes maximizing the total of both public and private investment under the prevailing constraints, since this determines actual aggregate saving. Although clearly a worthwhile objective, promotion of saving seems somewhat too narrow a goal for fiscal policy—even in a grossly underdeveloped country.

Broader Goals

In contrast to this limited objective, Walter Heller, in a United Nations report published in 1954, defined the goals of fiscal policy for the less developed countries as follows:

(1) to make available for economic development the maximum flow of human

[9]E.g., by an Indian economist, R. J. Chelliah, in his book *Fiscal Policy in Underdeveloped Countries* (New York: Macmillan Co., 1960), p. 44.

and material resources consistent with minimum consumption requirements; (2) to maintain reasonable economic stability in the face of long-run
inflationary pressure and short-run international price movements; (3) to
reduce, where they exist, the extreme inequalities in wealth, income, and
consumption standards which undermine productive efficiency, offend justice,
and endanger political stability. These objectives are not basically different
from the economic goals of allocative efficiency, economic growth, stability,
and optimum income distribution which guide fiscal policy in advanced countries on a free enterprise basis.[10]

The breadth of this statement of goals makes it difficult to find within
it unambiguous guiding principles for the application of fiscal policy in
less developed countries. Indeed, the United Nations report in which
the quoted statement appears contains few such guiding principles.

Lessening Inequality

The goal of reducing income inequality mentioned in the United
Nations statement, and found also in other views of how fiscal policy
should be applied in less developed countries, illustrates how difficult
the articulation of acceptable principles in the fiscal policy field can be.
The connection between greater equality and accelerated growth is
both indirect and tenuous.[11] It may consist primarily in convincing
people that there is a significant relationship between greater input of
effort and greater rewards. If the gains from economic development
accrue primarily to a few strategically placed individuals, ordinary
workers may not be motivated to make the extra effort that self-
perpetuating development requires.

Other writers have noted that fiscal policies aimed at greater income
equality have both good and bad effects on economic growth. For
example, Bauer and Yamey observe that:

> redistribution from the richer to the poorer members of a society is likely to
> strike at some of the most important sources of capital formation, and also to
> penalize, and hence inhibit, the exercise of special skills and initiative which
> are rare in all societies and particularly in underdeveloped ones. On the other

---

[10] *Taxes and Fiscal Policy in Underdeveloped Countries* (New York: United Nations,
1954), p. 1.

[11] For a discussion of some of the complications, see the essay "Macro-Economics of
Income Distribution," by H. G. Johnson, in *Income Redistribution and Social Policy*, ed.
A. T. Peacock (London: Cape, 1954), pp. 19–40. W. A. Lewis feels that an initial accelera-
tion in economic growth generally increases inequality, but that as growth proceeds this
inequality stabilizes and eventually begins to diminish. See his *Development Planning*
(New York: Harper & Row, 1966), p. 87.

hand, the beneficiaries of the process of redistribution, quite apart from their enlarged incomes, may become more efficient participants in economic life, although this effect is likely to be deferred.[12]

Perhaps the point that needs to be stressed is that redistribution of wealth and income may have a constructive role to play in conditioning people to make the changes necessary for economic growth. If redistribution can be confined primarily to wealth, and limited in its application to income, the negative incentive effects of this leveling may be avoided.[13]

In any country where agricultural land is an important form of wealth, and where ownership of this land is highly concentrated, the demand for land reform is apt to be urgent. This reform may be essential before any substantial improvement in agricultural productivity is possible. Without it the peasant cultivators may feel, with good cause, that additional effort merely increases the rents they pay and not their own incomes.

Many people in less developed countries are far more interested in land reform, which they can comprehend, than in economic development, which they cannot. Yet the former may offer far less scope for constructive action than the latter. The more overpopulated a country is, the greater the demand for land reform is likely to be, and the less there is to be gained from simply redistributing the available land area. By tying the two objectives of land reform and growth together, support for an economic development program may be solidified. The Nasser government has done this very successfully in Egypt, for example.

Although a fiscal policy that stresses wealth and income redistribution may conflict with one that strives to maximize savings and to give maximum encouragement to innovation, there are those who believe that all these objectives can somehow be harmonized.

---

[12]P. T. Bauer and B. S. Yamey, *The Economics of Underdeveloped Countries* (Chicago: University of Chicago Press, 1957), p. 168.

[13]W. A. Lewis takes a similar view when he notes that growth causes profits to rise, which in the past has created large fortunes in a few hands. Democratic governments, he notes, "are most suspicious of this process and very reluctant to let the capitalists make substantial profits out of economic development; on the other hand if profits are kept low, or taxed heavily, private saving will be small, and there will be little incentive for private enterprise. The Liberal way through this dilemma is to encourage private capitalists to make all the profits they can while alive, and to tax them severely when they die." See his *The Theory of Economic Growth* (London: Allen & Unwin, 1955), pp. 400–401.

Diversification

At least one other possible fiscal policy objective remains to be examined. A group of international experts meeting under United Nations auspices in 1951 defined the long-range goal of compensatory fiscal policy for the less developed countries as "the financing of developmental investments aimed at diversification of the national economy and at reducing the sensitiveness of the balance of payments."[14] According to this view, fiscal policy should be mainly occupied with encouraging the starting and growth of new industries. This approach is in harmony with the views of such students of the growth process as Kuznets, who sees a pattern of rapid expansion, followed by stabilization and decline, as the typical history of particular industries.[15] For an entire economy to grow rapidly it must have a sufficient number of new and growing industries to outweigh those in the later stages of stability or decline.

Concensus Lacking

It should be clear from the foregoing discussion (1) that the various possible guiding principles for fiscal policy in less developed countries cover a fairly broad range, and (2) that little unanimity of viewpoint is in evidence except on the broad principle that fiscal policy, in general, ought to promote investment. Nearly all students of the problem are agreed that there is less scope for contracyclical fiscal policy in underdeveloped than in more fully developed countries, and also that more emphasis should be put on longer-range objectives and on structural effects of fiscal policy in the poorer countries.

Most analysts also agree that less developed countries tend to have a chronic inflation problem—because of the sheer magnitude of public investment that is thought desirable and because of the limited fiscal capacity inherent in their traditional methods of taxation.

Incidentally, one of the more detailed problems of fiscal policy that has received considerable attention in the less developed countries is whether the budget of the central government should be separated into current and capital outlay. While many less developed countries have done this, and there are clearly some analytical advantages in it, the

---

[14] *Report of the Technical Assistance Conference on Comparative Fiscal Administration*, Geneva, July, 1951 (New York: United Nations), p. 40.

[15] Simon Kuznets, *Six Lectures on Economic Growth* (Glencoe, Ill: Free Press, 1959), pp. 33–34.

feeling among many outside observers is that this separation often furnishes an excuse for fiscal irresponsibility in a less developed country.

The income effects of public expenditure are broadly similar, whether outlay is for investment or for current operating purposes; the inflation problem, if one exists, is in no way changed by a divided expenditure budget.[16] Yet governments often take the view that there is less need to cover the capital budget by adequate taxation than to so provide for the ordinary budget. This lack of revenue cover for the capital budget is a prime contributor to chronic inflation in some countries that have adopted this budget division.

THE CHRONIC INFLATION PROBLEM

Regardless of whether they have, in fact, defined the correct goal for fiscal policy, many less developed countries do, in practice, run persistent budget deficits; these often do not lead to increasing utilization of available resources, but merely to rising prices, rapid loss of foreign exchange reserves, and flight of capital toward safer havens. Usually the underlying cause is the sheer size of the program for public investment in social overhead facilities, or what has come to be called infrastructure—in transportation, communications, power and water supply, educational facilities, public health measures, and all the other market-broadening and supporting services required for a modern industrial state.

These facilities are expensive; they do not readily attract private investment; and they are often not divisible into feasible small pieces into which strictly limited capital funds can advantageously be invested. Moreover, a balanced improvement in all these facilities is necessary to realize the full net social product they can yield.

The pressure in a country anxious to develop is always to move as rapidly and on as many fronts as possible in bringing this overhead investment up to desired levels. In this process it is easy to become overcommitted.

---

[16]Arthur Smithies, although an advocate of the split budget for less developed countries, makes the important point that what the capital budget obscures is that the government's ability to borrow depends on the relation of public to private indebtedness and on the productivity increase in the whole economy rather than on the productivity of government projects alone. Certain current expenditures may be more productive from this standpoint than some capital outlays. See his *The Budgetary Process in the United States* (New York: McGraw-Hill, 1955), pp. 459–62.

Conflicting Consequences of Inflation

It remains to examine some of the ways in which an inflationary process within a less developed country can affect growth sequences. The analysis quickly becomes confusing because we see that some effects of inflation are apparently benign toward growth while others are clearly malignant.[17] Both sets of effects are felt primarily in the private sector. Rates of public investment tend to be made according to plan, and continued more or less independently of their price consequences. The same cannot be said for the foreign-exchange consequences, which often require a reevaluation or rescheduling of development plans because of progressive deterioration in the international accounts.

When development planning is biased on the side of inflation, in the first instance rising prices will enlarge profit margins in the private sector, which will normally attract more investment. This investment, however, is quite likely to be concentrated increasingly in inventory of finished goods rather than in processes which will increase output continuously in the longer run. The more rapidly prices rise, the greater will be the pull toward quick turnover profits, against those requiring longer periods to be realized.

Traders who are experienced in the sequences of inflation may foresee future restrictions on imports which can only add shortage value to inventories, thereby increasing future profit margins on inventory investment.

The personal income increments generated by public deficits will be increasing demand broadly for all goods and services, but especially for those consumed as the level of money income rises. These are apt to be imported goods.

The upward pressure on prices may also be transmitted rather quickly to wages. Although unemployment may be substantial, there may be little or no labor surplus in particular skills or in certain geographic areas. Geographical mobility of labor may be low, owing in part to lack of information about job opportunities and in part to ingrained resistance to change.

---

[17]Dudley Seers, analyzing the inflation and growth experience of Latin American countries, concludes that "it is meaningless to set up a hypothesis that inflation helps or hinders growth. Growth and inflation are interrelated but not in any simple way." See his "A Theory of Inflation and Growth in Underdeveloped Economies," *Oxford Economic Papers*, 14, no. 2 (June, 1962):191.

Interest rates, already high in a chronically capital-scarce environment, may rise even more rapidly than final product prices, especially since the government may have to resort to techniques containing some element of compulsion in order to place the securities covering its budget deficits.

Thus a cost-push element to the inflationary process quickly develops because so few idle resources can be drawn into employment by the demand pull. Lack of supply elasticities may make the inflationary process more quickly cumulative than it is in a more advanced country.

Balanced or Unbalanced Growth?

Inflation not only raises prices unevenly; it also causes growth to become unbalanced, i.e., more rapid in some sectors, trades, and regions than in others. This is not, however, the kind of imbalance that some analysts believe to be desirable for an optimum growth process. The lack of balance they seek is among different industries.

Some students of the growth process have maintained that only a horizontally balanced improvement, occurring simultaneously in all industries, can be self-perpetuating.[18] Others have viewed the growth process as inherently and necessarily unbalanced and disorderly, in which marked improvement must first occur in one or more industries — to be subsequently diffused among the remaining, more stagnant sectors of the economy.[19]

It is not my purpose here to give a critique of the conflicting viewpoints that make up the balanced and unbalanced growth theories.[20] The balanced growth viewpoint has been instrumental in convincing many emerging countries of the need for a big push, i.e., for simultaneously developing a number of different industries, so that demand for all the newly produced goods can expand simultaneously.[21]

---

[18]One reasoned explanation of this point of view may be found in Ragnar Nurkse's *Problems of Capital Formation in Underdeveloped Countries* (New York: Oxford University Press, 1953).

[19]A good statement of the case for unbalanced growth may be found in Paul Streeten, "Unbalanced Growth," *Oxford Economic Papers*, 11, no. 2 (June, 1959):167–90.

[20]Such a critique is given by A. O. Hirschman in his book *The Strategy of Economic Development* (New Haven: Yale University Press, 1958), especially pp. 50–76. Hirschman is a critic of the balanced growth doctrine, which in general he feels has not actually been characteristic of successful growth sequences.

[21]R. Nurkse has pointed out that the idea of balanced growth is a limited one, confined to the horizontal pattern of supply and demand for consumables. It is not applicable to the relation between overhead facilities and the consumer goods sector,

continued on next page

By and large, this doctrine has exerted a strong influence for ambitious development planning, which increases the likelihood of persistent inflation. Unfortunately, the unbalanced growth doctrine, with its implied prescription to attempt a long technical leap forward in some particular industry, in hope that this will somehow pull the stagnant sectors of the economy along with it, has also been an influence for ambitious development planning.

The Strategy of Disequilibrium

There is an implication in the previous pages that mere size of a country's public investment effort is often a prime mover in generating a persistently inflationary sequence. This will be so only where a substantial part of the public outlay is deficit-financed, and where adequate inflation-repressing measures are not taken along with the expansion in public investment. If the investment is financed by adequate taxation, there will be no inflation to suppress; rather, this taxation, by falling heavily on consumption, will enable the necessary transfer of resources into investment to be made; but only rarely has the desire for development been accompanied by a correspondingly strong will to tax fiercely enough to make this development consistent with price stability.

It remains to inquire whether, by deliberate resort to the sort of disequilibrium systems that advanced countries have used for war finance, less developed countries can actually overcome the obstacles to more rapid development thrown up by unfettered operation of the price system.

The essence of this strategy of disequilibrium is to accept inflation as a necessary evil but to attempt to thwart most of its usual effects. This is commonly done by elaborating a network of direct controls—over use of foreign exchange, over prices, over investment, and over related variables that would otherwise change markedly during the inflationary process. The object is to defeat the normal economic responses to an unstabilized situation and to forestall some of the consequences, such as a rapid rise in consumer outlay or accelerated use of foreign exchange reserves.

---

[21] *continued*
which is essentially a vertical relationship. In the process of capital expansion a lack of balance in the vertical structure of production may be unavoidable or even desirable. See his essay "International Trade Theory and Development Policy," in *Economic Development for Latin America* (London: Macmillan & Co., 1962), p. 250.

Chapter 3

Effects of Direct Controls

The difficulty with this course of action is that it is frequently impossible to administer the required direct controls with reasonable equity; moreover, the mere effort to do so detracts attention from development itself, and from the changes that ought to accompany it. What value is there, e.g., in freezing relative prices when they ought to be changing because of the supply alterations that result from, and that need to accompany, growth? What is the value of limiting foreign remittances if funds seeking to go abroad are forced instead to take illegal channels?

In a war economy there is present a sense of dedication to a common purpose that insures a minimum level of compliance with direct controls, irritating as they may be. This same dedication to economic development is not usually present; moreover, opportunities to avoid controls are ordinarily greater in the less than in the more developed countries.

Despite the difficulty of repressing inflation, country after country has taken this route in its search for accelerated development. Perhaps some countries have done so because they have underestimated the amount of public investment necessary to start a cumulative growth sequence, or because they have overestimated their ability to raise taxes or to draw additional resources into employment by raising effective demand. Once caught in the inflationary spiral, there frequently remains the possibility of being rescued by foreign aid or, failing such a rescue, of seeking stabilization by devaluation and by cutting back public capital outlay.

Consequences of an Inflation Gap

Perhaps the worst feature of a development program financed by inflationary means is the damage that it does to a country's trade and financial position vis-à-vis the rest of the world. As internal prices rise, exporting becomes progressively less profitable, while imports are sought more eagerly because of higher incomes and rising consumption standards. Inflation turns the terms of trade against the inflating country in much the same way that a fall in export prices originating abroad would. As foreign exchange reserves decline, international credit becomes harder to secure on favorable terms, while capital outflow is encouraged, if a fixed exchange rate is maintained.

An inflationary process that is successful in raising the volume of investment must also reduce consumption, although not necessarily by an equal amount. Since the inflation produces a shift to profit, consumption by groups other than profit receivers is apt to be reduced by less than the investment expansion.[22] Moreover, the net investment induced by the inflation is only a fraction of the total investment financed by inflationary means. Some increase in net saving can perhaps be obtained, but it is only the difference between the additional saving of those groups benefiting from the inflation—which in turn is only a fraction of their additional income—and the dissaving of those groups injured by the inflation.

A policy of raising net investment by inflationary financing must also be successful in keeping wages down. This is largely the mechanism by which the necessary restriction in consumption is obtained. Whether workers can be persuaded or compelled to accept progressively lower real incomes without reducing their input into the productive process depends on how weak their bargaining position is and on whether retreat into the subsistence sector of the economy, which is injured relatively less by the process of inflation, is a practical alternative. One marginal effect of inflation is to draw labor back into the subsistence sector, already oversupplied with workers, at a time when the growth process itself requires a continuing shift of labor away from the subsistence- toward the market-oriented, money economy sectors.

The predisposition toward financing at least part of public investment by inflationary methods is undoubtedly present in many less developed countries, especially those that lack sufficient revenue flexibility in their tax systems. This predisposition results from the very human desire to invest enough to offset population increase and to begin catching up with the higher income countries. It also results from a tendency to view development too exclusively in terms of raising the quantity of capital formation, while neglecting other necessary ingredients of the growth process such as increasing skill, adaptation to more advanced technology, accelerated innovation, and improved mobility of resources.

CONCLUSION CONCERNING BUDGET RULES

It appears that, since the objectives of fiscal policy are not always the same in different countries, budgetary rules of thumb are not likely to

---

[22]Cf. E. M. Bernstein and I. G. Patel, "Inflation in Relation to Economic Development," International Monetary Fund *Staff Papers*, 2, no. 3 (November, 1952): 381.

be very helpful. Fiscal policy in less developed countries is properly oriented less toward the short-run, contracyclical objectives that guide this policy in advanced countries and more toward the longer-range goals, among which accelerated growth is prominent. This being the case, the microeconomic effects of fiscal policy, including the structure of the tax system and the character of public expenditures, are apt to be relatively more important than the overall balance between revenue and expenditure.

Keynesian deficit finance will not work efficiently in most less developed countries because supply inelasticities prevent the chief response to a rise in aggregate demand from taking the form of higher employment rather than higher prices. Underdeveloped countries are more prone to inflation than more advanced countries because of less flexible revenue systems, greater pressure for public investment, and greater dependence on international trade. Greater conservatism should therefore characterize the fiscal policies of poorer countries than those of nations with higher levels of income.

Instead of looking to deficit finance to underwrite large programs of public investment, less developed countries should rather be concerned to minimize budget deficits, chiefly by heavier taxation of consumption. This need not involve personal income taxation but may be accomplished by selective sales and excise taxes, with the highest rates applying to the least-necessary products. These taxes alone, however, are unlikely to build sufficient yield flexibility into the revenue structure. Other taxes are needed; some of the possibilities will be examined in detail in a later chapter.

If a budgetary rule is to be followed, and perhaps no such rule should be stressed overmuch in the essentially pragmatic search for growth, the old conventional rule of annual budgetary balance is perhaps the one best suited to maintain a self-perpetuating growth sequence. There would be advantages, from the standpoint of growth in the private sector, in occasional budgetary surpluses, provided these could be obtained without too radically limiting the amount of public investment; but few of the poorer countries have such productive tax systems.

Only countries that rely heavily on export taxation at progressive rates and that experience unusually favorable export markets can ordinarily expect to generate budget surpluses, and these only spasmodically. Budgetary surpluses, if realizable, do nevertheless constitute public savings that can offset larger private investment.

The annual balance rule has the additional merit of making clear the costs of development programs, since these costs must be financed immediately. A group of American economists, writing in 1949, put the case for a balanced budget this way:

> Annual budget balancing is thus both difficult in practice and unsound in principle (for the U.S.). But one great merit it does have; it provides a yardstick by which legislators and the people can scrutinize every activity of government, testing it both for efficiency of operation and for its worthwhileness in terms of cost. Every government program undertaken has to be paid for in a clear and unequivocal sense. The Legislature and the Executive are required to justify additional taxes equal to the cost of any new program. This is a principle every citizen can understand.[23]

This kind of discipline may be even more important for a less developed country than for one such as the United States.

Perhaps one should not expect to define a general budgetary rule that will give accurate policy guidance. According to one authority, such rules either turn out to be empty or arbitrary.[24] Especially for less developed countries, where conditions vary so widely, such rules are doubly hard to articulate. About all one can say is that no better rule than that of annual budgetary balance comes readily to hand, and that the less developed a country is, the more it apparently needs to practice a conservative financial policy.

Contracyclical fiscal policy is a luxury for the more advanced countries; it is not a practical way of accelerating the growth process in a country that is just getting cumulative growth started.

[23] *American Economic Review*, December, 1949, p. 1263.
[24] P. A. Samuelson, "Principles and Rules in Modern Fiscal Policy," in *Money, Trade, and Economic Growth: In Honor of J. H. Williams* (New York: Macmillan Co., 1951), p. 175.

4

Foreign Aid and Private Capital Imports

The only capital resources from outside a country that are normally available for financing economic development are those received from friendly foreign governments as aid (both grants and loans); from international institutions such as the IBRD as loans; or as private investment from foreign business firms in search of profits. There are other possible means of access to external development resources, such as successful wars of conquest, but I shall ignore these and proceed on the assumption that a country seeks to develop by peaceful means.

Aid, international loans, and private investment are sources not only of the capital necessary for development but also of the technical skill, or "know-how," which can be so vital in transforming a backward economy. One of the elements necessary for a takeoff into sustained growth (to use Rostow's somewhat unfortunate figure of speech), and to determine whether such a takeoff represents a real possibility for many emerging countries, is a series of demonstrations showing that newer methods are, in fact, significantly more productive than traditional methods. Foreigners are often in a good position to supply these demonstrations, although the appropriate lessons must be drawn from them by local businessmen and local workers in the developing country.

Political Basis of Foreign Aid

Foreign aid is at best a small and uncertain source of capital for economic development; in the past its availability has been relatively unrelated to the efforts a country is itself making for economic development. Aid has been extended on the basis of complex political considerations—in which resistance against Communism, strategic location, and other geopolitical or ideological factors have usually counted for

76

more than economic policy.[1] Those countries receiving the largest relative amounts of aid have been politically divided, actually engaged in hostilities, or on the brink of war. Without law and order, or stability of government, and lacking the possibility or the determination to give development a high priority in the scheme of things, little economic growth is likely.

The volume of foreign aid has been very unequally distributed among the different countries that are seeking to develop. This is clear from Table 2, which shows regional allocations of United States economic aid. Military assistance is excluded. Certain countries not strategically located have received only intellectual aid or technical assistance; others have had massive infusions of capital in the forms of grants or loans for general economic support; often this support has been unrelated to specific development programs but intended only in some general way to keep a troubled economy afloat. Certain neutral countries have accepted aid both from the West and from the Communist bloc, perhaps hoping thereby to get the best of both worlds and at the same time to retain their unaligned political status.

United States economic aid has been aimed primarily at preventing individual countries from falling within the influence of Communist

TABLE 2
UNITED STATES FOREIGN ECONOMIC ASSISTANCE
(In Billions of Dollars)

	Near East and S. Asia	Latin America	Far East	Africa	Europe	Other	Total
Total Postwar	17.3	9.4	16.2	3.0	30.3	4.9	81.2
1962–64 Average	1.8	1.1	.8	.5	.3	.4	4.9
1965	1.7	1.3	.7	.3	.2	.4	4.6
Loans	1.3	.8	.2	.1	.2	*	2.6
Grants	.4	.5	.5	.2	*	.4	2.0
Repayments and Interest							
Total Postwar	1.3	2.5	.8	.3	7.1	.1	12.2
1965	.3	.3	.2	*	.2	*	1.0

*Less than $50 million.
SOURCE: Agency for International Development. Printed in January, 1966, in *Economic Report of the President* (Washington, D.C.: Government Printing Office), p. 303.

[1] In a study of United States foreign aid George Liska describes the present allocation as one of "studied ambiguity and mutually contradictory declarations." Cf. his *The New Statecraft* (Chicago: University of Chicago Press, 1960), pp. 198–99.

dictatorships, and only secondarily at assisting growth within the recipient countries. The United States aid missions abroad have been unable to make the long-run commitments necessary for sustained growth, since United States aid funds are appropriated annually.[2] Recipient countries, for their part, have been well aware that their political orientation, rather than the improving of their economic prospects, has been the main object of economic aid from the United States and the other Western nations. Often, recipient countries have actively resisted efforts to plan in an orderly fashion for development and thus to lessen their dependence on aid receipts once they have progressed to a critical point (such as the takeoff into self-perpetuating growth) on their own. Countries that have voluntarily terminated foreign aid have done so either because they were temporarily prosperous (Burma) or because they have wished to be strictly neutral in the cold war.

VOLUME OF AID AND PRIVATE CAPITAL FUNDS

According to OECD tabulations, in the years 1956–59, total aid and private capital flows from the West to the underdeveloped countries ranged from $6 to $8 billion per year. Of this total amount, a little more than one-half has been provided by the United States; the remainder by the more than twenty other countries that adhere to the OECD. France has been the largest European contributor, closely followed by the United Kingdom. Germain aid to less developed countries has amounted to less than half that of France and to about two-thirds that of Britain. By 1963, free world countries other than the United States were contributing $2.5 billion annually through their own bilateral aid programs. Total free world aid to the less developed countries reached $8.4 billion, of which $1.2 billion was channeled through international agencies.[3] In 1964 the total figure remained about the same. The distribution by donor countries that are members of the OECD and that

[2]An AID mission director expressed United States participation in the development planning process of countries we are aiding in these highly revealing words: "The extent and nature of the American participation in the formulation of the country's development plans often is determined, not by any thoroughly considered doctrine as to the function of foreign advisors, but rather by the personal relations which exist between members of the American group and key national officials." Alvin Roseman, "An American Aid Mission Director's View of Technical Cooperation," *Annals of the American Academy of Political and Social Science*, 323 (May, 1959):4.

[3]*The Foreign Assistance Program*, Annual Report of AID to Congress for Fiscal 1963 (Washington, D.C.: Government Printing Office, 1964), p. 3.

TABLE 3
DISBURSEMENTS OF LONG-TERM FINANCIAL RESOURCES TO LESS
DEVELOPED COUNTRIES FROM NATIONS OF THE OECD, 1964
(In Millions of Dollars)

Country	Net Official Government Aid	Private Long-Term Investment	Private Export Credits of Over 5 Yrs.	Total
Austria	13.1	1.4	.8	15.3
Belgium	80.0	49.6	6.5	136.1
Canada	128.8	20.3	—	149.1
Denmark	11.0	2.2	8.1	21.3
France	841.4	334.5	99.9	1288.6
Germany	459.5	194.2	89.9	743.6
Italy	56.0	75.1	28.8	159.9
Japan	178.4	80.4	18.7	277.5
Netherlands	49.1	50.2	22.7	122.0
Norway	17.0	5.2	3.4	25.6
Portugal	62.8	—	—	62.8
United Kingdom	490.5	210.0	98.7	799.2
United States	3534.0	1303.0	12.0	4849.0
Totals	5921.3	2338.9	389.5	8649.7

SOURCE: Compiled by the OECD and reprinted in Seymour J. Rubin, *The Conscience of the Rich Nations* (New York: Harper & Row, 1966), Appendix.

coordinate their efforts through its Development Assistance Committee is shown in Table 3.

Table 3 includes long-term private export credits, which are not always regarded as resources for development proper. (Figures quoted for earlier years exclude these exporter credits.) The figures refer to aid and private capital exports in all forms (grants as well as loans); contributions through multilateral agencies such as the United Nations; and direct bilateral help. Both direct and portfolio investment are included in private capital exports.[4] Excluded are military assistance and also short-term loans made originally for periods of one year or less. The figures do, however, include loan funds disbursed by the IBRD and other worldwide lending agencies such as the IDB.

Although the flow of financial resources to less developed countries has increased somewhat in recent years, this increase has been less than

[4]OECD, *The Flow of Financial Resources to Countries in the Course of Economic Development* (Paris: OECD, 1961).

proportional to the expansion in gross national products of the aid-supplying countries. Thus they have fallen somewhat farther behind the 1 per cent of GNP target which has sometimes been used to fix a norm for development resources during the 1960's. The sum $6 to $8 billion per year is large, but when it is spread among all the recipient less developed countries it becomes, though still significant, a minor source of needed development capital.

Capital Requirements for Development

Development capital requirements of the less developed countries are clearly enormous and cannot be estimated with any precision; they must be fixed arbitrarily on the basis of certain stated assumptions. A group of United Nations experts in 1950 calculated that to transfer 1 per cent of the working population of less developed countries each year from agricultural to nonagricultural employment, and to invest each year 4 per cent of the national incomes of these countries in agricultural improvement, would take more than $19 billion of annual investment. This figure made no allowance for public utility investments such as transport, communications, and power and was therefore incomplete. It would also be considerably higher today.

An FAO report in 1949 placed the investment needs of less developed countries at about $17 billion per year, based on these countries' own development plans, which varied considerably in the amount of progress they envisaged. Most of these plans have since been revised upward so that this figure, if calculated today, would also be much larger. Pierre Moussa, a French economist, figures that $30 billion per year is a feasible minimum amount.[5]

Manifestly, the bulk of the funds to finance development have to be raised locally, through taxation or borrowing. Moreover, aid will not flow indefinitely. The United States Congress is increasingly reluctant each year to continue foreign aid appropriations, although each year it is solemnly assured by the Administration, whether Democratic or Republican, that this outlay is vital to United States foreign policy. Other western countries have somewhat analogous difficulties in securing aid funds via the legislative process.

Private Investment

Private portfolio and direct investment, which is also included in the annual $6 to $8 billion figure, has been considerably smaller than

[5]See his *The Underprivileged Nations* (Boston: Beacon Press, 1963), chap. 9.

government aid. In the years 1956–59, investments and loans by United States nationals in less developed countries averaged just over $1 billion per year, while investments by nationals of European countries averaged nearly $1.6 billion.

Much of private foreign investment is concentrated in the extractive industries, especially oil. This may be seen in the fact that about one-half the dividends and interest paid abroad to private interests by the less developed countries comes from the big three oil producers, Iran, Iraq, and Venezuela.

United States private foreign investment has fluctuated more widely than has that of European countries.[6] At the end of 1961 this private investment had a book value of over $55 billion and returned nearly $3 billion per year in earnings. The $55 billion gross value represented the net result of all past years. By the end of 1965, United States private investment abroad had increased to nearly $71 billion, and earnings to nearly $5.4 billion. Of this total, direct investment in operating facilities accounted for nearly $50 billion, while the balance of $21 billion was portfolio investment, largely in foreign securities.

The distribution of United States direct investment abroad, by region and by type of facilities, is shown in Table 4.

TABLE 4
U.S. PRIVATE DIRECT INVESTMENT ABROAD, END OF 1965
(In Billions of Dollars)

Region	Mining	Petroleum	Manu-facturing	Public Utilities	Trade	Other	Total
Canada	1.7	3.3	6.9	.5	.9	1.9	15.2
Latin America	1.1	3.1	2.7	.6	1.0	.8	9.4
Other Western Hemisphere	.2	.5	.2	*	.1	.3	1.3
Europe	.1	3.4	7.6	.1	1.7	1.1	13.9
Africa	.4	1.0	.3	*	.1	.1	1.9
Asia	*	2.4	.7	.1	.3	.2	3.6
Oceania	.2	.5	.9	*	.1	.1	1.8
International	*	1.1	*	.9	*	*	2.0
Totals	3.8	15.3	19.3	2.1	4.2	4.5	49.2

*Less than $50 million.
SOURCE: United States Department of Commerce, *Survey of Current Business*, September, 1966, p. 34.

[6] *Ibid. passim*

Chapter 4

It is apparent from Table 4 that United States private investment in less developed countries is extremely small. For example, aside from petroleum the total accumulated United States private investment in all the countries of Africa and Asia is only about $2 billion. Clearly, this is not a major source of capital for development.

Portfolio investment is even more highly concentrated than direct investment in the more industrialized foreign countries. This may be seen in Table 5.

TABLE 5
LONG-TERM PORTFOLIO INVESTMENTS ABROAD BY U.S. NATIONALS
AND ENTERPRISES, END OF 1965
(In Billions of Dollars)

Area	Foreign Bonds	Foreign Stocks	Banking Claims	Other Securities	Total
Western Europe	.9	2.1	1.7	.8	5.4
Canada	5.8	2.9	.1	.7	9.5
Latin America	.7	.1	1.2	.4	2.4
Other foreign countries	1.5	.2	1.3	.2	3.3
International institutions and unallocated	1.1	—	—	—	1.1
Totals	10.1	5.0	4.3	2.0	21.6

SOURCE: United States Department of Commerce, *Survey of Current Business*, September, 1966, p. 40.

Table 5 shows that investment in Canadian securities and claims accounts for about 45 per cent of all United States private portfolio foreign investment. Apart from banking institutions, few United States businesses or individuals hold foreign securities extensively.

Government Aid in Relative Terms

Although foreign aid has come to be quite a heavy burden on the United States, and also on the western European countries providing it, the amount of aid, in proportion to the gross development capital requirements of the less developed countries, is so small that it represents, at best, a marginal contribution to growth. As one writer has pointed out, apart from a few favored countries such as South Korea, South Vietnam, and Taiwan, external aid has averaged only $1 to $2 per year per head of population and no more than 1 per cent of national income in most of the recipient countries, small as their national incomes are.[7] These figures clearly reinforce the views, already stated, that the bulk of savings for economic development must be obtained internally, and that foreign aid cannot be expected to meet more than a very small fraction of total development capital requirements.

It has often been suggested that, since foreign aid is so small relative to the aggregate capital requirements for successful development, its amount should be increased; but this suggestion seems unrealistic. The political resistances in the aid disbursing countries to a massive expansion in help to the poorer countries are such that doubling the amount of aid, for example, which would still leave aid a minor source of capital for development, is quite out of the question. On the contrary, the trend in recent years has been to reduce aid and to put more of the reduced flow that has been provided on a repayable basis.[8] Loans have replaced grants not only in the United States aid program but also in the aid programs of other countries.

The small amount of foreign aid available to underdeveloped countries as a group should not cause us to overlook the fact that in certain countries aid has dominated the economy and has been an important influence in preventing either chaos or stagnation. Laos and South Vietnam, for example, have received far more economic aid in proportion to population or to growth potential than have most other countries.

Even where aid is not a major source of capital for development, it may be of critical importance as a catalyst in getting the development process started. Aid-giving countries never expected to do more than prime the pump, or start a process of investment that would eventually pick up its own momentum. Less developed countries, for their part, cannot reasonably expect any significant part of their development to be externally financed. The real mass of capital for development must come from internal savings, either generated voluntarily in the private sector or forced as public savings by taxation and use of the proceeds for public or private investment.

[7] Frederic Benham, *Economic Aid to Underdeveloped Countries* (London: Oxford University Press, 1961), p. 42.

[8] Robert Asher has pointed out that there is no necessary connection between the financial terms on which the United States makes aid available to a foreign country and the terms on which such aid subsequently becomes available to the business enterprises and private citizens in the country aided. Cf. his *Grants, Loans, and Local Currencies* (Washington, D.C.: Brookings Institution, 1961), p. 121.

Chapter 4

Problems of Aid Administration

The United States foreign aid program has been criticized on many scores—unclear objectives, maladministration, lack of a clear philosophy of development, not relating aid to the recipient country's own efforts, and so on. I have no intention of inquiring into these charges or the corresponding defenses. Some mistakes have certainly been made, as was perhaps inevitable in any large program of this nature, mounted with insufficient preparation and often on a crisis basis. The main purpose of aid programs has always been strategic and political—as already noted.

Measures of Effectiveness

There have been some notable successes in aid programs and some equally notable failures. So far as influencing the rate of economic growth in less developed countries, the total effect of foreign aid has undoubtedly been quite small. Given the magnitude of the task, no other result could reasonably have been expected.

When foreign aid has been received in large volume, some of the recipient countries have become dependent upon it; they have sometimes been slow to make the economic adjustments that would enable aid to be reduced and finally eliminated altogether. This dependence on aid is a danger that can perhaps be avoided by using the political leverage created by aid disbursements to persuade recipient governments of the necessity for following a consistent set of sound economic policies, so that the growth process can actually become self-sustaining.[9] Lacking adherence to these policies, any diminution in foreign aid will simply allow traditional societies to remain static, instead of generating the dynamism and making the shifts in resources that development demands. The United States is possibly less effective in its aid programs than it could be partly because it has hesitated to influence economic policies in recipient countries in a broad way, although individual aid technicians have not always exhibited similar scruples.[10]

[9] P. T. Bauer has noted that giving foreign aid necessarily draws the donor country into the internal politics of the recipient country. See his *Indian Economic Policy and Development* (New York: Praeger, 1961), pp. 120–21.

[10] Daniel Wit has suggested that "the critical test of a foreign aid program is not whether it has succeeded in bribing foreign governments of questionable effectiveness and uncertain local support, but whether it has been able to generate development and thereby to assist a country to achieve self-sustaining growth." See his article "A New Strategy for Foreign Economic Aid," *Orbis*, 7, no. 4 (Winter, 1964): 800–820.

If economic aid is actually designed to trigger a self-sustaining sequence of economic development, it ought to be based rather firmly on some theory concerning the operation of the development process; it ought also to be applied at points where multiplied effects of the aid infusions are most likely to be secured. When one looks at what has been done in the United States aid programs to particular countries, and within these countries by the aid missions, it is hard to avoid the conclusion that a general philosophy of growth has been lacking; too often aid has been granted on a patchwork, hit-or-miss basis in which considerable waste and lost motion have been inevitable.[11] There have indeed been individual country programs; but these have often been worked out as devices to secure appropriations, or in terms of what recipient countries think they needed or were prepared to accept, rather than what they actually required to start or sustain the development process.

Content of Aid Programs

Nearly every aid program which the United States has supported has contained some technical assistance for agriculture and public health as well as some outlay for education, often initially for teacher training, to be later supplemented by building schools, supplying instructional materials, and the like. Both agricultural improvement and basic education are essential to the development process; both are also long-range, relatively slow payoff investments that require many years to yield their full benefits.[12]

In countries where aid infusions have been relatively large, e.g., South Korea and Laos, aid has also taken many other forms—such as supplying essential imports of consumer goods, building factories, roads, electric power generating facilities, and other investments in infrastructure. Very often there has been little if any discernible relation

[11]J. D. Montgomery has made the point that in recent years we in the United States have presumed to offer advice to less developed countries only because we make a distinction between political and technical. This distinction is not appreciated in some other cultures so that advice we consider politically sterile sometimes sounds to the foreigner like an invasion of national sovereignty. This may be a common cultural barrier to effective intellectual aid. See his article "Crossing the Culture Bars," *World Politics*, 13 (1961): 544–60.

[12]Agricultural improvement may pay off both quickly and handsomely when new methods are actually adopted on a broad scale. The slowness comes in really bringing about changes in agricultural practice on this broad scale when producing units are relatively numerous. It is slowness in adopting new methods rather than the productivity of these methods that is the main problem.

between the amount of aid the United States has poured in and the resulting development. Inevitably, the United States taxpayer begins to wonder whether aid to certain countries, however much they may be threatened by a Communist menace, is actually a prudent investment.

As many writers have pointed out, there are two distinct categories of less developed countries—those that are overpopulated and those that are not. The policies that will work for the second group are not at all appropriate for the first group. Countries with excessive and rapidly growing populations need industrialization as an outlet for surplus labor forces that cannot constructively be employed in agriculture; countries with unused land, or land that could use more labor applied creatively to it, have less necessity to develop an industrial sector. Among countries with which the present writer is familiar at firsthand, Egypt is an example of an overpopulated country; Burma is not overpopulated in relation to the available natural resources (arable land, water, forests, minerals, etc.).

AID AND AGRICULTURAL PRODUCTIVITY

Even in countries where population pressure on resources makes industrialization a necessity, the path to industrial growth, as noted in an earlier chapter, may lie in the first instance through improvements in the agricultural sector. We have already seen that in the early stages of development a smaller agricultural labor force must produce more food and fiber if a growing industrial and urban population is to be sustained.[13] Failing this, part of the food supply must be imported at a time when costly imports of industrial equipment are necessary for the growing manufacturing sector. The result of this two-pronged advance in imports will almost certainly be a balance-of-payments crisis that will limit further development. Avoiding this kind of crisis is one reason for concentrating initial development investment heavily in the export sector.

Unfortunately, even the countries that are not overpopulated often entertain aspirations toward industrialization, similar to those found in the overpopulated countries; this in spite of the fact that some of the

---

[13]That there is a natural progression to economic development is a very old idea in economic thought. Jean Bodin, a French lawyer, political philosopher, and early writer on fiscal policy, observed in 1583 that "according to the natural course of things, therefore, the greater part of the capital of every growing society is first directed to agriculture, afterwards to manufactures, and last of all to foreign commerce." See his *The Six Books of a Commonweale*, trans. R. Knolles (London: G. Bishop, 1606), bk. 3, chap. 1.

highest income countries of the free world are strongly agricultural. Australia, New Zealand, Denmark, and Holland are obvious examples.

Barriers to Progress

Although United States aid programs have consistently recognized the desirability of organizing a rapid advance in agricultural productivity as an initial step toward sustained economic growth, they have usually found it very difficult to achieve this result. Less developed countries commonly lack well-functioning agricultural extension services, efficient marketing cooperatives, and adequate sources of farm credit; and the level of literacy among the rural population is usually low. Facilities should be built up, not according to the American pattern, but according to one that is specially suited to local conditions. This buildup necessarily takes considerable time.

The practices that will bring this spurt in agricultural productivity include better seeding and fertilizing techniques, improved methods of livestock culture, proper crop rotation, and the like. All these have a fairly low capital-output ratio, i.e., they require relatively little investment in proportion to the potential increases in output; but they raise marketing problems, especially when staple products are exported in competition with products of other countries. When world demand for a particular agricultural material is relatively inelastic, efforts to increase output of that material in one country that is an important supplier may merely reduce world prices to the point where investments in agricultural improvement have a relatively low payoff.

The remedy for this situation, so far as a single exporting country is concerned, is quality improvement and gradual diversification of agriculture so that the export earnings no longer depend exclusively on one or two staple crops.

Aid programs that seek to raise agricultural productivity have usually concentrated on relatively small-scale demonstration projects, designed to show farmers new techniques, new crops, and improved practices that will raise their incomes. It is necessary in such projects to organize convincing demonstrations that will appeal to relatively uneducated, conservative people and to show them to as many farmers as possible. Even when they are convinced of the advantages of the new methods, ordinary farmers cannot apply them without access to credit and necessary supplies.

In many overpopulated countries, the typical farm may be so small that mechanization and other large-capital methods are uneconomic.

United States agricultural practice today is designed primarily to economize on labor by employing more capital equipment. Less developed countries may well have more to learn from Japanese agricultural methods, which have remained relatively labor-intensive, than from the extensive cultivation practices of the United States, Canada, and other countries where agricultural land is relatively abundant. We come again to the point that transplanting the methods of an advanced country to one less advanced will simply not work. There must be constructive adaptation to local conditions and to the local price-wage structure.

AID AND INDUSTRIALIZATION

When industrialization is being planned, whether or not assisted by foreign aid, one initial problem is often the very limited home market for manufactured goods within the developing country. Another problem is the finding and backing of local entrepreneurs who can successfully "miniaturize" manufacturing processes so as to produce goods for local consumption at competitive prices.[14]

Although planners may assign rough priorities to specific industries to be developed in the private sector, and may provide incentives for particular kinds of investment, there must be adequate provision for local entrepreneurial initiative in factoring out business opportunities that may or may not correspond precisely with the planners' priorities.[15] Ideally, planning for the private enterprise sector should indicate priorities only in the broadest terms; it should assist the starting of new ventures with information, credit, and absence of regulation, consistent with the broad social priorities established, by anyone having the talent and the experience necessary to create a successful new business.

Development banks have an important role to play in this process. They may, indeed, be the principal institution of contact between the government and the emerging entrepreneurial class. The dangers of

[14]N. S. Buchanan and H. S. Ellis have pointed out that Japan's experience in industrial development provides a constructive example of how possession of a large sector of small scale enterprise may give an initial impulse to industrialization. See their *Approaches to Economic Development* (New York: Twentieth Century Fund, 1955), pp. 278–79.

[15]Milton Friedman remarked in the course of a general condemnation of United States economic aid, "If anything is clear from widespread experience with governmental economic activity, it is that a governmental venture, once established, is seldom abandoned. And surely it is almost as clear that governmental officials are less experimental, less flexible, less adaptive, than private individuals risking their own funds." See his paper "Foreign Economic Aid: Means and Objectives," in *The United States and the Developing Economies*, ed. G. Ranis (New York: Norton, 1964), p. 31.

overplanning for the private sector are very real and ought to be resisted, if this sector is to play a truly dynamic role in the growth process.

The pattern of foreign aid best calculated to help emerging countries develop economically appears to be one offering much intellectual assistance (of a rather discriminating nature), but relatively little money, which at best can amount to only an incremental portion of the needed capital. The politically oriented United States aid program has often reversed this emphasis—a fact which may partially account for the disrepute into which the program has fallen, so far as particular countries are concerned.

Deft technical assistance requires the recruitment of somewhat unusual persons, who combine missionary zeal with enough flexibility of mind to recognize that adaptation rather than transplantation is the task at hand. Needless to say, these qualities are not easy to find; nor have they always been embodied in the field personnel actually selected.

AID AND FISCAL POLICY

Since my main theme in this study is fiscal policy, the bearing of foreign aid upon this policy in the recipient country is a subject that needs to be examined carefully. Because fiscal policy lies so near the heart of the political program of a government, there is always a delicate question involved: how much and in what way is an aid-giving country justified in influencing the economic policies of a recipient country?[16] The promise to expand aid or the threat to withhold it can be a powerful force in influencing administrations, especially in poor countries.

Unresolved Issues

I am not suggesting that the United States should use its aid program to create economic colonies, foster a new imperialism, or influence arbitrarily the policies of recipient countries in order to advance United States interests. To do this would be to reinforce local suspicions that

---

[16]G. Ranis has suggested that the United States should require recipient countries to free their foreign exchange markets and allow all claimants to compete on an impersonal, price-determined basis for foreign currency. He feels that this and more nearly equal access to internal bank loans would enable small business in the developing countries to complete more effectively, and that consequently, more growth would be produced. See his article "The Crisis in Foreign Aid," *Yale Review*, Summer, 1964, pp. 522–32.

all United States aid has an underlying selfish motive. I am suggesting, rather, that if we used *Realpolitik* more discriminately, yet with greater vigor in the issues selected, we might at the same time obtain more credit for the substantial element of altruism that is actually present in United States economic aid to less developed countries, paradoxical as this statement may sound.

At any rate, the constant redirection and reorganization of United States aid programs through the years indicate we have yet to evolve a settled philosophy toward foreign aid and toward its place in our own foreign economic policy. The fact remains that, even with a flow of $6 to $8 billion a year toward the less developed countries, the induced growth in these countries has been both modest and uncertain; consequently the disparity in per capita income between the advanced and the less advanced countries is annually growing wider instead of narrower.

The United States cannot continue the present or a larger outflow of aid indefinitely without endangering its balance-of-payments position even more, or without generating a new isolationist revolt in its political orientation. We are in the unfortunate position of being neither able to do the job adequately nor able to desist from doing it inadequately. Our Western allies, particularly Germany, should properly be carrying more of the burden than they do; whether they can be brought to assume a larger share is an open question.

The United States, as a minimum, ought in its aid program to reward in a tangible way countries which pursue sound fiscal policies calculated to promote economic growth, and to penalize countries which openly embrace inflation and inadequate budgetary controls. Actually, we do almost the opposite. A country that has gotten itself into financial arrears can often count on our aid to extricate it; indeed, to perpetuate the faulty arrangements that led to the problem in the first place. We have done little to promote fiscal rectitude in Laos or Korea and have given only minimal aid to countries such as Malaysia which have tried to steer a conservative financial course toward sustained growth. On balance this accords ill with the image we seek to create—that the United States is actively trying to help the developing countries to progress through their own efforts.

In setting up intellectual assistance to less developed countries, the United States has been far more prompt to provide grazing experts, teachers, or soil classification specialists than it has budget analysts or tax policy advisers. This is not to deny that all kinds of experts can be useful and can have a productive place in the scheme of technical assistance. It does suggest, however, that it is possible to be overly concerned with the details of economic development and to neglect the central policy measures that establish the framework within which such development becomes plausible. The government structure and policies in a poor country may be even more of a barrier to growth than peasant conservatism or lack of a vigorous entrepreneurial class. Iran is a case in point.[17]

Shortcomings in Financial Policy

In each of the four less developed countries in which I have worked as an adviser, economic development was the avowed goal of the administration, and development plans had been drawn up. I was much impressed, however, by the facts (1) that the Ministries of Finance had little understanding of the role finance should play in facilitating the growth process, and (2) that these Ministries even displayed some lack of empathy for the aspirations of the administration. Only in Iran was the Ministry served by foreign technicians with a broad appreciation of development finance or fiscal policy. The only request to the United States government for technical assistance in the financial area made by any of the other three countries (Egypt, Burma, and Costa Rica) during the period of my experience was for help in customs administration.

I do not know whether these particular countries were typical of less developed countries generally; hopefully they were not. None has made noteworthy progress toward its economic goals, although failure to take financial advice is merely one among many reasons for this lack of progress. The point to be stressed is, rather, that each country was receiving considerable technical assistance from the United States, and two of the countries were receiving substantial grant aid in addition; yet no direct effort was made by the United States government systematically to influence fiscal or budgetary policy in the recipient country, although in each case this policy was palpably inadequate to the demands of economic development.

[17]Iranian government procedures are unnecessarily complex, resulting in an unusually large bureaucracy. For example, the Iranian Ministry of Finance, in proportion to population, is about 15 times as large as the United States Treasury Dept. To receive payment for supplies routinely provided the Iranian government, vouchers and other documents must pass through more than 100 individual hands, resulting in considerable delay and an inevitable increase in the cost of government purchases.

The view that the developing countries need financial advice is further buttressed by the United Nations' appraisal of development programming and administration in Latin America, where, in virtually every country, it found the budgetary process to be inadequate, antiquated, incomplete, or lacking in some other significant respect. Repeated attempts have been made by the United Nations Technical Assistance Administration to supply advisory help in government finance. In this respect, at least, they appear to be more forward-looking than the United States government.

Countries that have newly attained their independence may be somewhat reluctant to ask for help in financial policy formulation and administration, because they are emotionally prone to associate supervision in finance with colonial status. Yet these same countries have shown no reluctance about asking for help in establishing and operating central banks; these institutions are at least as sensitive in some policy respects as are Ministries of Finance. The fault, if fault there be, probably lies as much with the United States, for failure strongly to urge help in financial administration upon the countries it is assisting, as it does with the recipient countries themselves.

The financial aspect of economic development is so important that countries which follow unsound financial policies risk their entire development effort in the process. I am not speaking solely of inflation in this connection. We have already seen that some countries are able to grow in spite of rapid inflation while others stagnate with monetary stability. Still other countries have experienced rapid inflation and no growth while yet a fourth group of countries has combined rapid growth with stability. All intermediate combinations of results are also to be found in recent experience. I am speaking, rather, of the whole complex of tax and expenditure policies which may either accelerate growth or retard it. The appropriate kind of tax system and the proper expenditure programming can contribute greatly to growth whether or not the overall budget is in balance.

Needed Reforms in Expenditure and Tax Policies

Many less developed countries have an important job to do in rationalizing public expenditure, so that necessary investment outlays and essential social services will actually receive proper priority and less essential public expenditures will be cut or eliminated. There is often to be found, also, an excessive degree of formality in routine government operations in less developed countries that serves no real purpose.

In some countries government employment is more a kind of work relief for the educated classes than it is a necessary adjunct to the efficient conduct of public business. Responsibility for allowing this situation to continue falls largely on the Ministry of Finance, within which the budget process is normally located. It has been my experience that Parkinson's first law, i.e., that work expands to fill the time allotted to it, works rather more effectively in less, than in more advanced, countries.

Whenever a large-scale program of public investment is started, there is need, in spite of the most rigid economy in routine or traditional government services, for a massive increase in tax revenue. This extra revenue must be extracted in a tolerably equitable manner if the majority of the electorate is to remain convinced that the benefits of development are worth their price. Part of the price is higher taxation, first in the agricultural sector—which must generate the bulk of public savings, since no other sector has the capacity to do so—and later in other sectors as they also grow. It is not enough to depend on the traditional sources of revenue, even where these show some flexibility of yield. New taxes must be developed, put into operation, and administered fairly alongside the older taxes.

There is a venerable and rather cynical cliché in public finance to the effect that only an old tax is a good tax. The sense of this maxim is that understanding, acceptance, and administration of a tax inevitably improve with time. But an inequitable or highly regressive or badly designed tax does not always acquire merit with age, however well economic arrangements may adjust to it. Witness some of the United States federal excise taxes that were still in effect until mid-1965, although originally designed to limit consumption during World War II.

The Scope for Intellectual Aid

Although there are many stubborn problems of tax policy that a developing country must face, it is in budget formulation and administration that many of them can perhaps best use technical assistance at the present time. The Latin countries as a group admittedly have very deficient budgetary structures and practices. Many of the Asian countries, although they may have formally good budget systems inherited from their colonial days, need modernization of these systems as well as imaginative thinking in financial administration. I am less familiar with the African nations, but it is hardly possible for

93

most of them that are newly independent to have more than a rudimentary budget mechanism. Budgeting would seem to be a most promising field for technical assistance—which the United States has hardly begun to exploit effectively. Hopefully the International Monetary Fund will soon also be in a position to offer constructive help to its members in the budget and public administration fields.

While a certain amount of technical assistance in the field of taxation has already been provided to the less developed countries, this has not been done in a consistent nor an adequate manner. The United Nations has sent missions to a number of countries in response to their requests; but the terms of reference for these missions have varied and have usually been less than comprehensive. The United States Agency for International Development has also sent a number of missions, sometimes staffed with personnel from the Treasury Department. These have generally stressed administration more than policy. Private consultants have been employed by still other countries.

Recently the IMF has established a new Department of Fiscal Affairs, but the department is too new to have had any significant impact as yet. The IMF does offer perhaps the most promising framework within which technical assistance in the field of finance can be provided; it is to be hoped that the developing countries will make extensive use of this service, which can help them greatly.

The kinds of tax policies that are most appropriate for less developed countries will be explored in a later chapter and need not concern us here. The point now is simply that, as the volume of financial aid tapers off, as it surely will, the need for technical assistance will continue; hopefully a much better job can be done with this assistance in the future than has been done in the past. This assistance costs relatively little but can help a good deal to rationalize and accelerate the development process.

Control of Consumption

One of the principal purposes of more effective taxation during a development sequence is to limit the rise in consumption during this period. The late Professor Nurkse hypothesized that developing countries would usually have a bias toward overconsumption because of what he called the "demonstration effect" of higher living standards in other countries. As he saw it, the more a country progressed, the more its people would become aware that people in other countries lived better, and consequently the more they would attempt to increase their own consumption. This explanation accounts in part for the high propensities to consume so often observed in less developed economies.

At the same time it is apparent from our analysis that a relatively low marginal propensity to consume is needed if the saving necessary for development is to be obtained. In the opinion of many governments, the easiest way to get the necessary additional saving is by forcing it, i.e., by having the government seize a substantial slice of income by taxation and use the proceeds either for public investment or for lending to private entrepreneurs. Seizing incomes for public saving by taxation is probably more realistic in many countries than hoping these savings will be made voluntarily from the enlarged incomes that are attributable to development outlays.

CONCLUDING REMARKS

Apart from the macroeconomic problem of generating enough saving, whether public or private, to finance development, foreign aid can be used to get improved budgetary procedures, a more equitable tax system, and a system of financial incentives designed to promote private investment more effectively. Details of these programs will have to be tailor-made for individual countries, making due allowance for the prevailing institutions and the financial history of each country. The annual consultations of the IMF with member countries seem to offer a suitable vehicle for this sustained help in fiscal policy. To date these consultations have been limited largely to the bearing which domestic financial matters have on a country's international position.

It appears that the eventual payoff in foreign aid, both to the giving and the receiving countries, is not solely in the capital that is transferred, but in the technical help that ought to accompany the money. The record of the United States government in effectively serving both these objectives has not been wholly successful. The foreign aid multiplier, i.e., the relation of growth in national product achieved to foreign aid received, is not as high as it might be.

The distribution of aid among recipient countries has reflected the political policy of containing Communist influence and offsetting it where it has appeared to be strongest. Although political considerations cannot be neglected and will doubtless continue to dominate the United States aid program, there is need in our long-range strategy to relate aid more closely to the efforts that individual countries are making toward their own development, and also to use the leverage resulting from aid to obtain more realistic financial policies in recipient countries. As a device for building goodwill, foreign aid has not been wholly successful; as a device for promoting development, its success could possibly be a little greater. Self-help should have been stressed more strongly from the beginning of our aid program. In our present programming we are giving belated recognition to the soundness of this principle.

5

Investment Incentives in the Private Sector

It is apparent to all who have studied the process that rapid economic development requires a large amount of public investment—in transportation, utilities, agriculture, education, and other areas of economic activity; but public investment alone will not assure a successful growth sequence. Increases in other factor inputs than capital are also needed.

Public investment is basically ancillary to the necessary private investment in new or expanded business enterprises that provide additional jobs and add both volume and variety to the flow of finished goods and services.

We have seen in an earlier chapter how development planning, if skillfully conducted, can direct public investment into the spheres most likely to help economic growth. Planning for the private sector should be less a matter of directing investment into predetermined sectors and preconceived enterprises than of publicizing business opportunities that will arise from the benefits of public investment programs, collecting and disseminating data on business intentions to invest, and generally helping private investors to coordinate their own plans with one another and with the official plans for public investment.

To plan public investment properly is not easy, because in the public sector a functioning system of market prices, in which consumers vote their preferences, is not available. Some methods of appraising the potential social productivity of public investment possibilities is needed; the one I have suggested is benefit-cost analysis, which requires that all decision-related data be quantified. Those projects with the most favorable benefit-cost ratios are the ones toward which public investment should first be directed. Benefit-cost analysis is no substitute for judgment; it is merely a framework within which judgment may be exercised systematically.

THE ORGANIZATION MIX

Our concern in the present chapter is with private investment in the less developed countries. The private investment of which I am speaking is primarily that by nationals in their own countries, only secondarily that by foreigners in less developed countries.

Investment incentives may be designed either to stimulate local investment or to attract foreign capital or both. Less developed countries in recent years have engaged in considerable competition to attract foreign investment, offering tax and other incentives in that competition. These incentives have sometimes been generally available to any business that qualifies; in other cases they have been offered only in specific contracts between the host government and the new investors. Terms for these individual contracts can and do vary over a broad range.

A Word of Caution

The whole problem of investment incentives should be approached rather cautiously by the government of an emerging country—among other reasons because it may be unwise to create discrimination between local and foreign investors (or among different groups of local investors); because the potential amount of foreign investment that may be attracted is so small; and because tax equity, which concessions to investment nearly always violate, is an asset generally worth preserving.

Even if national policy decrees that incentives are to be offered to private investment, these need not take the form of tax concessions. Direct subsidies may be employed or credit may be offered on favorable terms. Overt subsidies may well be preferable to those given covertly through the tax system, in that the cost is more readily made a matter of public knowledge, and the overt subsidy may be easier to remove once the compelling need for it has passed.

Private investment which countries seek to stimulate should normally run considerably larger than the amount of public investment, although the mixture of public and private enterprise varies greatly from country to country. Malaysia, for example, believes in a broad scope for private enterprise and in only a limited area for public investment. Burma, close by, believes in broad public investment in all sorts of business enterprises, which reduces considerably the scope for private investment.

Importance of a Proper Economic Climate

An economic climate in which private investment can flourish is vital; this climate is composed of many elements which contribute to confidence in the security of, and continuing profitability of, investment. Law and order, respect for contracts, and assurance of private property against confiscation and arbitrary restrictions that amount to slow confiscation are all obvious requirements, as is freedom to organize and to manage business so that the search for profit is not unreasonably hampered. Equitable application of prevailing laws is imperative, as is sufficient access to credit for normal business purposes.

All these elements are not incentives to private investment so much as preconditions for continuous expansion of this investment. Prospective rates of return must be high enough to compensate for the risks involved, the difficulty of saving, and the alternative uses of capital, such as passive moneylending to consumers or exporting funds to other countries, that contribute less to development than active investment.

Improvements in the investment climate stimulate investment by reducing the risks involved, thus altering the balance between prospective rates of return on alternative uses of funds. Risk may be regarded either as a deduction from rates of return or as a cost of investment.

Taxes obviously have a bearing on the ability and willingness of savers to employ their funds in business ventures. The more onerously these taxes bear on business income, the less, broadly speaking, will be the inducement to employ funds in business pursuits. The taxes are of no more importance in this respect, however, than the government expenditures which the taxes finance. These expenditures, if productive, can widen the opportunity for business to grow and to sell its products or, if unproductive, can narrow this opportunity by profligate outlays and restrictive policies.

We come up against that venerable problem the optimum relation of government to business on which so much has been written. It is not my intention to discuss that problem here. It would nevertheless seem an elementary proposition of logic that, if private enterprise is to make the larger part of the investment needed for economic development, the government should facilitate business and not undertake to hamper it by overzealous regulation. Yet in virtually all countries, advanced as well as less advanced, the trend in recent years has been toward more regulation of business in many areas. I do not argue that this trend is mistaken nor that it can or should be reversed. The logic of history

seems to give it inexorability as it creeps on like a glacier. I only suggest that a relatively rapidly moving glacier may be somewhat more destructive than a slower moving one.

Varying National Attitudes

The less developed countries of the world hold all shades of opinion concerning the proper mixture of public and private enterprise for carrying on their people's business. At the one extreme are the Communists, Socialists, and State capitalists, who want the government to run virtually everything, leaving only a few crumbs of opportunity for the private businessman. Illustrative of these crumbs, Russia still has its free markets, a few unliquidated kulaks, and numerous part-time market gardeners. Burma, although it rejects the Communist ideology, is moving steadily toward State Socialism.

At the other extreme are a few countries, more conservative in their economic policy orientation, who want development but want it without replacing or limiting private enterprise.[1] Mexico is one such country.

The third bloc of countries of the low-income world falls somewhere between these extremes, with respect to the mixture between public and private enterprise they desire in their economic organizations. Some wish growth to emerge primarily from the private sector; others, and I suspect there are more in this group than in the one just mentioned, look primarily to the public sector to provide the dynamism that will drive the growth process forward.

My purpose is not to examine the relative merits of public and private enterprise in an abstract way; it is, rather, to elaborate the point that a country's choice concerning the mixture between public and private enterprise it wishes to foster is not unrelated to the fiscal policies that must be adopted to make growth successful, given the choice concerning enterprise. The less public enterprise an emerging country chooses, the lighter can usually be the burden of taxation, with a correspondingly greater reliance on the private sector's ability to generate savings by voluntary means. Another possibility is that the government may assemble public savings and relend these savings to private business ventures. Few countries do this in other than a limited way.

---

[1] Eugene Black makes a strong plea for an expanding and dynamic private enterprise sector in his paper "The Future of Economic Development," in *Private Investment*, ed. James Daniel (New York: McGraw-Hill, 1958), pp. 1–10.

Not only the amount of taxation but also the different forms of taxation depend on what we may call, for simplicity, the economic organization mix, i.e., the relative portions of public and private enterprise.

RELATION OF THE ORGANIZATION MIX TO DEVELOPMENT POLICY

Let us assume that the political choice is an organization mix relatively heavy on the side of private enterprise. Fiscally, this means a preference for voluntary as opposed to coerced saving—in the hope that because of this choice aggregate saving will be larger and development, therefore, more rapid.

A Broad Concept of Saving and Capital Formation

The saving discussed here is that used to finance all forms of capital formation, regardless of whether they are counted as such in the national income and product statistics. Capital embodied in people, whether called accumulated skill or some other name, is essentially the matter at issue. In conventional national product accounting, investment in human capital, if I may use this term, is not ordinarily counted in capital formation but is scattered between consumer and government expenditure, depending on whether the outlay is private or public. Moreover, there is not even an expenditure equivalent for certain types of human capital formation. Inventions and innovations may arise spontaneously, as it were, without specific expenditure equivalents in the social accounting sense. Although very substantial capital investment may be required to make these new techniques effective, they contribute a net product over and above this implementing investment.

One of the troubles with social accounting, as with financial accounting, is that it proceeds according to accepted conventions which are as rigid as those defined by Emily Post—if somewhat less useful. For example, the services of housewives in the home are not conventionally counted in the national product; this gives rise to Pigou's well-known paradox—that the bachelor who marries his cook thereby diminishes the national dividend, as Professor Pigou preferred to call it. A son's college tuition is counted as consumer expenditure rather than as capital formation in United States national product accounting as well as in most other countries, because they follow a similar convention.

Without laboring the point, it is sufficient here to note that there are many kinds of capital formation, not all of which are counted in the statistics. But virtually all require corresponding saving because they are merely the counterparts or mirror images of capital formation.

The saving may be done privately or publicly, voluntarily or under coercion. The question is under what economic organization mix and what other policy constraints this saving can be brought to an optimum and maintained at an optimum flow over a sustained period. The essence of the growth process is that it is not possible without saving by some groups; expressed otherwise, failure to generate enough saving will inevitably slow the growth process down.

The product generated by economic activity is dependent on both volume and quality of inputs of effort, skill, resources, and capital into the productive process. These inputs depend on incentives to put forth work, utilize skill and knowledge, and invest capital—in order to improve production techniques and to lower costs.

THE ROLE OF INCENTIVES

It is customary for economists to discuss financial incentives, since these are the chief wellsprings to activity within their competence; sometimes they even go so far as to assume implicitly that financial rewards, obtained or only sought, are the primary or even the only significant drives that motivate people. Yet it is well known that hope of material gain is only one among many forces that drive men to pour forth additional effort. The desire for distinction, the instinct of workmanship (so dear to the heart of Veblen), and the urge to conform are psychological constructs that are often used to explain the variety and vigor of human activity.

I have no desire in this work to enter into a discussion of what causes people to behave as they do. The relevant point is simply that their motivation is complex and that the desire for economic gain or financial reward is only one among numerous interrelated human drives.[2] Given this difficulty, can an economist say anything of unusual insight about what systems of incentives within the private sector are best calculated to promote economic growth?

Nature of Investment Incentives

The focus of this chapter is on incentives to private investment. These have the common property of raising the prospective net rate of return from such investment; they are effective insofar as the volume of

[2] J. S. Furnivall has suggested that less developed countries tend to be "plural societies" in which different segments of the population are not motivated in the same way, and that custom plays an important role in economic behavior. Cf. his *Colonial Policy and Practice* (Cambridge: At the University Press, 1948), pp. 303–12.

this investment actually responds favorably to the incentives in an amount that outweighs the cost of the incentives in foregone revenue or in some other form.

If the incentives take the form of favorable tax treatment, their character obviously depends on the tax system in force. Many well-developed countries that rely heavily on income taxation provide investment incentives in the forms of accelerated depreciation, investment credits, and generous depletion allowances. Less developed countries may use these same techniques if they have income taxes; but they may also provide incentives through favorable customs duties, reduced property tax assessments, or in other ways outside the tax system. In a number of African countries standstill tax agreements are popular. These guarantee qualifying enterprises against future tax increases for specific future periods, sometimes running as long as twenty-five years.

PUBLIC AND PRIVATE BUSINESS

We are often told that the purpose of private business is to make a profit by performing a public service, i.e., by providing something that people want and for which they are both willing and able to pay. If this objective is accepted, it would seem logically to follow that a government desiring to encourage growth should intervene in the business process only to insure that business does indeed provide a public service instead of simply a private one, and also that it does this within reasonable standards of employment and other legitimate concerns of public policy. Illegal activities may be highly profitable; but they are illegal simply because they are adjudged to contravene established public policy in some significant respect.

Government Monopoly and Government Regulation

Public policy toward business varies greatly from country to country. In the United States it is illegal to organize monopolies in restraint of trade; but many other countries see nothing wrong in this procedure and indeed regard it as normal business practice. In Costa Rica it is illegal for private business to manufacture wines or liquors, because this trade is a state monopoly; other countries monopolize other commodities such as cigarettes, matches, arms and ammunition, and salt. Central banking services, coinage of money, delivery of mail, and transportation by rail are other examples of services that are widely conducted as state monopolies.

Numerous other forms of production, not actually monopolized by the state, are conducted by private enterprise only under stringent government regulation. Commercial banking, insurance, brokerage, manufacture of habit-forming drugs, etc. are closely regulated by nearly every country through some instrumentality of government. The public-interest attribute of these businesses, and the palpable opportunity for conflict between private profit and the public interest, causes few people any longer to question the desirability of close government regulation over these industries.

Licensing

Many other businesses, trades, and occupations operate under a system of licenses and licensing that implies still a lesser degree of government regulation. In the United States one cannot be a public barber, a real estate broker, a public accountant, a surgeon, or an attorney without being properly licensed.

There is always presumed to be a public interest in licensing or in doing business under a license. Practicing medicine without a license is a serious offense because the public interest in treatment only by qualified physicians is obvious. Yet quacks earn lucrative incomes if they can keep ahead of the law. Barbers are presumably licensed in the interest of sanitation, while real estate brokers are licensed largely to prevent fraud.

The difficulty with licensing is that it is sometimes not easy to determine just where the public interest ends and restrictive practices designed to raise incomes of the licensed practitioners begin. This is especially difficult when the licensing authority—a board, or whatever it may be—is composed largely of members of the trade or profession being licensed.[3]

My purpose, however, is not to scrutinize the merits of licensing a particular occupation in a certain way; it is to make the point that licensing is a peculiarly pervasive form of government regulation over business activity, and one that can vitally affect the standard of business practice and the incomes attainable in particular occupations. In this light, the economic consequences of licensing become rather important.

In the less developed countries in which I have served as an adviser, the close regulation of business activity (through licensing or other

---

[3]In his classic study of property rights, R. H. Tawney observes that "all professions have some rules which protect the interests of the community and others which are an inposition on it." Cf. his *The Acquisitive Society* (New York: Harcourt, Brace, 1920). Reference is to the Harvest ed., pp. 92–93.

methods), which was locally regarded as the normal standard of government practice, has impressed me strongly and generally unfavorably. While this may be indicative of sheer private enterprise bias, I find it difficult to forget—when confronted with the network of controls, permits, and restrictive conditions under which business must be conducted in many developing nations—that the countries that have already become industrialized have generally done so under a frontier psychology that abhorred restraint on the individual.

Japan is a significant exception. Industrialization there came under the aegis of the state—with state capital and state direction.[4] Many countries now striving to industrialize believe state capital and state direction to be imperative in their own situations. Japan may, therefore, be a more suitable model for many of the poorer countries with aspirations toward industrialization than is England, Germany, or the United States.

Preconditions for Effective Incentives

Whether a country, in its development strategy, elects to depend much or little on private enterprise, it should understand the growth incentives in the private sector. These may be financial or nonfinancial, opportunity-defining or opportunity-concealing—an actual disservice, on balance, to the cause they seek to advance. The main tasks for the incentives, whatever they are or whatever form they take, are actually to expand total capital formation and to widen job and business opportunities.

The role of education in this process is extremely important.[5] A first result of education, formal or informal, is the creation of constructive dissatisfaction with things as they are. Successful revolutionaries are often recruited from university student bodies; many politicians get their basic training on college campuses—in elections for the student council or other campus offices—or in army schools.[6] But no college that I know of gives a course in how to start a business on your own:

Some years ago, a small-business office of the Department of

---

[4]G. C. Allen, *Modern Japan and its Problems* (London: Allen & Unwin, 1928), chap. 5.

[5]T. W. Schultz has advanced the thought that outlays which are considered investments in human capital should include expenditures for health facilities and services; for migration, so that workers can take advantage of changing job opportunities; and for formal schooling, on-the-job training, and adult education. See his paper "Investment in Human Capital," *American Economic Review*, March, 1961, pp. 6–9.

[6]U Nu in Burma is a good example. So is Nasser in Egypt; the army was his school.

Commerce, which subsequently became the Small Business Administration, did provide this training, not in classrooms but through publication of a series of booklets. These were aimed chiefly at returning veterans of World War II and the Korean War who sought to establish businesses of their own.

These booklets were quite useful and still sell steadily, if unspectacularly. They deal with obvious factors in business chance, e.g., how to pick a location; how to estimate capital requirements and obtain capital; how to build on previous work experience; how to select and train help.

A Specific Suggestion

One useful technique in promoting economic development might be for the countries exporting capital and providing intellectual aid to translate these booklets into Thai, Bantu, Farsi, and Urdu and to distribute them abroad. To my knowledge this is not being done, although the United States government has technical assistance missions in countries where all these languages are spoken.

Naturally, such a program assumes that people can read. Where they cannot, it is necessary to begin with reading instruction. There are, of course, many people who can read but do not or will not. How are these to be reached? Plainly through some other medium than the printed word. Picture books are one possibility of which some limited use has already been made; but the best one would seem to be films.

In virtually all the less developed countries films are popular; indeed, with music they are among the most widespread cultural contacts among peoples. I have learned at firsthand, as have many other American advisers, that the image which many foreigners have of the United States has been shaped primarily by American movies. Not all these exports are without merit, but the typical Hollywood film hardly gives an accurate impression of life in the United States. The commercial film, after all, is meant to entertain rather than to instruct.

Educational films have been made on almost every subject from blast-furnace technique to gardening. My suggestion is, simply, that serious thought be given to the preparation of a series of training films in local languages on practical subjects such as crop rotation, insect control, keeping accounts, packing for export, and the like. Some of this has been done; but much more intensive use of the technique could be made. As an educational tool this audiovisual method has practically no limits to its possible applications.

The first step in providing incentives to private investment is, therefore, to open up to people living in traditional societies some vision of the modern world—showing what variety, challenges, and opportunity it offers, as well as what problems. Education, largely informal, can help to provide this vision.

In the less developed countries that I know from personal experience, USIA libraries have been in the forefront among effective forms of technical assistance. It is because they offer a window to the modern world that they are both popular and effective. They should be equipped with more films than books, but with educational material of all sorts.

I have personally seen people in low-income countries spend hours pouring over the Sears Roebuck catalog. They had simply not previously realized what volume and variety of consumer goods were available in higher-income nations. Once they realize this, their desire to participate more actively in economic development is often stimulated.

Skills for Development

Once education has played its initial role in creating constructive dissatisfaction, it should offer practical training in those trades, crafts, and occupations that will be increasingly needed as development proceeds. I am a strong advocate of adult short courses in such disparate subjects as truck maintenance, bookkeeping, sanitation in the home, nursing, inventory control, and the like—to mention only a few at random. Development requires learning many new skills for new occupations. It requires also the unfolding of a forward-looking viewpoint that will encourage people to innovate in any way they can.[7]

What part should financial incentives play in this process? They can be rather important. If people see that training in new skills pays, they will be encouraged to seek this training and to acquire the skills. Of course, if too many people try to become tractor mechanics there may soon be a surplus of such artisans. For this reason the menu of educational opportunity should offer as many choices as possible.

Priority ought naturally to be given to the teaching skills, e.g., to the

[7]Peter Kilby makes a case, based on evidence collected in Nigeria, that a rapid increase in productivity in industrial establishments in less developed countries is possible through relatively simple changes in physical organization of plant processes. He believes that this increase can be realized largely by teaching managerial skills. Cf. his article "Organization and Productivity in Backward Economies," *Quarterly Journal of Economics*, 76 (1962):303–10.

training of teachers, nurses, and foremen, because such training spreads in a kind of chain as the trained teach others. After the teaching skills, attention should be given largely to training for the new occupations that will be necessary as development proceeds. If an irrigation project is being built, dry farmers need to be taught how to farm with sufficient water. If a hydroelectric plant is being built, the training given should be in industrial applications of electric power, i.e., in how to motorize processes that were formerly done by hand.

The training process should be carefully scheduled in time and in volume with the rest of the economic development process, so that trained workers will be on hand when they are needed but so that no large backlog of skills inappropriate to the production to be carried on will be accumulated. Many less developed countries, for example, have far too many lawyers, not because they need them, but because people are traditionally trained in the law as a prestige form of education. Much bitterness and revolutionary fervor can arise when trained lawyers or other professionals are unable to establish practices or find employment which is suitable to their training.

This discussion of education and training in a chapter devoted to private investment may seem a digression. In reality it is not, because the accumulation of human capital may contribute as much or more to growth as may the formation of fixed capital in plants, machinery, and tools. Incentives to investment should embrace stimulation of outlays on education and training as well as on equipment. These incentives may take such forms as subsidies to educational institutions, student allowances and loan funds, wage advances geared to the completion of specified training courses, and tax concessions for educational expenses met privately. The form and design of these incentives for education and training raise many technical questions that will not be examined here.

SPECIFIC INCENTIVES TO INVESTMENT

Turning now to the problem of incentives to private investment in the usual sense, these may also take many forms. A good investment climate is essential, including equitable treatment of both local and foreign capital, stability of economic policies, and confidence among businessmen that these policies are actually well conceived and will work to assist growth. Credit should be adequate, though not at artificially low interest rates, since these can distort the appropriate investment structure. Especially important is a general feeling of confidence that development is about to occur and that the process will actually be accompanied by broadening markets and the emergence of new profit opportunities.

Design of Investment Incentives

Use of the term incentives to investment sometimes connotes the grant of some special privilege or concession. It may not be necessary actively to dispense special treatment through a tax concession or in some other way, but merely to remove prevailing deterrents. Improvement of the investment climate may be accomplished without necessarily giving investors special advantages. Some less developed countries have perhaps erred in giving too much attention to special incentives and too little to bettering the prevailing investment climate.

Private investment can sometimes be encouraged without special inducements merely by government assistance in pinpointing investment opportunities that emerge from the many-sided process that economic development involves. Encouraging business participation in the planning process, publicizing the specifics of public investment projects, collecting and disseminating statistics and other information on market potential, and giving guidance as well as credit though development banks can help to strengthen the confidence of local entrepreneurs and to guide their efforts in constructive directions. Contrary to the belief of some observers of development efforts, I do not consider local entrepreneurial talent to be in short supply in most less developed countries. Given a reasonable chance in an openly competitive environment, I believe that in most cases this talent will come forward in abundance and will function as a force for progress.

Building institutions for the mobilization of private savings and their direction into investment is essential. Savings banks, stock exchanges, and other financial intermediaries need to be promoted in order to encourage saving and to give businessmen access to funds beyond their own resources and their ability to get bank credit. Persuading savers to look to equities rather than to traditional fixed-income investments is an important part of the overall process of stimulating private investment.

Special incentives to attract investment by foreigners may be considered desirable, because this investment is essentially a net addition to the resources for development otherwise available to an emerging country. The relative positions of foreign and local investors need to be weighed carefully, however; in some cases past prejudices against foreign investment need reexamination. Joint ventures between foreign and local private interests may be attractive, although those between foreign private and local government interests may be less advantageous.[8]

Discussion of investment incentives has so frequently run in terms of special tax treatment that I turn now to this aspect of the subject.

TAX CONCESSIONS

Most countries that aspire to develop regard industrialization as an important part of the progress they hope to make; consequently their development plans assign a relatively high priority to the creation of new industries as net additions to their economic base. Sooner or later the question arises whether tax concessions, tariff protection, or other forms of artificial aid to profit in these new industries are in the national interest. Many countries offer investment incentives only to pioneer industries, i.e., those that are totally new to the country in question. Other countries make their incentives more generally available to new investment which may be merely for the expansion of an existing industry.

A Basic Problem

A general difficulty among countries having income taxes arises from their assertion of the right to tax both income originating within the country, regardless of to whom it accrues, and income received by all residents of the country, regardless of where it originates. This means double taxation of income from foreign sources, and either statutory or treaty provisions, or both, are required to provide relief. If nations could agree on a rule that all would apply, such as taxing only income originating within their borders, this problem could be avoided and the international flow of capital would undoubtedly be promoted.[9] The likelihood of such a rule's being adopted cannot be regarded as very great. The problem of differing national rates of tax, of course, would remain.

The methods employed by capital-exporting countries to relieve double taxation of foreign-source income vary. Some countries exempt

[8]For a well-balanced appraisal of these joint ventures see W. G. Friedmann and G. Kalmanoff, *Joint International Business Ventures* (New York: Columbia University Press, 1961).

[9]The International Chamber of Commerce has advocated such a rule and has worked out in some detail how it might be applied. See their brochure *Taxation Policies in Relation to International Investment* (Paris, 1961).

it from tax in whole or in part; others allow the foreign tax as a deduction in domestic tax computation; still others, including the United States, permit crediting the foreign tax against the domestic tax. This varying practice creates some complex problems for developing countries that are anxious to install income tax concessions, especially in the form of a tax holiday for new industries.

Many countries feel that new industries should have such a temporary tax holiday for several years, until they become established on a profitable basis. Many other countries actually grant either reduced income tax rates or total exemption from income taxes for a period, such as five years, to any new industries established in the country pursuant to their overall development plans. Some countries provide investment incentives on a case-by-case basis; others offer these incentives generally to any enterprises that qualify. The incentives are sometimes graduated with the size of investment or with the amount of new employment created. To qualify, a certain percentage of final product value must sometimes be added within the country offering the investment incentive. This rules out assembly operations that avoid tariffs without actually fostering local manufacturing. The question to be asked is whether such tax concessions are a desirable form of financial incentive.[10]

Pros and Cons of Income Tax Concessions

Proponents of such tax concessions claim that without them the new industries would not be established; therefore, the concessions are justified because their effect is to increase the size of the tax base and thus to produce more revenue after the concession period has expired than if no such concession had been granted.[11] Opponents of the concessions,

[10]For a more extended discussion of income tax exemptions as an investment incentive, and of the features of the exemption laws of various countries, see K. M. Kauffman, "Income Tax Exemptions and Economic Development," *National Tax Journal*, 13 (1960):141–62. George E. Lent of the IMF has also examined in some detail the investment incentive plans of thirteen countries. His paper "Tax Incentives for Investment in Developing Countries" was published in the July, 1967 issue of the IMF *Staff Papers*, pp. 249–323. This is an excellent catalogue of present practice among the emerging countries.

[11]P. B. Richman has developed models of the increases in the investment necessary to pay out for tax sparing at various rates. These show, as might be expected, that the higher the rate of tax foregone, the larger must be the induced increase in investment. The models she develops are perhaps a little misleading because she assumes that tax foregone would otherwise be spent for public-capital formation in the capital-importing country. See her *Taxation of Foreign Investment Income* (Baltimore: Johns Hopkins Press, 1963), chap. 5.

on the other hand, argue that tax concessions favor investment in new industries over investment in established industries, which is not always in accord with social productivity, and that these concessions sometimes encourage the expansion of uneconomic enterprises that may have difficulty in meeting the test of competition once they are on a full taxpaying basis.

Much depends on the size and nature of the tax concession and on the period of time it is allowed to run. A concession of three to five years may do relatively little harm, whereas one that extends for ten or fifteen years is more likely to be attended by the sort of problems that opponents of tax concessions have in mind. A tax concession may not be an efficient method of stimulating the activity desired. If the concession is too broad, the revenue loss may be large relative to the increase in investment obtained. If it is too limited, requiring case-by-case dispensation, it may be inhibiting to investment as well as administratively troublesome.[12]

Tax concessions to investment need not take the form of an exemption, or of a holiday for a limited period, even where income taxes are involved. Investment credit provisions may be incorporated into an income tax, thus reducing the amount of income otherwise taxable. Special investment reserves may be allowed, on which tax is deferred for a definite period. Accelerated amortization may be permitted, either by an initial year allowance or by use of a declining balance formula. This has the effect of postponing tax liability, as opposed to straight-line depreciation. All these devices have been used by the advanced countries. Their common difficulty is that they are all more complex than outright exemption, and hence make heavier demands on tax administration.

Non-income Tax Incentives

In the event the developing country does not have an income tax, or that this tax is relatively unimportant, tax incentives to investment may take still other forms. Many countries grant preferences in customs duties to materials, equipment, and supplies for new industries they are attempting to encourage, often coupling these with high punitive duties on the final products of the new industries to limit foreign competition.

---

[12]Panama has, for a number of years, granted tax concessions to investment projects on a contract or case-by-case basis. The *Fiscal Survey of Panama* concludes that the terms of these contracts might well be shortened, the qualifying activities limited, and the degree of administrative discretion reduced.

Local assembly of manufactured goods may be promoted, and in some cases forced, by high duties on finished products but low duties on parts or components for local assembly. In some instances foreign interests can be compelled by such rules, plus fear of losing markets, to establish local assembly plants they might otherwise prefer not to invest in. There are definite limits to the extent to which foreign investment can be forced in this manner; moreover, the whole process may be basically shortsighted for the developing country.

Low property tax assessments or even property tax holidays may be used to direct investment to particular areas. This technique has been much used by local governments in the United States and elsewhere to draw investment to distressed areas. In some cases facilities are even constructed with public funds and leased on a subsidized rental basis to private interests for the sake of the jobs to be created by a new plant or new facilities.

Incentives may thus be provided either in lower direct or indirect taxes. Greatest interest nevertheless attaches to those incentives which involve income taxation, especially the temporary exemption from such taxes. This is true even when income taxes are not important and when the investment incentives might better involve other taxes.

United States Tax Treatment of Foreign Source Income

We cannot in a rounded way discuss tax concessions, particularly the sparing of income taxes, without pausing briefly to inquire into the system that prevails with regard to taxation of foreign source income between the United States and other countries. In United States tax law the subsidiary of an American corporation or an American branch plant first pays income tax in the country where it is located and then is allowed to credit that tax payment against its United States tax liability. Thus if the foreign tax rate is as high as the United States tax rate, the foreign tax payment completely offsets any United States tax liability. If the foreign tax payment is less than the United States tax payment, then the foreign country takes its tax first and the United States gets only the residual amount up to the difference between the foreign and the United States tax rate. This provision is known as the foreign tax credit.[13]

[13]The nature and operation of this credit has been described in great detail by Elizabeth Owen in *The Foreign Tax Credit* (Cambridge, Mass.: Harvard Law School, 1961). There are, of course, special features to the credit such as limitations, qualifications, etc., which I have not mentioned.

113

Foreign branches of American companies incur United States tax liability on their profits as earned, since these are considered part of the parent's profits. Subsidiaries, being incorporated abroad, could until 1962 defer the United States tax on their profits until these profits were repatriated as dividends. The Revenue Act of 1962 ended this tax deferment for certain investments in advanced countries, but continued it for investments in less developed countries. Consequently, there is now in United States tax law a built-in incentive for investment in less developed countries. As yet this has not produced any marked upsurge in private capital outflow toward these countries.

In addition to the statutory provision for a credit of foreign taxes against United States taxes, the United States has a system of international tax treaties with a number of countries for the relief of double taxation. These treaties occasionally specify that certain foreign taxes, which are not strictly income taxes, will nevertheless be treated as though they were income taxes for the purpose of obtaining the foreign tax credit.

The Tax Sparing Issue

As various foreign countries have legislated tax holidays, the question whether United States treaties should give credit for tax sparing in foreign countries has arisen repeatedly. To illustrate the problem, if India grants a five-year exemption from income tax to a new business enterprise financed by American capital, the result at present is that India gives up its tax but the credit against United States tax liability is reduced; the United States government simply takes up the concession which the Indian government has granted. If India spares the tax, however, and the United States can be persuaded to spare the tax also, then the new investment has an actual tax holiday until it can be established on a profitable basis.

Opponents of tax sparing point out that a limited tax holiday for new business may be illusory if profits during the initial years of operation are small. To the extent that this is true, the revenue loss is also small. They also point out, with greater force, that sparing encourages the repatriation of profits, compared with the present rule under which tax is only deferred, not forgiven, on reinvested earnings.[14] Finally, sparing involves revenue losses to both the capital-importing and capital-exporting country and creates inequities in both countries.

[14]S. S. Surrey, "The Pakistan Tax Treaty and Tax Sparing," *National Tax Journal*, 11 (1958):156–57.

Although provisions for tax sparing have been written into the drafts of several treaties between the United States and foreign countries, the United States Senate has yet to ratify any treaty in which credit is given for foreign tax foregone.[15] Whether such treaties should be ratified or not is a question I do not propose to discuss here. Other capital-exporting countries have also negotiated tax sparing treaties.[16] The fact remains, however, that one obstacle to the spread of tax concessions is the fact that these concessions may merely increase the amount of tax liability owed abroad by reducing the foreign tax credit. The concessions may nevertheless be effective for stimulating local investment, if not for drawing in foreign capital.

Thus there is a technical problem: how to give tax concessions to new business enterprises financed by foreign capital. This problem is separate from the policy question whether such tax concessions are a sound idea for economic development.

Experience with Investment Tax Incentives Uneven

Puerto Rico has often been cited as a leading example of rapid industrialization assisted by tax incentives. These incentives were undoubtedly strategic because, through a unique combination of circumstances, it was possible to obtain virtually a complete holiday from both United States and Puerto Rican business taxes and yet remain within the tariff area of mainland United States.[17] Other countries do not have this unique opportunity to gain such relatively large capital imports through tax concessions.[18]

---

[15]These draft treaties are with India, Pakistan, Israel, and the United Arab Republic.

[16]United Kingdom treaties containing tax-sparing features have been concluded with Pakistan, Malta, and Israel. West Germany has such treaties with India and Israel; Japan with India, Pakistan, and Singapore; and Sweden with Ireland and Israel. See L. Mills and H. J. Gumpel, "Taxation of Foreign Source Income by Other Countries," in *Federal Tax Treatment of Foreign Income* by L. B. Krause and K. W. Dam (Washington, D.C.: Brookings Institution, 1964), p. 137.

[17]See M. C. Taylor, "What Happens When Exemptions End: Retrospect and Prospect in Puerto Rico," in *Taxation and Operations Abroad* (Princeton: Tax Institute Inc., 1960), pp. 170–86. In Taylor's view the end of Puerto Rican tax exemption will not be accompanied by marked migration of new plants to other locations.

[18]S. G. Ross and J. B. Christensen, in their study of Mexican experience with tax incentives, concluded that "a realistic appraisal of the economic history of tax exemption in Mexico seems to show that the program has reflected rather than influenced the course of Mexico's industrial development, since it was never directed at any object more specific than general industrial development. For the most part the only criterion for benefits was that the beneficiary's product be 'new' or 'necessary.'" See their *Tax Incentives for Industry in Mexico* (Cambridge, Mass.: Harvard Law School, 1959), p. 152.

Many developing countries have modified their investment incentive schemes to make them more restrictive than originally intended, thus admitting that some of the incentives plans were too generous in the first instance and that others have failed to generate the amount of additional investment initially hoped for. Competition among countries to attract foreign capital has resulted in an initial inflation in the generosity of tax concession schemes, followed in a number of instances by reconsideration and a closer look at the actual benefits obtained. This more hard-headed approach to investment incentives now augers well for a more intelligent use of these fiscal devices in future development planning.

The United States has long used tax incentives to encourage activities of a developmental nature. Canal companies, railroads, banks and insurance companies, and airlines have all received incentive tax concessions. The difficulty with use of the tax system for this purpose is that incentives, once written into the law, are extremely difficult to remove at a later time when they may be less urgently needed. For example, in the United States we have oil depletion, which was originally intended to encourage prospecting for oil when it appeared in danger of becoming scarce. At the present time, this activity does not need so much encouragement, but the tax concession is politically impossible to remove.

As a general principle of public administration, it is certainly better to subsidize particular activities deemed essential to development by appropriating funds and paying a direct subsidy than by installing a tax concession. In most less developed countries it is probably better to concentrate on improving the investment climate than to rely on tax and other incentives to stimulate private investment. It seems probable, however, that tax subsidies will continue to be used, with varying degrees of success, by countries that are anxious to encourage industrialization and other forms of economic development.

Some countries employ incentives to stimulate reinvestment of business earnings. These incentives include special allowances for investment financed in this manner, lighter taxation of reinvested than distributed earnings, and in a few cases complete exemption of ploughed-back earnings. These incentives raise a number of problems. They do not mesh well with temporary tax holidays; they often raise difficulties about the sources from which a particular investment is financed; and they are quite costly in revenue, because they are more generally applicable than other investment incentives. Despite these problems, capital-scarce countries will undoubtedly continue to experiment with this method of stimulating private investment. It does reward success and involves less explicit state direction of private investment than some other incentive plans.

TRADE RESTRICTIONS, TARIFF BARRIERS, AND OTHER IMPEDIMENTS TO COMMERCE

Trade restrictions and tariff barriers as well as other impediments tend to expand profits by creating monopoly conditions; businesses receiving monopoly treatment are able to earn larger incomes than they would in a more competitive environment. The temptation to use restrictions of this kind to encourage industrialization is strong, particularly in countries that do not have a competitive tradition in business activity. It is natural for the Burmese, for example, to turn to monopoly situations and to government enterprise because they have in the past steadily lost out in competition with Indian and Chinese traders and because they see opportunity for themselves largely in terms of restrictive practices against these foreign interests. Other countries have similar traditions.

The Trouble with Restrictions

The difficulty with expanding profits by creating monopoly situations is that such policies do not expand the entire economy but only certain sections of it; moreover, the aggregate expansion is apt to be less than if business were conducted on a more competitive basis. Monopoly does not necessarily lead to increased efficiency, which is particularly needed for economic growth. Therefore, any country which desires to expand the private business sector of its economy ought to be wary of artificially limiting competition in an effort to expand profits for certain producers.

It will be difficult for countries that do not have a competitive, free enterprise tradition to understand this point of view; indeed, to them it may appear contrary to common sense. The mere fact, however, that the growth of these countries has not matched the business growth of the free world ought to give them pause when deciding on their economic policies with regard to monopoly and competition.

Tax concessions, protective tariffs, and the like are primarily devices to attract investment into manufacturing activities. Yet manufacturing may not be the sector in which additional investment is most urgently needed. We have already observed in another chapter that encouraging industry necessarily means that productivity in agriculture must rise. As one writer put it,

> if you do not change agriculture you will not change the economy; this is I think one of the safe rules one can lay down for developing communities. At the same time agriculture is the most difficult sector to change for the simple reason that agricultural methods are thousands of years old and people prefer on the whole to go on in the ways of their fathers.[19]

Instead of giving up revenue through tax concessions and protective tariffs, in an effort to encourage manufacturing, it may be better strategy for an emerging country to collect at least some of this revenue and to use it for agricultural extension, roadbuilding, or public health programs.

CONCLUSION

Enough has been said to indicate that the problem of providing appropriate incentives to investment in the private sector is a complex one. We know what needs to be done: namely, that opportunities for profit need to be expanded and that individual businessmen need to have freedom to seek out and capitalize on these opportunities. There are many effective limitations on their ability to do so—lack of trained labor; capital and transportation; poor understanding of business methods; little information about markets; and insufficient demand within the home market. These are all reasons why the growth of industry may be extremely slow.

Financial incentives such as tax concessions, opportunities to make profits, and artificially low wages are important in spurring business investment in the private sector, but by themselves they may not be enough to bring about the large expansion in business investment which economic growth requires. Governments in emerging countries need continuously to be on the alert for techniques to expand industrial opportunities. They should also take the attitude that their primary job is to encourage private businessmen to undertake new investments which, in turn, can be a powerful factor in stimulating economic growth.

[19]Barbara Ward, *The Rich Nations and the Poor Nations* (New York: Norton, 1962), p. 106.

6

Tax Policy

The principle has been developed in earlier chapters that an emerging country requires an adequate revenue—one that will mobilize necessary savings and hold reasonably in check the inflationary pressures that a marked acceleration in investment tends to generate; such a country should also work steadily toward a flexible tax system, in which total tax yield will increase more than proportionately to the rise in national product that successful development brings.

Numerous other canons of taxation and criteria for tax policy have been advanced at various times and by various scholars with different value systems. Adam Smith's canons of equity, economy, certainty, and convenience are well known. More recently, D. T. Smith has remarked that a tax structure should be appraised from the standpoints of equity, economic consequences, and simplicity.[1]

The goals set for tax policy in a developing country may be described in either general or specific terms. K. E. Poole, favoring the general, remarks that the objectives of taxation are revenue, regulation, and economic control.[2] John Due, favoring the more specific, says that the functions of the tax system in a developing economy should be (1) curtailing consumption, (2) reallocating resources from less to more beneficial investments, (3) providing a flow of funds to government, and (4) providing incentives to alter behavior so as to facilitate growth.[3] More specifically still, the Planning Commission of the Government of Pakistan says flatly that "tax policy will be directed to mobilizing resources for development and allocating them according to Plan

---

[1] *Alternatives to Present Federal Taxes* (Princeton: Tax Institute, Inc., 1964), p. 3.
[2] See his *Public Finance and Economic Welfare* (New York: Rinehart, 1957), p. 115.
[3] See his *Taxation and Economic Development in Tropical Africa* (Cambridge, Mass.: MIT Press, 1963), p. 146.

priorities."[4] Clearly the objectives of tax policy can be as varied as the imagination and ingenuity of policymakers.

Measured against accepted criteria, the tax systems of most less developed countries will be found to be highly inadequate. This chapter will explore some aspects of actual tax structures in a few selected countries and will examine means whereby these structures may be brought more nearly in line with the requirements for development. Effects of tax systems and tax administration upon the development process in action will also be discussed briefly.

My plan in this chapter is to examine separately the different forms of taxation on which less developed countries rely and to suggest ways of improving them and combining them in a structure conducive to growth. It is obvious that less developed countries exhibit a great diversity in their tax structures and taxing practices. Differences are attributable to past history, varying philosophies of government, different administrative traditions, and numerous other factors. Despite the differences, there are some common threads running through the tax systems of many countries. These common threads furnish the framework for the discussion in this chapter.

Taxable Capacity

A concept often encountered in the current literature is that of the "taxable capacity" of different countries. Although a useful concept for descriptive and general appraisal purposes, taxable capacity does not lend itself to precise measurement, but permits only qualitative judgments concerning the fiscal performance of particular countries.[5] There are political and administrative as well as economic limits to taxable capacity. Despite lack of precision in the concept, most fiscal surveys of less developed countries conclude that not all available taxable capacity is being utilized. An optimum tax structure for a given country at a particular time will be one that is within the limits of that country's taxable capacity; but this capacity should grow steadily as development proceeds.

Let us turn now to some of the major revenue sources on which developing countries often depend.

[4]See *The Second Five Year Plan, 1960–65* (Karachi: Government of Pakistan, 1960), p. 47.
[5]See S. Plasschaert, *Taxable Capacity in Developing Countries*, mimeographed (Washington, D.C.: IBRD, 1962).

CUSTOMS DUTIES

Practically all countries tax imports; revenue from this source is often a large part of the total tax yield in a less developed country. The wide variation in relative reliance of different countries on import taxation may be seen in Table 6.

TABLE 6
IMPORT TAXES AS A PERCENTAGE OF TOTAL CURRENT REVENUE OF THE CENTRAL GOVERNMENT

(Averages for 1957–60)

Italy	.6
U.S.A.	1.2
France	2.2
Germany	5.2
Belgium	5.8
Norway	8.8
Netherlands	9.5
Mexico	13.8
Peru	14.2
India	16.7
Sudan	20.9
Portugal	22.8
Malaya	23.3
United Kingdom	27.6
Ceylon	28.1
Thailand	28.8
El Salvador	35.6
Togo	42.4
Honduras	44.1
Costa Rica	52.7

SOURCE: Adapted from Plasschaert, *Taxable Capacity in Developing Countries*, p. 46.

Variations in size among countries, as well as in the degree of their development, help to explain the ratios in Table 6. Generally the smaller countries as well as those less fully developed rely more on import taxes.

Imports are a convenient object of taxation; collection of customs duties does not make such heavy administrative demands on a developing country as, for example, an individual income tax or a retail sales tax would. When customs duties are high, prevention of smuggling can become an important preoccupation of government as well as an administrative headache, but this headache is closely related to the general problem of maintaining law and order, which will not be discussed here. Naturally, no tax system can successfully meet the requirements of development unless it can be enforced with tolerable equity and unless it is accepted by the populace as necessary to achieve agreed objectives.

Means of Improvement

The structure of import taxation in some countries is quite complex, with numerous individual duties often being applied to the same products. Where this problem exists, the tariff structure should be simplified and unified, to free administrative resources for the other obligations which a changing, more aggressive import tax policy will involve. Many customs procedures also need modernizing before duties can effectively be strengthened. This modernizing includes techniques such as sampling of shipments, simplifying of documents, and more accurate valuation methods.

Import taxes may be either specific or ad valorem. Although specific duties are easier to apply, they are apt to become outmoded over time. Ad valorem taxes keep up automatically with price changes and thus possess the right basis for yield flexibility. Developing countries will generally be well advised to move steadily toward ad valorem duties in their import taxation.

It is common in many systems of import taxation to exempt, or to tax at only nominal rates, essential imports such as food products, in a country not self-sufficient in food production; fuels; required raw materials for local manufacturing industries; and capital equipment for new industries in process of development. Maintenance materials such as lubricants, spare parts for durable goods in use within the country, medicines and drugs, and similar essentials may also be exempted or taxed at only nominal rates.

Rates on other products are often graduated on the basis of some concept of essentiality, with luxury products—automobiles, high fashion clothing, furs and jewelry—taking very high rates. Semi-luxury goods, such as household appliances, radios, and the like, take medium rates. Often, however, these medium rates are quite high.

It will be apparent that with proper classification and selection of rates, customs duties can, in effect, amount to a progressive tax on consumption; this is the way these duties are actually used by a number of countries.[6] Customs duties are, in fact, the administratively simplest

---

[6] I am speaking here of a revenue tariff on imports, not of a protective tariff designed to preclude these imports.

method of taxing consumption progressively in a small country that lacks manufacturing capacity.[7]

A progressive tax on consumption accords rather well with the economic requirements for early stages of development. We have already seen in an earlier chapter why development requires both an increase in saving and the expanded import of capital equipment. A progressive tax on consumption of imported goods is congruent with both these requirements.

Obstacles to Improvement

Despite the suitability of customs duties to the financial requirements of an early stage of development, a number of countries have shown reluctance to use these duties in the aggressive manner that accelerated development makes desirable. Raising import taxes may encounter strong resistance from the higher income groups within a country, since these groups are the principal consumers of imported goods as well as the most potent force politically. As the development process raises personal incomes, there is a natural aspiration on the part of those whose incomes advance to consume more imported products; this aspiration will of course be thwarted in various degrees by rising customs duties.

In spite of the potential unpopularity of this course of action, a first principle of tax policy for a country aspiring to develop should be to use import taxes vigorously—in order to restrain consumption and to increase savings. If savings do not increase voluntarily in the private sector, the additional flow of tax revenue will constitute public savings which can be used to finance development.

Examples of Poor Import Tax Policy

That many countries fail to grasp the first principle of tax policy will be clear from a few examples. In Iran, although the financial requirements for development are large—because public development expenditure is large and is only partially covered by oil revenue—import tax

[7]Richard Goode takes a similar view when he writes: "As a means of taxing consumption in the less developed countries, excises and customs duties seem more practical than an income tax with saving exempt or an expenditure tax. . . . At the present time ingenuity and energy can be more fruitfully employed in the improvement of indirect taxes and other conventional sources of revenue than in the introduction of an expenditure tax or a broad exemption for saving in the income tax." See his article "Taxation of Savings and Consumption in Underdeveloped Countries," *National Tax Journal*, 14 (1961): 321.

yields have not increased significantly. Moreover, many imported products, instead of being taxed heavily, are simply banned, thereby yielding no revenue. The reasons for import prohibitions, as they are called, and the results of such prohibitions are rather curious. Consider the following example:

Foreign cigarettes are on the prohibited list but are extensively smuggled and sold fairly openly on the streets of Tehran. The ostensible reason for the prohibition is a desire to protect the domestic cigarette industry, which is a government monopoly. At the time of this writing (1964) smuggled foreign cigarettes sold for roughly double the price of legal local cigarettes, which were of inferior quality. Yet the Ministry of Finance was unwilling to exchange the prohibition of imported cigarettes for a stiff duty, on the ground that such a change would further increase the volume of smuggling and thus in time diminish the market for locally manufactured cigarettes, because consumers generally prefer the imported variety.

In other words, confessing inability to control smuggling, the government sought to minimize it by a zero duty. The remedy would seem logically (at least to a non-Persian mind) to be better customs enforcement efforts rather than an attempt to buy off the smugglers at the expense of the revenue. This case illustrates once more how difficult the application of even rudimentary fiscal principles may be in practical situations.

In Burma during the year 1956, when the country was critically short of foreign exchange, the import of automobiles was banned completely. This ban was imposed in spite of the fact that the duty had been 51 per cent of the selling price before the ban. Potential smuggling was controllable and therefore not a factor in the prohibition. The government decided that it would rather give up the 51 per cent duty in order to save the 49 per cent foreign exchange outlay, which it thought nonessential.

During this period the Burmese kyat was considerably overvalued at the official rate of exchange. This overvaluation was accomplished by stringent controls over foreign payments. The decision was, therefore, to forego a good revenue source in order to maintain the exchange control.

I shall have more to say on decisions of this nature in a later chapter, which will treat the relations between fiscal policy and both trade and exchange rate policies in more detail. The immediate point, however, is not simply the fact that tax policy is often subservient to other aspects of economic policy; but rather that the whole constellation of policies is not actually very favorable to economic growth.

Costa Rica in 1961 had a dual-exchange rate system. Exporters were required to surrender their proceeds at one rate, while importers had to pay a higher rate for exchange to buy nonessential imports. This secondary rate amounted, in effect, to a generalized customs duty on all nonessential imports, and, in addition, these imports were subject to specific duties graduated on the basis of essentiality.

The government of Costa Rica was then under considerable pressure from the International Monetary Fund, as well as from friendly foreign governments, to unify its exchange rate. One trouble with the dual-rate system was that the export rate gave inadequate incentive to exporters, since it amounted to a kind of generalized export tax. The government was unwilling to raise the export rate and thus to give up the premium it collected on export proceeds, but was equally unwilling to lower the import rate, since this would have increased the volume of import of consumer goods. An equilibrium unitary rate would have been somewhere between the two rates.

A possible remedy in this instance clearly would have been to raise customs duties somewhat, to compensate for a more favorable import rate. Assuming that a dual foreign exchange rate was necessary, which in my opinion it was not, the exporters should have had the more favorable rate and the importers the less favorable one. This would have improved both the export and import sides of the country's trade account. In this particular case inadequate fiscal policy had to be bolstered by a patched-up exchange rate policy. Both policies were wrong and the errors in one merely compounded the errors in the other.

Countries that are now well developed once made extensive use of customs duties during the earlier stages of their growth. In the United States before the Civil War (1861–65), import taxes were the most important source of revenue. Great Britain, Germany, and Japan also depended heavily on import taxes during the early stages of their industrial growth, in spite of the fact that neither Britain nor Japan was self-sufficient in food at the time.

Conclusions Concerning Import Taxes

Customs duties are comparatively easy to understand and to enforce, making their use highly practical for countries in which the internal revenue system is not as yet well developed. These duties can be arranged, as I already noted, to amount, in effect, to a progressive tax on consumption, since they are commonly assumed to be largely passed forward into finished product prices.

125

It follows, therefore, that developing countries should, in the course of gearing their revenue systems to the requirements of development finance, first strengthen, simplify, and where necessary, raise in effective rates their system of import duties. The imposition of stiff import duties, rather than exchange controls, should be the chief method of limiting consumption and of conserving foreign exchange for the necessarily larger imports of capital equipment that development calls for. Tax advisers to less developed countries should make certain that the full potential of import taxation is being utilized before recommending other, more complex, revenue sources such as a personal income tax.

The principal obstacles to using customs duties as a progressive tax on consumption are (1) that this course necessarily means imposing an arbitrary standard of essentiality for rate-setting purposes, thus interfering with consumers' freedom of choice, and (2) that it may work unfavorably on incentives to produce.

If people are, on the one hand, to be motivated to work harder and more effectively in order to consume certain imported products and if, on the other hand, these products are to be put beyond their reach by high import duties, the input of effort so necessary for development may suffer. At the same time some people may be motivated to work even harder by virtue of stiff import duties, since luxuries become more expensive. The net effect on work incentives may be complex and uncertain.

TAXATION OF LAND AND OF AGRICULTURAL PRODUCTION

In addition to taxing imports, practically all less developed countries tax agricultural output or capital employed in agriculture in some fashion. The methods used are sometimes a mixture of property and income tax principles.[8]

Alternative Principles

As used here, property tax principles refer primarily to taxing wealth as an index of income, rather than to making income itself the object of taxation. The theory is that wealth taxes are easier to administer than other kinds, since wealth is not easily hidden; also, wealth taxes

[8]The leading reference on this subject is Haskell Wald's *Taxation of Agricultural Land in Underdeveloped Economics* (Cambridge, Mass.: Harvard University Press, 1959). Wald distinguishes three general types of land taxes, namely (1) those assessed according to land area, (2) those based on a rental value concept, and (3) those based on an income concept. He favors the income concept in his recommendations.

make less severe demands on taxpayers in accounting, record keeping, and voluntary compliance than income taxes.

The practice in less developed countries varies considerably in the relative reliance on property and income tax principles in land taxation. In some countries, agricultural land is taxed essentially on a property or wealth basis, while in other countries it is the income from land, whether actual or constructed, on which the initial burden of the tax falls. The latter system is often used where land records are incomplete or faulty but where current yield from land can readily be determined, either because the government provides the principal market for agricultural crops or is a principal processor of these crops.

Agricultural land taxes obviously depend on and must be geared to the prevailing system of land tenure. In parts of Africa where rural land is communally owned, such taxation is virtually impossible. African land taxes are imposed primarily on urban property.[9] In other areas where government ownership is common, ground rents often take the place of land taxes.

Need for an Increased Burden

It is common knowledge that less developed countries are primarily agricultural. We have already seen that a sharp increase in agricultural productivity is a necessary precursor, or adjunct, of industrialization, and also that agricultural taxation may be the chief technique for mobilizing the initial savings necessary for financing a development program.[10] It follows, therefore, that any country aspiring to develop rapidly must at an early stage face the necessity of greatly increasing agricultural taxation, if its development is to be financed by other than purely inflationary means. This increase in agricultural taxation can operate both as a spur to additional input into the agricultural sector and as a means of mobilizing capital for investment in nonagricultural pursuits.

[9]Due, *Taxation and Economic Development*, p. 102.
[10]Land taxation in Japan after 1870 provided the principal revenue of the government for the expansion of industry. Before 1870 Japanese land taxes were collected in kind and were used primarily to maintain the warrior class. After the Meiji restoration they were collected in cash and spent more productively. The land tax was fixed at 3 per cent of the value of the land, which amounted to about 35 per cent of the value of rice output; however the tax did not grow proportionately as farm production increased. For a description of this tax and use of the proceeds see the FAO paper "The Role of Agricultural Land Taxes in Japanese Development," reprinted in Bird and Oldman, *Readings on Taxation in Developing Countries*, pp. 436–49.

We have also seen that less developed countries in general are exporters primarily of agricultural materials and of products of the extractive industries. These exports must be sharply increased to provide the external finance both for expanded capital-goods imports and increased imports of consumer goods that will follow the income-raising effects of successful development. Hence the necessity for restricting imports by a system of customs duties that amounts to a progressive tax on consumption.

Heavier land taxes can also help to discourage consumption, since land owners may be among the wealthiest citizens of a developing country, and since they may also have the highest propensity to consume imports. For example, Egyptian landowners before the Nasser government were big spenders on luxury imports of all kinds.

Areas of Resistance

Land tax increases may be militantly resisted in countries where the landowners have substantial political power. Peasant cultivators, already close to the margin of subsistence, may also resist heavier land taxation because they fear this taxation will be directly reflected in their rents and will thus diminish their already inadequate net incomes from farming. Countries that are overpopulated, and therefore have the classic Malthusian problem of pressure of population on resources, will naturally distrust any precept which says their land taxes should be increased.

Nevertheless, it is still essential to strengthen agricultural taxation if development is to be assured. The problem is to find the least painful and most practical method of getting this higher tax yield from the agricultural sector.

Paths to Improvement

The form which agricultural taxation takes may also depend partly on the relative importance of local and national government within a country. The property tax is peculiarly adaptable to local assessment and collection, making its use by local government logical. The income tax principle is more suited to use by national government, which is in a better position to apply the tax uniformly. Most countries in early stages of development have highly centralized governments, with only the most rudimentary public functions being exercised at the local government level. Therefore, we often find use of the income principle in agricultural taxation in these countries.

When I speak of the income principle I do not mean use of actual net income as the basis of taxation. Rather, the tax usually attributes an arbitrary or constructed income to a given piece of land and bases the tax on this. This system is usually justified on the ground that farmers do not keep proper records and therefore only an attributed income is a practical base for taxation.

Unfortunately, a system of this kind, where tax collectors have considerable independent authority to make assessments, lends itself to collusion and independent deals between collectors and taxpayers. In practice such arrangements detract greatly from the equity of the tax, and also limit its capability as a revenue source.

It would seem, then, that land taxation in less developed countries could most practically be improved by reorganizing it along property tax lines, while perhaps providing for some sharing of the revenue between the local and the national government. Such improvement may come slowly because it requires, first of all, fairly systematic and complete records of land ownership which many countries lack. Aerial and cadastral surveys, plus modernizing the records of land ownership and transfer, may be necessary preliminary steps.

The essentials for a good tax on real property are well known. Complete tax rolls are needed. Assessment must be uniform and must reflect the consistent application of some well-recognized principle of valuation. Reassessments to keep abreast of changing valuations must be continuous. Promptness in collecting liabilities and in dealing with delinquencies is necessary. Administrative requirements for a comprehensive real property tax are not simple. Progressive rates based on the value of property holdings may be applied; they have been by some countries.

Property tax assessment and collection should be conducted primarily by the local offices of the national tax collecting organization but should be subject to uniform standards laid down by the national government. The land tax may actually serve as an important vehicle by which to decentralize the internal revenue service and to prepare for greater reliance on direct taxation at a later stage of development. When both local and national governments share the revenue there is a built-in incentive at both levels not to permit gross underassessment or undervigorous collection to impair this tax's potential yield.

There is, incidentally, a kind of rough equity in a stiff real-property tax for the purpose of financing development, since one consequence of successful development will almost certainly be a considerable rise in land values, especially in urban areas but also in the countryside. This is most certain to occur when population is rising rapidly; but it will also happen to some degree even where there is no severe population pressure. Without actually going back to the Ricardian theory of economic rent or to the Henry George principle of the single tax, there is plainly some direct association between economic growth and rising property values which should provide a convenient basis for taxation. Numerous countries have experimented with systems for capturing a part of the rise in land values attributable to population growth, urbanization, etc. by taxation.

Property taxes need not be limited to real estate but may extend also to personal property, tangible or intangible. While intangibles are sometimes difficult to reach, such tangibles as automobiles, household goods, and business equipment are often convenient objects of taxation.

Export Taxes

Export taxes are in use in a number of countries, probably in some cases on the mistaken theory that they can be shifted forward and will therefore fall, in part at least, on the foreign consumers of the exported products. While there is some evidence of partial forward shifting of the tea and jute export taxes levied by Ceylon, India, and Pakistan, export taxes are most typically passed backward to producers of the exported products.[11] Both flat rates and progressive rates are to be found in export tax practice. Malaysia, for example, levies a progressive export duty on natural rubber, with the rate geared to the price of rubber in the world market. All or part of the proceeds from export taxation are sometimes earmarked for expenditures that primarily benefit the export sectors. Thus, some of the Malaysian rubber tax is spent to replant areas with higher-yielding trees.

The extent of reliance upon export taxation by various countries is uneven, as Table 7 shows.

Export taxes have been most commonly adopted as fiscal expedients during export booms. Although their use during such periods may partially sterilize the rise in export incomes, continued reliance on them may have some important disadvantages, particularly on long-run export performance.

---

[11]For an appraisal of export taxes see K. L. Rothwell, "Taxes on Exports in Underdeveloped Countries," *Public Finance*, 18 (1963): 310–26.

TABLE 7

PERCENTAGE OF CENTRAL GOVERNMENT REVENUE FROM EXPORT TAXES
(1953-61)

Ghana	33.9
Ceylon	23.9
Uganda	23.4
El Salvador	21.1
Malaysia	20.1
Haiti	17.8
Mexico	12.5
Guatemala	12.4
Sudan	11.4
Venezuela	8.3
Ecuador	7.8
Bolivia	7.1
Thailand	6.5
Peru	6.4
Costa Rica	4.7
Honduras	4.6
India	2.9
Indonesia	1.5
Brazil	0.4

SOURCE: Rothwell, *Taxes on Exports in Underdeveloped Countries.*

Benefits and Costs of Export Taxes

For a single country to tax its principal exports heavily means to place itself at a competitive disadvantage compared with its rival suppliers. This loss of cost advantage limits the feasible reliance on export taxes unless all competing countries follow similar tax principles. Countries that rely on export taxes are understandably in the forefront in pressing for international commodity agreements that will cartellize production and support prices of such products as tin, rubber, coffee, wheat, jute, or other primary commodities which form their principal exports.[12]

The effect of progressive export taxes may also be secured by state

---

[12]G. Haberler has concluded that rather than trying to promote commodity price stabilization and buffer stock schemes, the less developed countries "would be better advised to learn to live with a certain degree of cyclical instability in their terms of trade and balance of payments. . . . There is no reason why the central bank should not accumulate foreign exchange in good years, sterilizing at least part of the proceeds, and then maintain imports for development and other purposes by dipping into the accumulated reserves." See his essay "Terms of Trade and Economic Development," in *Economic Development for Latin America*, ed. H. S. Ellis (London: Macmillan & Co., 1962), pp. 293-94.

marketing board arrangements. In Burma, for example, the government has become a monopsonistic buyer of rice for export. Peasant cultivators are required to sell to the government at fixed prices, while the government enters into wholesale export contracts at whatever prices the traffic will bear and pockets the difference as trading profit. In Burma, during and for several years following the Korean war, when rice prices were extremely high, these marketing board profits were the largest single source of revenue to the central government.[13]

The disadvantage with this system, which is, in effect, a 100 per cent tax on exports above the base price, is that it provides inadequate incentive to expand cultivation of the taxed commodities and thus to increase exports. In Burma, for example, the annual export of rice under this policy has been consistently below two million tons, whereas before World War II, under an open price policy and private trade in rice, the annual export trade had exceeded three million tons regularly and in certain years had reached 3.5 million tons. It is difficult for an outsider to see why even a Socialist government should choose voluntarily to limit its foreign exchange earnings in this manner.[14]

Unless a country has virtually an assured monopoly position in the supply of a needed product (as South Africa does with diamonds, for example), it should be chary of relying too heavily on export taxation. The long-run effects of such a tax policy are likely to be harmful to its balance-of-payments position as well as to its competitive position in the world market.

Consumers will naturally look to alternative sources of supply or to substitutes in an effort to avoid these commodity taxes. Natural rubber, which has for some years been burdened with high export taxes levied by the supplying countries, has steadily lost ground to the synthetic product. Copper, also heavily taxed, has likewise lost ground to aluminium in electric power applications and other uses.

I conclude, then, that export taxes are not a very fertile source of revenue for development finance. Countries needing revenue to finance

---

[13]For an appraisal of the operation of the Burmese rice marketing board see J. V. Levin, *The Export Economies* (Cambridge, Mass.: Harvard University Press, 1960), chap. 5.

[14]L. J. Walinsky, in his book on Burma's economic experience during the 1950's, writes: "Objections from the paddy cultivators to the fixed purchase price were strangely lacking. They did not realize, perhaps, how great was the Government's profit margin and how disproportionately they were contributing to the cost of the development effort." See his *Economic Development in Burma, 1951–60* (New York: Twentieth Century Fund, 1962), p. 500.

development would do well not to look to export taxes permanently to solve their problem.[15] Nevertheless, these taxes can be temporarily quite useful during an extraordinary export boom.

SALES AND EXCISE TAXES

Sales and excise taxes are employed by virtually all countries, developed as well as less developed. In part, their purpose is sumptuary, i.e., to limit consumption of certain products—such as liquor, tobacco, and narcotics—that are considered injurious to public health, safety, or morals. In part their purpose is purely fiscal, i.e., products which consumers consider necessary or highly desirable are without question good revenue producers; demand for these products is fairly inelastic with respect to price; therefore the taxes are largely shifted forward to ultimate consumers.

The United States, for example, in addition to taxing liquor and tobacco, until recently taxed by excise a long list of consumer durable goods including household appliances, musical instruments, luggage, phonographs and records, and jewelry. Although the original reason for these taxes was to discourage consumption of these products during wartime, when their production necessarily had to be limited, as well as to raise revenue, the taxes persisted well beyond the time of their original *raison d'être* simply because they were productive, and hence convenient revenue sources to the government.

Advantages and Disadvantages

In less developed countries, although many of the manufactured consumer goods are imported and hence can be reached by customs duties, there is still considerable scope for excise taxation. Passenger transportation by rail or bus; gasoline; local telephone and telegraph service; locally grown sugar, beer, tea and coffee; admissions to theaters and to sporting events; and club dues are potential candidates for excise taxation. Documentary stamp taxes on checks, notes, conveyances, and the like are extensively employed and are often substantial revenue producers.

Any system of excise taxation necessarily interferes somewhat with consumer freedom to exercise choice in a free market; thus it penalizes

[15]A. R. Prest concludes, similarly, "that it is now accepted by many that the disincentive effects of export taxes are so great that undue reliance should not be placed on them as a fiscal instrument." See his *Public Finance in Underdeveloped Countries* (London: Weidenfeld & Nicolson, 1962), p. 68.

those who choose to consume the taxed products, as against those who do not. While it is perhaps socially acceptable to penalize smokers and drinkers in this manner, there is no good reason for penalizing a housewife who uses an electric washing machine, which is taxed, as against one who prefers an old-fashioned washboard, which is untaxed. In fact, the effect of such a tax is actually inimical to economic growth, one feature of which is constantly greater variety and technical improvement in consumer products.

Underdeveloped countries have sometimes used excise taxes to good effect when these taxes fell on necessary products such as tea, coffee, salt, matches, and bread. Even at low rates, excises on necessary commodities produce large amounts of revenue; are comparatively easy to police and enforce; and are reasonably equitable horizontally, i.e., among those with similar incomes, if quite regressive vertically, i.e., among those with unequal incomes. Excises on necessities are largely shifted forward into final product prices and thus may be the only practical method of reaching the great mass of taxpayers with low incomes.

If a country industralizes by replacing imports with home manufactures, import duties must be replaced by other tax sources. Sales and excise taxes may be good candidates for this replacement function. They are comparatively easy to enforce but do inhibit growth of the new manufacturing industries which policy is encouraging. Thus products of already established industries should be the prime candidates for new excise taxes.

To advocate higher excise taxation in a poor country with the great bulk of the people close to the margin of subsistence is a harsh doctrine, requiring great political courage on the part of those leaders who espouse this policy. Governments have often fallen on the issue of the price of bread; many political leaders exhibit an understandable reluctance overtly to favor higher living costs as an imperative to development. Nevertheless, leadership has its obligations, and development has its price; the people must be brought to realize that this price has to be paid in one way or another, if effective support for development efforts is to be won.

If the process of economic growth were costless, there would be far fewer less developed countries than there are; only lack of resources, poor organization, or bad policies would be excuses for lagging in the competitive race toward higher living standards. In reality, all discerning politicians know that development is not to be easily gained, but that sustained effort and sacrifice by all elements in the population are necessary. Only by saving more and consuming less can development be paid for.

Excise taxes on the necessities produce one incidental result that may be favorable to development; this is the forcing of more of the total productive activity into the money economy and out of the subsistence sector. If peasant cultivators must pay higher prices for the few things they buy, they may be compelled to seek more cash income. Although there may be no practical method except property tax of reaching food produced and consumed at home, excises on products they take from the money economy will insure that they bear at least some tax burden.

Countries that are developing manufacturing industries for the first time may be reluctant to impose excise taxes on home-produced products for fear of retarding the growth of manufacturing activity. This is indeed a real danger; but excises on new manufacturing activities would not be productive of much revenue anyway; such taxes can be foregone without great loss to the fisc. Perhaps the best policy would be to grant temporary exemptions, for five or more years, to the new industries, and thereafter to tax their products at gradually rising rates after the industries have had time to become established.

General Sales Taxes

Whenever excise taxation becomes widespread there is always a question whether such taxation should not be generalized into a comprehensive sales tax. There is much to be said for this course, since selective excise taxation does distort consumer choice and does affect relative profitability of different businesses. A general sales tax, however, whether at the wholesale or the retail level, is a bit more difficult to administer than a system of excises; it may also, because of its flat rate, be more regressive in effect than a network of excises; a system of excises can have rates based on some concept of essentiality and thus can be even mildly progressive in effect. A general retail sales tax may be impractical in some developing countries because of the large number of small retail outlets; but a wholesale sales tax may be quite feasible. Such a tax, with food exempt, would be at worst only mildly regressive.

Excise and sales taxation thus offer a fairly fertile field in which less developed countries may expand their revenue systems without encountering impossible administrative problems. It is no accident that the more developed countries have used such indirect taxes as customs duties, property taxes, and excises at very early stages in their own development, and have gradually progressed from these levies to the more sophisticated and difficult forms of direct taxes, such as personal and corporate income levies.

The Value Added Variant

One type of general sales tax offers considerable potential for the less developed countries. This is the value added tax. Such a tax is used by France and also in modified form by Brazil and Argentina. In the United States it is used by the state of Michigan. A value added tax was legislated by Japan during the period of United States occupation following World War II; but it never actually went into effect. In recent years many countries have given increasingly serious consideration to this kind of tax.

The value added tax is a generalized tax on business gross income less purchases from other firms. It is measured by the "value added" by a particular firm, and thus is distributed roughly in accordance with each firm's contribution to national productive activity or net national income. Value added is considerably simpler to determine than net income, since the only allowable deduction from gross receipts may be outside purchases. It is more difficult to administer than a wholesale or retail sales tax because it covers all business enterprises rather than only those engaged in trade; but it is simpler than a net income tax, which assumes the existence of fairly complete books and records.

It is usually assumed that the value added tax will be levied at a low flat rate; the French tax, however, has classified rates, with the most essential products taxed least, and the least essential most. These classified rates are naturally the source of numerous complications.

The principal advantage of the value added tax is that it has, potentially, an extremely broad base; therefore it is capable of yielding substantial revenue at low rates. Even if an exemption is given to business receipts below a minimum size, thus reducing the number of taxpayers, the revenue potential is still high.

The value added tax is generally assumed to be largely passed forward into final product prices and therefore to be closely analagous to a kind of generally diffused sales tax. In practice, naturally, the possibility of forward tax shifting differs considerably between one industry and another, depending on competition, available substitutes, and numerous other factors. The value added tax is also neutral toward the form of business organization, not penalizing corporations as compared with proprietorships and partnerships, as many believe the corporation income tax does.

For a well-developed country with a sophisticated system of business income taxation, the value added tax is a rather retrograde alternative; but for an underdeveloped country with no adequate system of business taxation and a clear need of substantial additional revenue, the value added route may be quite attractive. Indeed, such a system may be better than proliferation of a number of excise taxes on domestic production, since it deals less harshly and in a less discriminatory way than the excises with various businesses vis-à-vis one another.

It should be clear from this brief discussion that sales, excise, and value added taxation offer real possibilities to countries in need of additional revenue to finance development. Strengthening these taxes should clearly precede in time, for most countries, the installation of broad-based personal or corporate net income taxes, because the administrative requirements for these indirect taxes are simpler.

A Brief Recapitulation

So far the burden of my argument has been that accelerated development, as planned by emerging countries today, requires in almost all cases a massive increase in tax revenue (public sector saving) and that this increase should be obtained by the fiscal authorities in almost any feasible and tolerably equitable manner. Some of the tax increases must necessarily be regressive in incidence and unpopular in application; but the only alternative is the crueler and more haphazard tax of a deliberately inflationary financial policy; in the end such a policy may well negate much of the real progress made in capital formation, as well as pave the way for all sorts of revolutionary political movements which may undermine the development efforts.

It may not be necessary to tax so aggressively that per capita consumption in absolute terms is reduced more than temporarily; but the rise in this consumption in real terms must be limited to but a fraction of the increase in total output, if the development effort is to gain momentum.

Governments have an obligation to be candid with their citizens about the price of development, as well as about its advantages. Great prizes are not easily won. In a war sacrifices must be expected. So should they be in the war against poverty and low productivity.

137

Income Taxes

Income taxes logically belong to a fairly advanced stage of economic development; yet they are found in operation in a large number of less developed countries. Usually they are narrowly based, incomplete, poorly administered, and in general not as productive and flexible as they are in more advanced countries.

General Features of Income Taxes

In many countries both corporate and personal net income are taxed, with or without some relief for corporate dividends. Corporate income tax rates are usually either flat or only mildly progressive, while individual income tax rates may be steeply graduated. Even in countries as yet little developed, there may be significant sectors of corporate business, perhaps engaged in foreign trade, in plantation agriculture, or in services such as banking, shipping, and insurance. These sectors may be well managed, may keep adequate records, and in general may be ready for income taxation long before a personal income tax is feasible.

Taxation of net income is complicated by numerous problems relating to permissible business expenses, including treatment of depreciation, exemptions and credits, capital gains or casual profits, and loss offsets. These problems are treated extensively in general works on income taxation and will not be discussed in detail here. For this discussion it is sufficient to note that measurement of net income for tax purposes is difficult; it requires a complex law and a high standard of administration for tolerably equitable results.

Among the more advanced countries, England has had a personal income tax in continuous operation for 120 years; the United States personal income tax has been effective for just over fifty years; France has yet to evolve the personal income tax as a major revenue source, relying instead much more heavily on indirect taxation.

The difficulty with personal income taxation is that it requires each taxpayer to keep fairly complete records and to file an annual return detailing his computations in arriving at taxable net income. In effect, each taxpayer is his own assessor, subject to general review by the tax collecting agency. The tax depends on a high standard of voluntary compliance with the prevailing law, since it is clearly impossible for each individual return to be audited in detail. In the United States, for example, more than sixty million individual income tax returns are filed with the federal government each year.

In a number of Latin American countries, personal income taxes are on a schedular basis, with different sources of income taxed at different rates and under varying rules. Such a system not only discriminates against certain sources of income but also makes impossible the application of proper family allowances, consistent rate progression, and other features of equitable personal income taxes. Where systems of this kind exist, it is important that they be integrated into a single tax on net income from all sources.

Some Drawbacks

In less developed countries that have an income tax, it is customary for tax collectors to audit each return each year and to infer net income fairly arbitrarily when records are incomplete. There is little uniformity in the way different collectors construe and apply the law, and much negotiation between taxpayers and collectors over the ultimate tax liability. Possibilities for collusion, bribery, and wholesale tax evasion are rampant under such a system.

Personal income taxes in less developed countries may be reasonably effective in reaching wage and salary income, where concealment is difficult, but far less effective in reaching business income, where concealment is much easier, especially when many business transactions are conducted in cash rather than through check payments. Property income may also be difficult to reach where bearer shares are common or where tax evasion is sanctioned by tradition and customary behavior among certain groups. The net result may be that an individual income tax bears more heavily on income from work than from ownership, whereas the opposite relationship might actually be more conducive to development.

In advanced countries the personal income tax is a powerful weapon for redistributing income and for reducing economic inequality. In less developed countries the objective of lessening inequality is ordinarily less prominent. As we have already noted, reducing inequality of income from work may not be a good thing in a developing country, although reducing inequality of income from property may have beneficial effects upon productive input. Business profits, which are income from work and from property in combination, should not be reduced too sharply by taxation in a society where private investment is expected to contribute importantly to development.

Less developed countries have often adopted income tax statutes which were beyond their effective capacity to administer equitably.[16] The result of this premature adoption of income taxation has sometimes been to discredit this tax before it could reasonably have been expected to work properly. Advisers who urge income taxes on countries not yet prepared for them do no service to the countries they are advising.

Many of the complications in an individual income tax derive from the progressive rates. If this tax is levied only at a flat rate there is little need to be concerned about bunching of income in particular years, timing of deductions, capital gains, and other features which occupy a disproportionate share of the statutes in countries with progressive income taxes. A flat rate income tax has the advantage of possessing at least some revenue flexibility, although less than would be desirable, and of being adaptable to withholding on several types of income.

Non-income Personal Taxes

There are certain forerunners of a general progressive tax on personal income that may be useful in themselves and may also help to pave the way for an income tax at a later stage of development. A number of African countries use what is called a personal tax; this is essentially a cross between a poll tax and an income tax. This tax usually relies on local assessment, although there may be some sharing of revenue with the national government. The tax is not based on returns but on personal knowledge of more tangible evidences of affluence such as size of household or known spending habits. The rate is commonly flat, although progressive rates are applied in a number of countries.[17] This tax offers distinct advantages, in that it prepares the way for personal income taxation as we understand it and also, since it must be paid in cash, forces people out of the subsistence sector and into the money economy. The African countries which use this tax have, as yet, only rudimentary fiscal systems.

When To Rely on Income Taxation

At what point in a country's economic development experience does a personal income tax become appropriate? It is impossible to specify

[16]It has been pointed out that in Panama, although the income tax is fairly low, there is evidence of widespread evasion. Poor enforcement of the tax may be seen from the fact that a penalty for negligence or fraud had never (until 1964) been levied. See *Fiscal Survey of Panama* (Baltimore: Johns Hopkins Press [for the OAS/IDB], 1964), p. 6.

[17]For a good description of African personal taxes see John Due, "The African Personal Tax," *National Tax Journal*, 15, no. 4 (December, 1962):385–98.

an answer to this question in purely economic terms. A review of the less developed countries that have personal income taxes shows, in effect, that these taxes are not very broadly based. The personal or family exemption is sufficiently high in comparison with average family income to exclude the bulk of the population from the income tax rolls. Nevertheless, the limited income taxes in these countries serve an important purpose in preparing the populace for heavier reliance on this tax at a later date, when family income is higher.

The history of personal income taxes in advanced countries reveals that these taxes nearly always began as class taxes on the higher-income groups and were only much later generalized, by reduced personal exemptions, to strike the mass of income recipients. In the United States, for example, it was not until World War II that the personal income tax became a mass tax. England depended more heavily on personal income taxation from World War I onward. In neither country would the income tax have worked on a mass basis without the earlier years of administrative and compliance preparation.

It seems, then, that less developed countries should install personal income taxation only when they are politically, administratively, and socially ready for this step. There should be concensus that reducing income inequality will promote social progress; a minimum standard of orderly record keeping by business; and a confidence by the public in the integrity and objectivity of the revenue service. Lacking these essential conditions, a personal income tax will be inequitable, poorly administered, and generally unsuccessful. Even when the conditions for a successful income tax are present, the tax must be kept on a limited basis for a number of years and therefore can not immediately become a major revenue producer. It is an untenable theory that any less developed country can finance development simply by installing a personal income tax similar to that of the United States or the United Kingdom.

DEATH TAXES

Death taxes are in general use in more advanced countries, less widely used among less developed countries. They offer some scope for fiscal productivity and even more for reducing extreme inequalities in wealth such as are to be found in many poorer countries.

Alternative Forms

Death duties may take the form either of estate taxes, which are levied on the entire estate prior to distribution and regardless of the number of heirs, or of inheritance taxes, which are collected from individual heirs on the basis of amounts received. Each tax has a certain philosophical basis. The estate tax may be regarded as an excise on the privilege of transferring wealth from one generation to the next; the inheritance tax is a kind of wealth accessions tax, reaching accretions that are not touched by the income tax, at least until a later date.

By Anglo-Saxon tradition the state has an equity in the property of a decedent which death taxes express. Death taxes commonly employ progressive rates on the theory that no intolerable effects will result from taxing large accumulations of wealth heavily; on the contrary, by making it harder for heirs of wealthy men to live without working, death taxation may serve a useful social purpose.

The form death taxation takes naturally depends on the prevailing legal system in a particular country. In India and some other countries of the Far East, property is regarded as belonging to the undivided family rather than to particular individuals. The number of persons with claims to the wealth of an undivided family is constantly changing through births, deaths, and marriages. Under this system a periodic wealth tax, say every five years, may be more appropriate than making death and inheritance the taxable event. In the Near East, Muslim law specifies almost exactly how a decedent's property shall be divided. It would seem that in countries where this custom prevails, the estate tax principle would be more appropriate than the inheritance tax principle; either may be used, however.

Pros and Cons

Death taxation raises fewer administrative problems than income taxation, since the number of returns is fewer and since death ordinarily means a property accounting anyway, whether or not a tax is levied. The chief problems in death taxation are location and proper valuation of property. The latter is sometimes difficult when the property is not marketable or has not been transferred for a long time. Locating all intangible property included in an estate may also be difficult.

Death taxation can be a significant source of revenue for less developed countries, although it is not as yet widely used; it can be employed to break up large aggregations of property that have the effect of limiting economic opportunity for the great mass of citizens. Countries not yet able to operate progressive income taxes may attack the distribution of wealth through graduated rate death taxes.

Taxation of property passing at death usually also means that *inter vivos* gifts must be made subject to tax. Otherwise it would be easy to avoid the death tax by giving property during life. In the United States, gift tax rates, which are imposed on the donor, are 75 per cent of the corresponding estate tax rates. This differential is thought to be justified on the ground that gift tax is paid earlier than estate tax. Despite the rate differential, however, most wealthy taxpayers do not take full advantage of the tax savings possible through *inter vivos* gifts.

OTHER TAX SOURCES

Net Worth

Wealth, or net worth, taxes are in use in a number of countries including Sweden, Norway, the Netherlands, West Germany, Colombia, and India. The Indian tax, for example, uses rates ranging from $\frac{1}{2}$ per cent to $1\frac{1}{2}$ per cent above fairly high exemptions. It applies to net worth of corporations as well as to that of individuals, but not to wealth invested in agricultural land.

It has sometimes been contended that properly designed wealth and either income or expenditure taxes can complement one another, both functionally and administratively. For example, a common return might be used for both a wealth and an expenditure tax, or cross checking of returns filed by the same taxpayer might help to uncover avoidance or evasion.[18] While this is theoretical advantage of interlocking taxes of this nature, the administrative requirements of the combination are more complex than they would be for a straight income tax producing equivalent revenue. The expenditure tax is essentially a variant of income taxation in which saving is exempt.

Excess Profits

Excess profits taxes are in use in a number of countries including India, Uruguay, Colombia, and Mexico. Usually these taxes have an invested capital base, i.e., the tax applies only to profits in excess of a stated rate of return on invested capital. These taxes can at times be highly productive of revenue, but they tend to penalize success and thus are not especially appropriate for a permanent place in the tax structure of a country that is anxious to develop.

[18]This was a feature of the tax recommendations made to the Indian Government in 1956 by N. Kaldor. B. Higgins has also recommended a similar scheme to the government of Indonesia.

Building a Tax System

It remains to mention briefly how the different types of taxes that have been discussed in the preceding pages can be put together to create a system that will be (1) capable of reaching most taxable sources; (2) equitable—both horizontally and vertically; and (3) responsive to changing economic conditions. In general, a developing country should obviously build on the tax system it already has, making sure that its major taxes do not get seriously out of date, are progressive in effect wherever possible, and are within its administrative capability. Obvious gaps in the revenue structure should be filled, so that all groups within the population will be contributing their fair share to the necessarily heavy costs of public investment.

As a long-run goal the reliance on direct taxation should gradually increase, but progress toward that goal may require both institution building and new public attitudes. These naturally take considerable time. Meanwhile, indirect taxes can be employed that are progressive in effect and flexible in yield.

The review in the preceding pages of the various revenue sources, and the way in which each may be used, indicates that any country which is truly anxious to finance development in a fiscally responsible way can find the revenue, given the will to tax adequately and to risk some political unpopularity in the process. Support for a program of adequate taxation must be based on broad public understanding of the benefits and costs of development and on public acceptance of the conclusion that the benefits are really worth the costs. Without this public understanding and acceptance, economic development will remain either a vague aspiration or merely another method of exploiting the many for the benefit of the few.

Structural Effects of Taxation

So far, this chapter has developed the themes that successful development, which in most poorer countries means a stepped-up program of public investment, requires a fairly massive expansion in tax revenue, and that this revenue should be sought in any manner which is both feasible and tolerably equitable. It must be recognized, however, that any tax has economic effects and that those which are harmful to development ought to be minimized as tax burdens become heavier.

Some General Principles

Harsh taxation of business profits, for example, will not stimulate business growth and may cause shortfalls in private investment compared with plan targets. Likewise, taxes that bear too heavily on wage differentials between one occupation and another will not encourage the mobility of labor that economic growth requires.

On the other hand, progressive taxes on consumption, whether by import duties or excise taxes, work positively, for the most part, by encouraging saving and conserving foreign exchange for the necessary import of capital goods. Such taxes also help to prevent prices from rising too rapidly when ongoing investment is increasing personal incomes faster than the output of finished goods and services is rising.

Without adequate taxation too much strain has to be put on monetary policy and on direct controls over prices, foreign payments, and wages. These direct controls ossify the economic structure and impede the shifts in resources that development requires. They are also likely to be highly inequitable in application and to divert attention from expanding output to evading or circumventing the controls. Price movements have a definite role to play in facilitating economic adjustments and resource shifts. Unnecessary interference with the price system will not ordinarily be helpful to development.

Proper taxation can be used to encourage economic adjustment rather than to impede it. Temporary tax holidays for new industries, although in one sense unfair to industries already established, may enable these new industries to flourish and thus to expand the future tax base. If used properly, these holidays should be strictly temporary and should not be allowed to become embedded in the tax structure as permanent special concessions.

Finally, the case for heavy taxation of agriculture in an economy aspiring to develop rests on the grounds (1) that agriculture is the one industry capable of furnishing the gross savings needed for development finance in many countries, and (2) that this taxation may provide an impetus to the improvement of productivity in agriculture, and also to the shifts in labor and other resources out of agriculture into the secondary industries such as manufacturing and distribution.

The Continuing Task

A country's tax structure must be reviewed periodically as development proceeds. The relative dependence on various taxes and on evolving revenue administration must be continually modified. The aim should always be a tax structure that will be adequate, flexible, and harmonious with the emerging pattern of economic activity. Tax barriers to progress must be removed promptly as they develop; tax incentives must also be removed as soon as they have served their primary purpose. At the same time there is need for a stable, continuing base tax structure within which expansion can proceed, free from uncertainty about the form of future tax levies.

7

Fiscal Policy in Relation to
Other Economic Policies

Although important in its own right, and the main concern of this monograph, fiscal policy is only one of the many tools a government has available for encouraging economic growth. In the present chapter I propose to look briefly but broadly at the entire complex of government economic policies—in particular the relation between public finance and the monetary, trade, and international economic policies of less developed countries—to determine how these policies might fit together in order best to stimulate development. The optimum blend of economic policies will obviously vary from country to country and from one stage of growth to another; but there are general principles that may be articulated.

Role of the Private Sector

I assume, for purposes of the present chapter, that the economy is not altogether centrally directed and that the private business sector has an essential role to play in the total development effort. The relative sizes of the public and private enterprise sectors clearly vary from country to country, depending on the nature of each country's development program and the prevailing philosophy about the appropriate spheres of public and private enterprise, respectively. As the Clay Committee stated in its report:

> Sound governmental planning consists of establishing intelligent priorities for the public investment program and formulating a sensible and consistent set of public policies to encourage growth in the private sector.[1]

It may be taken for granted that much of the social overhead investment—in education, transportation, power and water supply, and health—will be publicly financed. Likewise, certain of the programs for

---

[1] *The Scope and Distribution of the U.S. Military and Economic Assistance Program* (Washington, D.C.: U.S. Government Printing Office, 1963), p. 16.

improvement of agricultural productivity, especially those utilizing demonstrations that require extension agents, will also be publicly financed. Industrialization, which is a component of virtually all national development programs of the emerging countries, may be either publicly or privately financed. Even if publicly financed, the ultimate control over the new industries may either be kept in public hands or allowed to pass gradually into private ownership.

We have already observed that investment planning for the private sector should, if efficient, be less a matter of deciding and directing what shall be invested where than it is of creating conditions favorable to the sorts of investment that will perpetuate and magnify themselves for the benefit of all. In encouraging private investment, fiscal policy may be less important than the other economic policies which define more fundamentally the investment climate.

FISCAL AND MONETARY POLICIES

By monetary policy I mean the measures taken by central authority to determine the supply of means of payment and to adjust this money supply continuously to the needs of trade. A variety of instruments, ranging from blunt changes in reserve requirements or credit ceilings to delicate and subtle variations in interest rates, may be used to implement monetary policy. The more highly developed the financial structure, the subtler monetary policy techniques are likely to be.

Role of the Central Bank

Monetary policy is primarily the responsibility of the central bank; this bank may be nominally independent of the government, but it is actually close to the center of power in both economic policymaking and execution. In virtually all countries the chief executive of the central bank is an important economic policy officer who occupies a strong position of influence in the councils of government. This position depends less on the source from which the central bank draws its capital than on general recognition that the actions of the central bank have broad economic repercussions which may promote or retard growth.[2]

[2] In his well-known book *The Art of Central Banking* (London: Longmans Green, 1932), R. G. Hawtrey wrote at length on the "enlargements and compressions" of consumers' income and outlay effected by central banks and concluded that "if this fundamental causal sequence were generally understood, the public would hardly acquiesce in the central banks proceeding, from their position of complacent detachment,

continued on next page

If the government runs a deficit, the central bank must be prepared to help finance this deficit; if foreign exchange must be conserved, the central bank will undoubtedly help develop the program for conservation and may actually administer it. Central banks in less developed countries also have a hand in developing the information and statistics necessary for formulating and executing public investment plans.

The primary responsibility of central banks is regulating the money and credit supply and influencing interest rates by their monetary operations.[3] As lender of last resort, the central bank influences the lending policies of commercial banks and thus indirectly determines how easy or difficult the access of private business to credit shall be, and at what rates of interest. In lending to the government the central bank can influence the budget and perhaps also the taxation policies.

Harmony and Conflict between Fiscal and Monetary Policies

Fiscal and monetary policies together make up a team or combination that can influence the volume of economic activity both directly and indirectly. A blend of loose fiscal and monetary policies can incline the economy toward an inflationary spiral; this may induce a fever of development for a time, but it will also certainly induce a reaction when the fever has burned itself out. In contrast, a combination of overtight fiscal and monetary policies may stifle the normal impulses toward growth by restricting investment in virtually all sectors. A loose fiscal policy in combination with a tight monetary policy may also slow growth.[4]

---

[2] *continued*

to generate depression, unemployment, bankruptcy, budget deficits and defaults, with all the resulting political and social convulsions. . . ." Today the sequence is better understood, and central banks are, in fact, much less detached in their policy prescriptions.

[3] According to A. Harberger, the money supply is typically smaller in relation to national income in less developed than in more developed economies. Accordingly, a given public deficit of 1 per cent of national income means a larger relative expansion in money supply, and more inflation. See his paper "Some Notes on Inflation," presented at the Conference on Inflation and Growth, Rio de Janeiro, January, 1963 (mimeographed).

[4] A Guatemalan economist, Michael Zuntz, concludes that, if it is possible to levy sufficient taxes to cover the internal direct cost of an investment program, it is always wiser to do so than to use monetary expansion or fiscal deficits, since the optimum use of foreign exchange reserves will be assured. He also believes that efforts by less developed countries to employ artificially low interest rates will fail because of foreign exchange effects. See his paper "Some Observations on Monetary Policy in Underdeveloped Countries," *Economic Development and Cultural Change*, no. 4 (December, 1952), pp. 273–85.

The argument in an earlier chapter was that developing countries should aim generally at annually balanced budgets, not so much because of the intrinsic merit of this rule, but because alternative rules do not logically serve less developed countries nearly as well as this old rule aimed more at price than at employment stability. Surpluses and deficits are essentially contracyclical weapons for the maintenance of relatively full employment in advanced countries. Less developed countries have a more structural unemployment problem; the cyclical problem they do have is not so amenable to financial remedies.

Examples of nonoptimum fiscal and monetary policy mixes in less developed countries come readily to mind. In Costa Rica in 1961, for example, tax revenue was inadequate and the deficit in the government's budget considerable. Prices would have risen rapidly and speculation would have increased, had it not been for the tight lid which the central bank maintained on the supply of credit—by setting ceilings on the amounts which the government-owned commercial banks could lend in various loan categories. The result was a cumbersome system of selective credit restriction in which individual exceptions to the ceilings determined which enterprises could expand.[5]

These credit ceilings stultified private investment rather generally, substituted an administrative method of rationing credit for a price system, and gave the government an unfair advantage in access to resources, compared with private businessmen. They also diverted the attention of businessmen from productive investment to a search for ways of circumventing the credit ceilings. In effect, the central bank, by controlling the access to credit, became the development planning agency, except that it had no comprehensive plan. It merely dealt with a multitude of applications for credit on a hit-or-miss basis, without an underlying philosophy.

I have already commented, in an earlier chapter, on some of the unfortunate effects of a nonoptimum fiscal and monetary policy mix. It is

[5]That this particular system of selective credit controls was cumbersome does not mean that such controls may not have a place in development policy. It has been argued by some economists, e.g., J. Pesmazoglu of the Bank of Greece, that such controls may be used constructively to direct investment into socially more productive but privately less profitable sectors. See his paper "The Relation between Fiscal and Monetary Policy," presented to the OECD Conference on Government Finance and Economic Development, Athens, December, 1963 (mimeographed). The difficulty in practical application of this position naturally lies in accurately measuring differences between social and private marginal productivity. I remain rather skeptical about the likelihood of wise use of selective credit controls in planning private investment.

sufficient here to note once more that little self-perpetuating development occurred under this particular policy combination.

The opposite combination, a tight fiscal policy and a fairly easy credit policy, has, in my opinion, more logic behind it for a developing country. The tight fiscal policy insures that an ample volume of public saving will be generated to finance public investment, while the easy credit policy insures that private investment will not be starved for want of loans. Such a policy combination may be less inflationary than the opposite combination, since private investment generally adds to output more quickly than public investment. Adding to the money supply through private loans may therefore be less dangerous than adding to it through a government deficit. Also, there may be less risk of disequilibrium to the balance of payments when private rather than public credit is being expanded. Private bankers can be relied on to see that loans are for productive purposes; government officials who plan public investment programs may be less hard-headed in this respect.

The combination of laxity in both fiscal and monetary policies may be illustrated by the situation in Iran at the present time. That country has a large foreign exchange income from the export of oil, which accrues to the government. Most of this is set aside and programmed for economic development. The problem comes in financing the local currency component of development outlay.

Iran has a grossly inadequate and inflexible system of taxation which is so poorly administered that a good portion of legal tax liability is never collected. Consequently, the consolidated budget of the national government shows persistent deficits year after year. These deficits are financed by the central bank on essentially open-book credit.

There is no established market for government securities and hence no real alternative to financing the deficits through the central bank. As the government goes on piling up deficits, commercial bank deposits expand, while bank reserves expand also, since the commercial banks have easy access to the central bank discount window. The only tightness of any sort in monetary policy comes when the central bank from time to time raises commercial bank reserve requirements; this is at best a crude method of dealing with the excess of liquidity that is constantly being generated by the government's fiscal policy.

The result is a rapid advance in prices which is tacitly accepted by the Iranians as an inevitable concomitant of development. In reality, the government is relying on inflation to do the taxing it is too timid to do directly.

This process redistributes income upward, i.e. in favor of the higher-income groups, instead of downward, and means that the mass of people are deprived of most of the benefits of development before they occur. In such a situation it is not surprising that the populace at large is, at best, rather apathetic about development as a national goal.

Burma in the years during and immediately after the Korean War was in a somewhat similar position. A world shortage of rice caused the price to skyrocket, which assured Burma of an unusually large foreign currency income, since rice is the country's chief export. Moreover, under the marketing board system then in force, the increment in foreign exchange income accrued entirely to the government. With large foreign exchange reserves in hand, and a bland confidence that the price of rice would remain high for some time, Burma embarked on an overambitious program of public investment.

The Socialist government then in power did not recognize any immediate administrative limits to enlarged public investment, with the result that the gestation period of public projects steadily became longer and longer. The investment program itself was too capital-intensive in nature and was poorly balanced among the various sectors of the economy, doing virtually nothing for agriculture, for example, and far too much to encourage electrification and new manufacturing industries. The local currency component of development outlay was not matched by tax increases but instead by deficits which were largely financed by the central bank.

In this disequilibrium system, imports for consumption increased very rapidly. When these imports began to use foreign exchange too quickly, they were curtailed administratively by exchange controls and import prohibitions. No sooner had this been done than domestic prices began to get out of hand; these were temporarily slightly restrained by administratively untenable direct price controls, which quickly became unenforceable. Such private investment as occurred was concentrated mainly in stocks of finished goods, which were virtually certain to advance in price.

This situation indicated a clear need both for a stronger tax policy and for more credit restraint by the central bank. The real villain was simply the size and nature of the public investment program. The program was excessive both from the standpoint of finance and from the standpoint of administrative capacity to carry it through successfully.

The situation was eventually righted by an emergency transfusion of foreign aid plus a sizeable reduction in the scope of the public investment program. The latter necessarily meant a considerable waste of resources, because complements of projects already finished were not carried out promptly; it also contributed to the downfall of the Nu government.

In Costa Rica, Iran, and Burma, inadequate tax policy was obviously a strong contributor to the stalling of the development sequence. Weak tax policy either placed an intolerable burden on monetary policy (Costa Rica) or underwrote an inflationary spiral in which sustainable growth could not flourish (Iran and Burma). This is not to claim that, with a sufficient weight of taxation, development would have proceeded smoothly in these three countries; merely that the combination of fiscal and monetary policies was wrong in each case, although for somewhat different reasons.

Obstacles to Policy Harmony

A proper combination of fiscal and monetary policies for a developing country obviously requires continuous coordination and cooperation in the policy evolving process. This is not always easy to secure. Ministries of finance in less developed countries may not fully appreciate either the logical interlocks between various financial policies or the need for admitting the central bank to the economic policy councils of government. The Central Bank of Burma, for example, never had an effective voice in the budget considerations which determined the size of the government's deficit; yet it was regularly called upon to finance this deficit, although its own lending powers were strongly limited by legislation. Neither does the Central Bank of Iran have other than the broadest and most perfunctory participation in the budget process.

As has been noted, monetary policy is especially important in determining how well private investment does its part in the development effort. This is also the sector of investment that has seemed to lag in so many less developed countries. Government can always, in some manner, find the finance it needs to conduct its programs, even if it squeezes the private sector somewhat in the process.

The real danger in so many development programs is that public investment will increase while private investment stagnates or declines. The devices used by governments to secure their own finances, whether foreign exchange controls, restrictions on private lending, price controls, or whatever, inevitably constrict the private sector. Net development is the sum of both private and public investment. Fiscally more responsible policies are needed, to see that one does not rise at the expense of the other and thus inhibit growth.

The blend of fiscal and monetary policies that will be most favorable to development cannot be prescribed in specific terms; it must be evolved in each developing country on the basis of its own institutions and its own problems. It appears, however, that developing countries are prone to err in adopting too weak a taxation policy, coupled either with a necessarily expansionist monetary policy or with a tight credit policy that permits public investment to grow partially at the expense of private investment. My suggestion is that a tighter taxation policy (to insure the noninflationary finance of public investment), coupled with a relatively easy credit policy (to insure the continued expansion of private investment), is the combination best suited to the needs of most developing countries. This rule of thumb can be applied, obviously, only when appropriately adapted to the current situation in any particular country.

CAPITAL-OUTPUT RATIOS

It has become fashionable, in discussions of development, to speak of capital-output ratios. These ratios are merely shorthand expressions for the nexus between an amount of investment and the ensuing rise in value of output. Capital-output ratios of, say, 2 to 1 or 5 to 1 are supposed, in some esoteric manner, to indicate whether a development program has been well conceived or is being properly executed.[6] Intercountry comparisons of capital-output ratios are also quite fashionable.

Uses and Abuses of the Ratios

I have no fault to find with the use of capital-output ratios in statistical contexts where they may be useful. One should employ these ratios with caution, however, both in the planning process and in program appraisal.[7] Such ratios, if calculated *ex post*, reflect essentially the combined marginal productivity of all increases in productive inputs, not merely of investment; if used *ex ante*, as indicators of the

[6]F. T. Moore has shown that in fifteen country missions sponsored by the IBRD the implied capital-output ratios for the investments recommended range from just over 2 (Mexico) to more than 5 (Guatemala). Moore believes that, generally, an investment program which stresses rapid industrialization will show a higher capital-output ratio in a less developed than in a more advanced country. See his article "The World Bank and Its Economic Missions," *Review of Economics and Statistics,* 42 (1960):85.

[7]Some of the limitations on the use of capital-output ratios in development planning have been stated by H. B. Chenery in his article "Comparative Advantage and Development Policy," *American Economic Review,* 51 (1961):18-51.

amount of output expansion to be expected from given schedules of investment, they are at best crude macroestimating equations and at worst, downright misleading.

A rather obvious misuse of capital-output ratios may be found in the preparatory work for the third Indian five-year plan of development. Starting from desired output increases based primarily on population growth and per capita income targets, the Indian planners worked back, via capital-output ratios that were essentially arbitrary, to investment schedules. The flaw in the process was that, since the capital-output ratios employed were consistently too low, the investment schedules (although well beyond India's own financial capacity) could not possibly produce the amounts of income and output expansion that were desired. The result of this oversanguine and crudely mechanical planning technique will inevitably be a mass disappointment with the outcome of development planning, when the plan period has been completed and the actual accomplishments are measurable against the initial projections.

Capital-output ratios are not the same in all sectors of the economy. I have already indicated that such ratios may be quite low in the agricultural sector; but they are almost always very high when industrialization is the field toward which investment is directed. Therefore, intercountry comparisons of capital-output ratios may reflect nothing more than the varying emphasis put on different fields of investment in different country plans. Such comparisons may not be indicative either of development performance or of the extent of self-help being mobilized in individual country situations.

This digression on capital-output ratios in a chapter devoted to interrelationships between broad areas of economic policy has been introduced primarily because these ratios are influenced by the blend of prevailing economic policies.[8] If this blend is for any reason not the optimum one, the capital-output ratio will be higher than it would be if based on a more suitable policy mix. When comparisons are made between capital-output ratios in different countries, the interpretation of the results ought to take into account these differences in economic policy mix. This is not always done.

FISCAL AND TRADE POLICIES

The international trade policies of a developing country strongly

[8]Chenery, *Comparative Advantage and Development Policy.*

influence, and in turn are apt to be influenced strongly by, its fiscal performance. Many less developed countries are monocultures with only a single important export. This exposes their economies to the vagaries of the world market and makes development planning difficult, since foreign exchange earnings are uncertain.[9]

Less developed countries are prone to point out that the terms of trade are often disadvantageous to raw material producers, which most of these countries are. Although it is highly questionable whether over the last fifty years there has been a fundamental shift in the terms of trade in favor of manufactured goods, it is undeniable that from time to time raw material producers have been in a weak trading position.[10]

The remedy often sought by less developed countries with only one or two exports is international commodity agreements which will place price floors under their export commodities. These price floors, to be effective, often must be accompanied by production restrictions, to keep stocks from accumulating to excess proportions, and by financial provisions, to keep stocks off the market for extended periods. The alternative to commodity agreements—export diversification—is much more difficult to achieve.

Interplay of Trade and Fiscal Policies

Export taxation is one point at which fiscal and trade policies often meet and where wrong combinations from the standpoint of long-run growth have sometimes been evolved. I have already commented, in an earlier chapter, about the dangers of depending too heavily on export taxation, a dependence that often results when a country behaves in a more monopoloid manner than the facts justify. It is difficult to see why Malaysia, for example, clings so resolutely to its progressive export taxes on natural rubber when the competition from synthetics is so intense. Surely other revenue sources could be found that would be less damaging to the country's long-term trading position. Similarly, Chile, with its export taxes on copper, has done much to undermine its commercial position in the world economy.

[9]A. K. Cairncross has pointed out that less developed countries as a group have a narrow range of exports, a large portion of which consists of gifts of nature. He also notes that their exports are in fairly intense competition with one another and that as a group their imports of primary products are roughly half as large as their exports. See his *Factors in Economic Development* (London: Allen & Unwin, 1962), pp. 214–38.

[10]For a balanced view of this question see T. Morgan, "The Long Run Terms of Trade between Agriculture and Manufacturing," *Economic Development and Cultural Change*, October, 1959, pp. 1–23.

With import taxes such an important source of revenue in many less developed countries, changes in trade patterns or in trade volume may have important fiscal consequences. A barter deal, for example, in place of previous normal commercial trade, may be disruptive to the revenue flow and therefore unbalancing to the budget. Secondary effects should be considered when barter offers are being appraised. Burma, for example, in 1955 made a large barter agreement with Russia. The Burmese got a high accounting price for their rice, only to be charged very stiff prices for the Russian commodities they agreed to take in return. In retrospect the agreement looked very much less favorable than it had in prospect. Because of the marketing board system then in force the excess price of rice became government revenue while the excess price of the return goods came out of the pockets of consumers. The net effect of the barter agreement was to levy a hidden tax on consumption of imported products, as though customs duties had been raised. This was quite a different effect than the Burmese initially expected.

Attention has already been called repeatedly to the fact that a new or enlarged public investment program means a two-ply increase in imports. Capital goods imports rise because of the high import content of public projects, while consumer goods imports rise because of the income-generating effects of the expanded public investment. Unless the rise in consumer goods imports is somehow forestalled by higher taxation, a squeeze on foreign exchange reserves is inevitable. Less developed countries all too commonly respond to this squeeze by import licensing or some other direct control over access to foreign exchange. This step has the incidental effect of weakening the revenue position, since fewer imports at the high duty rates are permitted.

Most less developed countries are more dependent on international trade than are the advanced countries—with the exception of the United Kingdom and Japan.[11] If imports are restricted, countries may face retaliation from their trading partners, which can easily render their efforts to conserve foreign exchange unsuccessful. Trade restriction is a game which in the end no country can hope to win.

We noted, in an earlier chapter, that changes either in a country's terms of trade or in the volume of its exports can affect its fiscal position. The conclusion reached there was that it was usually undesirable to try

---

[11]G. Haberler, *International Trade and Economic Development*, National Bank of Egypt Fiftieth Anniversary Commemoration Lectures, Cairo, 1959, pp. 5–14.

to compensate, by means of fiscal policy, for exogenous changes in international economic position. Such efforts at compensation run the risks both of bad timing and of overcorrection, with the result that the scale of public investment may have to be altered too often, causing some inevitable waste of resources.

Desirable and Less Desirable Combinations

An underdeveloped country will usually be wiser to allow its foreign exchange reserves to fluctuate in a residual way and to keep its tax and expenditure policies steady, rather than to endeavor to gear these policies to its temporary international trade position. Some variation in fortune in foreign trade must be expected; trouble comes when temporary changes are regarded as permanent, and development plans formulated accordingly.

Another point at which trade and fiscal policies may touch concerns the sheltering of infant industries which are created as a result of development programming efforts. The classical case for protective tariffs justifies such levies for development purposes when new industries are just getting started and foreign competition is properly to be feared. The problem always is whether the new industries really have the capacity to become competitive after an initial period.[12] If they do, protective tariffs of a temporary nature may well be thought necessary. The difficulty arises, of course, in deciding just when the infant industries are sufficiently mature to face world competition. The healthy infants with the capacity to grow to robust adulthood undoubtedly deserve sheltering, but the sickly infants are perhaps better off being allowed to perish early, if they can never face the world market with comparative advantage. It is sometimes rather difficult to judge how healthy a new industry will be several years hence.

Numerous examples of uneconomic industries, deliberately created for national prestige or by poor development planning, can be cited. The Egyptian steel industry is a good example.

Egypt has neither coal nor iron ore as a domestic resource; yet the Nasser government has been determined from the time it seized power

---

[12] J. R. Hicks has commented that less developed countries must, in their search for development, reach the point where they can export some manufactured goods as well as raw materials. He suggests that each country specialize in one or two manufactured consumer goods and that they form face trade areas in which they can export manufactured consumer goods to one another. At present the volume of this type of trade is very small. See his *Essays in World Economics* (Oxford: Clarendon Press, 1959), pp. 180–88.

to create a steel industry. It has actually done so on a small scale. Anyone who has studied the geography of steelmaking knows that it is primarily a materials handling business; hence, cheap transportation of the materials is a most important cost factor. Egypt can never hope to enjoy a comparative advantage in steelmaking but will always be a high-cost producer because of excessive transport costs, compared with other countries. Yet for reasons of military posture and national prestige, a steel plant from the first enjoyed a priority in Egyptian development planning; one was actually constructed at high capital cost and is now operating with excessive running costs. Other fields of investment, many with greater financial possibilities or more substantial social benefits, were sacrificed to make room for the steel plant.

The Egyptians knew steel was a bad investment by all rational economic calculations. That they went ahead anyway indicates both the political content of development planning and the propensity, found in many less developed countries, for making poor estimates of the relative marginal efficiencies of investment in different spheres of activity. In a sense, Egypt's initial error was in trade policy—making steel instead of buying it more or less permanently from other countries —a clear case of disregarding comparative advantage.

Conclusion Concerning Trade Policy

It remains to inquire just what kind of trade policy a less developed country should pursue, once it has decided on industrialization as a major component of its economic development effort. Some changes in the composition and in the geography of trade are inevitable if this effort at industrialization is to be at all successful. If the industrialization effort is well conceived, trade gradually ceases to be entirely an exchange of raw materials for manufactured goods and becomes more an exchange of manufactured goods for other manufactured goods. This is the character of trade between well-developed and highly industrialized countries—the United Kingdom and Japan, for example.

This kind of trade change results from continuous attention to export possibilities and assiduous cultivation of new export markets. It is well known that the volume of a country's imports follows the indicators of its economic activity, such as national product. Therefore, as countries develop, they become increasingly important as export markets for other nations. Whereas the more advanced countries clearly have the lead in export sales of manufactured goods, many less developed countries enjoy advantages—good location and low wage scales, for example—that could be turned to profit if their industrialization efforts were effective.

For this reason I have urged that investment efforts in less developed countries should be oriented more toward export expansion than toward import substitution. Import substitution invites retaliation from trading partners, diminishes international trade, and raises productivity less on the average than would a more balanced development effort. Possibilities for export expansion are to be found largely in adding more value to already successful exports and in diversifying economic activity from the monoculture model too often found. This course requires substantial attention to agricultural improvement as a prelude to successful industrialization, a fact which numerous other writers have noted.

I conclude, therefore, that the kind of trade policy most conducive to successful economic development is an active one—that provides strong incentives for producers to seek new foreign markets; that avoids barter agreements and other arrangements that artificially limit the channels of trade; that uses protective tariffs very sparingly and then only for strictly limited periods; and that does not employ artificial exchange rates. This is, if you will, a conservative trade policy; a conservative fiscal policy, too, has been demonstrated to be most compatible with sustained economic growth over the long pull.

FISCAL POLICY AND EXCHANGE RATE POLICY

A foreign exchange rate is merely a price of one currency in terms of another; it is subject to the same influences as other prices. Foreign exchange rates differ from other prices, however, in that they are not free to fluctuate but are fixed by convention and international agreement. Countries may define their unit of account by a quantity of gold (thus establishing gold parities, with other currencies similarly defined), or in relation to reserve currencies such as the United States dollar or the British pound. Countries that adhere to the International Monetary Fund accept an obligation to define a par value for their currencies and to maintain actual exchange rates within 1 per cent of this par value. A few countries still stubbornly maintain flexible or "floating" exchange rates, but they are in the minority.

Variables and Constants

In a country that adheres to a fixed exchange rate, changes in its international payment flows will be reflected in movements of its foreign exchange reserves. Less developed countries customarily keep these reserves as current balances with the central bank of a reserve currency country, such as the United States or the United Kingdom.

There is a mutual interaction between changes in fiscal policy and changes in the balance of payments. If taxes are increased, though government expenditures are unchanged there should, normally, be fewer international payments and a consequent rise, *cet. par.* in foreign exchange reserves. If foreign payments should rise because of increased imports, tax revenue will also rise because of the additional customs receipts. If government expenditures rise while tax revenue is stationary, foreign payments will increase and foreign exchange reserves will tend to decline, because of the income effects of the additional government expenditure.

During the 1920's much was heard of the "purchasing power parity" of different currencies. This concept defined a kind of equilibrium in foreign exchange rates which equalized the relative prices of internationally traded commodities in different countries. Currencies were said to be over- or undervalued in relation to their equilibrium values or purchasing power parities. Nowadays little is heard of international price comparisons of this nature; currencies are said to be overvalued when foreign exchange reserves are persistently being drawn down and undervalued when there are persistent surpluses in the international accounts. The comparison is with a variable or floating rate used in these circumstances.

If foreign exchange rates were free to move, the price of foreign currencies would rise when a given country's reserves were declining and would decline when its reserves were rising. If the exchange rate is fixed, some other mechanism must be found to balance the international accounts.

A case for floating exchange rates as a normal feature of planned economic development is made in the following quotation:

> To avoid having its development program fall into a balance of payments trap, a country ideally should adopt a floating exchange rate. The argument commonly advanced against adoption of a floating rate is that it encourages resort to inflationary means of financing development and will therefore result in continual depreciation of the exchange rate. The weakness of this objection, however, is that countries planning economic development by that very fact are under strong pressures to resort to inflationary financing, and that if they adhere to a fixed rate in these circumstances, they will have to combat the resulting balance of payments problems by direct or fiscal means that are certain to introduce significant distortions in the allocation of resources. The

choice is therefore not between price stability and inflation but between two methods of offsetting the adverse effects on the country's international competitive position of the domestic inflation that accompanies development planning. A floating exchange rate achieves this offsetting automatically, without interfering with the allocation of resources according to comparative advantage as modified by development planning.[13]

Despite the alleged advantages of floating exchange rates, relatively few developing countries have followed this course.

Although a few less developed countries, chiefly the oil producers, have persistent surpluses in their international accounts, most of these countries suffer from payments deficits and from shortages of varying severity in foreign exchange. As has already been pointed out, one effect of a step-up in public investment that is not balanced by increased taxation is an increase in foreign payments and a decline in foreign exchange reserves. If the corrective mechanism for this situation is not to be found in a rise in price of foreign currencies, it must be sought in some other way. The method most commonly chosen by less developed countries in financial difficulties is foreign exchange control, i.e., in administrative limitations on access to foreign currencies. This course of action deals temporarily with the balance-of-payments difficulty but does nothing fundamental to correct it. As the public investment program picks up momentum, the controls over foreign exchange usually must be progressively tightened.[14] Foreign aid can also bridge the balance-of-payments gap temporarily but this merely papers over the cracks in the underlying economic structure.

Consequences of Outdated Parities

Many less developed countries cling to par values for their currency that have become outdated and that no longer reflect true equilibrium rates. They reason, correctly, that devaluation would increase the cost of the public investment program, since its import content would become more expensive. This is a shortsighted view because the government can always command the resources to complete its own program,

---

[13]Harry G. Johnson, "Fiscal Policy and the Balance of Payments in a Growing Economy," OECD Third Study Conference on Problems of Economic Development, Athens, 1963, pp. 10–11.

[14]J. R. Parkinson has argued for import surcharges or auctioning of foreign exchange as alternatives to devaluation for Pakistan, faced with a severe foreign exchange shortage in about 1960. In his view these techniques would have fallen more heavily on the profits of traders and less on consumer prices than devaluation would have. See his article "The Balance of Payments and Fiscal Policy in Pakistan," *Scottish Journal of Political Economy*, 9 (1962):99–109.

although private investors may not be able to do so because of the exchange controls. Public investment is therefore made partly at the expense of private investment.

In many less developed countries overvaluation of their currency in terms of foreign currencies is reflected in a gap between the official rate of exchange and the free or illegal market rate. Individuals and business firms that cannot get foreign exchange through the official channels resort increasingly to the illegal channels, both in anticipation of further currency depreciation and to complete necessary foreign payments.

Currency overvaluation also robs exporters of adequate incentives to increase the volume of their exports, since they are required to surrender their exchange proceeds at rates which do not compensate them for their costs and leave normal margins of profit. As imports are progressively limited by exchange controls they naturally rise in price, levying a hidden charge on consumers and adding to business costs. This hidden charge compensates, in a sense, for the failure of the government to tax in order to protect its foreign exchange position, in the face of rising public expenditure. The lesson is obvious: in economics there is no free lunch.

The dangers of becoming committed to an unrealistic exchange rate are real ones, which can easily thwart other efforts at development. Countries that aspire to develop should therefore maintain unitary exchange rates and should keep these rates realistic. An adequate fiscal policy can help to do this.

There remain the dual and multiple exchange rate systems that many less developed countries have employed. Generally these multiple rates are a substitute for an adequate fiscal policy, since they amount to taxes on foreign exchange for various purposes.[15] The International Monetary Fund opposes multiple rate arrangements and has repeatedly urged its member countries to unify their rates, offering at times special credits for this purpose.

Multiple rates restrict international payments, cause needless administrative difficulties, and create structural problems within the economies where these multiple rates prevail. For example, the normal

[15]W. Baer and M. E. A. Herve point out that multiple exchange rates may be used to promote a specific structure of imports and exports to fit into a general development program devised to bring about desired changes in the economic structure of the country. See their note "Multiple Exchange Rates and the Attainment of Multiple Policy Objectives," *Economica*, 29 (1962):176–81. Most multiple rate systems are not well enough designed to be effective in promoting development over the long run.

relations among the agriculture, trade, and manufacturing sectors become distorted. The differentials in the multiple rates seldom correspond exactly with the cost and price differentials among the various sectors.

When a country has allowed its exchange rates to become unrealistic, i.e., when its currency has depreciated far below the official rate, devaluation may be the only remedy. In this instance the devaluation should be sufficient in amount to restore equality between the official and free rates and should be accompanied by a stabilization program that will forestall further depreciation.

Such a stabilization program will probably involve a combination of tax increases and cutbacks in the development program. The former is hard to achieve politically, and the latter will mean shortfalls in plan targets. Devaluation is merely recognition of the fact that financially the development program has been out of balance for some time; otherwise the currency depreciation would not have occurred.

International agencies and aid-dispensing governments are eager to help countries which make a real effort at self-help in solving their financial problems; they are understandably reluctant to give emergency transfusions when efforts at self-help are negligible.

In conclusion, it appears that a realistic exchange rate policy is the one best calculated to keep the sequence of economic growth in motion. Without an adequate fiscal policy such an exchange rate policy is difficult. An aggressive tax policy can sometimes bolster a sagging exchange rate, and will often be a feature of stabilization efforts following a devaluation made necessary by persistent balance of payments deficits.

8

Fiscal Advice to Less Developed Countries

The term fiscal advice, as it is used in this chapter, covers both policy advice and all other intellectual or technical assistance (largely in the form of administrative help) that pertain to the revenue and expenditure processes of the central government in a developing country. Therefore the term comprehends budget and tax advice as well as help in central accounting and auditing, revenue administration, and financial procedures. The discussion will cover only fiscal advice provided by foreigners to a host government, not that received by a government from its own nationals.

Less developed countries have sometimes sought fiscal advice from abroad; at other times it has been urged upon them. When sought, it has often been for administrative rather than for policy matters; when urged, it has often concerned policy in the first instance, with administrative help provided as a follow-on once the policy suggestions have been accepted or at least considered. I do not mean to imply that less developed countries never seek policy help; they often do, but they also frequently wait to seek this help until a crisis has arisen. To be most useful, fiscal advice, like medical attention, should be given early.

Fiscal advice is available from international agencies such as the United Nations and the International Monetary Fund, and also from individual governments of well-developed countries such as the United States, which offer technical assistance in this as in many other fields. The United Kingdom has provided considerable technical help in the fiscal area to Commonwealth countries, as has France to her former colonies. Other European countries have also helped emerging countries.

Arrangements for Fiscal Advice

Seldom does fiscal advice cover the entire field of government revenue and expenditure. Usually it is just a segment of the problem

Chapter 8

that engages the attention of foreign advisers. This segment may be the budget, a muddled tax administration, or a development plan that is not working according to expectations.

Often the terms of reference given foreign advisers are not broad enough to enable them to get to the root of the problem.[1] There are understandable reasons for this situation. Questions of tax policy are naturally politically sensitive, as are many questions relating to the size and program distribution of the budget. Governments may be reluctant to entrust such sensitive political issues to foreign hands.

Much fiscal advice to less developed countries has taken the form of short-term missions composed of several experts, who make a survey of the situation and leave a report containing recommendations. Unless coupled with adequate follow-up, such missions often accomplish very little. It is fairly easy for an outsider to spot flaws in the fiscal structure of a given underdeveloped country and to recommend corrective action. These suggestions often do not take proper account of the special local conditions and ingrained resistance to change, nor do they necessarily generate the initiative needed to carry through reforms. Moreover, such recommendations quickly become outdated unless acted on promptly—as frequently they are not.

Instead of a full-scale survey mission it is often better for a single person, with considerable breadth of viewpoint, to work with a host government for some time on current problems in order to make that government aware of the areas in which additional intellectual assistance should be sought. This person should be a generalist rather than a specialist—able to function competently with budget or tax problems, monetary or trade policies. An appropriate background would be training in economics or law, plus broad experience.

Tours of duty abroad, when arbitrarily fixed in duration, frequently yield technical advice that is of only minimum value. It may take an orientation period of several months before an adviser, new to a given country, can confidently offer suggestions that will fit properly the country's institutional and political structure. He cannot simply put

[1]Dudley Seers has given a number of reasons why foreign economists advising local governments are less than wholly successful. His comments are not directed specifically to fiscal policy but apply generally to economic advice to less developed countries. See his article "Why Visiting Economists Fail," *Journal of Political Economy*, 70 (1962): 325–38. In Seers's analysis, failure is as often attributed to vague terms of reference or inadequate organization, within the host country, to employ advice, as to short-comings of the foreign advisers themselves.

166

forward, as appropriate to the local situation, the experience and techniques of more advanced countries; instead he must adapt these to the special circumstances of the country he is advising.[2] His suggestions must also take into account the personalities of host government officials, the prevailing power structure of the government, and the background of previous laws and institutions.

Amenability of Host Government Officials to Advice

Foreign advisers should not expect all their recommendations to be accepted, but they must keep pressing for enough acceptance to make their program substantially effective. In this process they may easily become unwelcome, and isolated or unpersuasive, after a time. If this happens, the adviser should not be committed to a fixed tour of future duty but should be repatriated and perhaps replaced by someone else. A tour, in other words, should last only so long as the adviser is reasonably influential. To be effective he must often be expendable.

An elementary principle of fiscal advice to less developed countries is that no standard or ready-made solutions to problems can or should be prescribed for all countries. In particular, adoption of a progressive tax on personal income is not a sovereign remedy for all fiscal ills. At a proper stage of development such an income tax may be appropriate; before this stage is reached it may be inimical to development as well as administratively impossible and politically unacceptable.

Foreign advisers repeatedly fail because of inadequate appreciation of the economic structure and prevailing cultural attitudes peculiar to the country they are advising.[3] The advisers may also not fully appreciate the administrative and organizational limitations of the developing country they are trying to help. A personal income tax, if poorly administered and poorly complied with, is one of the most inequitable and inefficient taxes that can be devised. Even though well drafted, it inevitably diverts some attention away from business improvement toward tax minimization and avoidance. Likewise, a method of increasing land taxes that fails to take proper account of the traditional

[2] A similar point is made by W. Beckerman in his article "The Economist as a Modern Missionary," *Economic Journal*, March, 1956, pp. 112–13.

[3] Guy Hunter writes that "the most general single cause of difficulty lies in the attempt to transfer political systems, social institutions, technical methods, and educational patterns straight from the developed to the developing countries. For all of these are essentially the end-product of being a developed country, not the recipe for becoming one." See his article "Independence and Development," *International Affairs*, 11, no. 1 (January, 1964):48.

patterns of land tenure or of crop marketing will obviously not work well.

Among the reasons why an income tax may be ineffective is that it is impossible to make a detailed yet uniform audit of each income tax return; furthermore, this would be undesirable even if it were practical. It would imply an intolerable degree of inquisition into personal affairs and the expenditure of too much time and effort on negotiation leading to final settlement of liability. It would also open the door to wholesale bribery and corruption.

The collection of income taxes in the United States, the United Kingdom, and other well-developed countries depends primarily on citizens' self-assessment, supplemented by strictly limited spot checking by revenue officials. No less developed country can afford to invest more of its limited personnel resources for fiscal administration than this in tax collection; therefore, a system of direct taxation will work well only if the underlying law imposing these taxes is fairly well comprehended and accepted by the public. Acceptance is likely to be a gradual thing, owing to wide adherence to the maxim that only old taxes are good ones.

Once a foreign adviser begins to offer suggestions to a host government he will inevitably meet a varying response. Some of his ideas may be quickly accepted; others may encounter stubborn resistance. Still others may be acceptable in principle but their adoption in practice may be delayed. Sometimes host government officials will take particular ideas advanced by an adviser but will reject related suggestions logically linked with those they have accepted. Erratic as this may appear, there are sometimes good reasons, from their standpoint, for the choice. They may not always reveal these reasons to their foreign advisers.

Although his advice will probably grow more valuable, the more he learns about the country in which he is serving, a foreign adviser's effectiveness may diminish as he becomes better known to host government officials and as his views lose some of their novelty. They may trust the adviser more, personally, when they come to know him better, but may be less influenced by the substance of his advice.

Need for Strict Objectivity

Advisers cannot always court popularity in the countries where they are serving and expect to remain truly effective. The adviser is there primarily to inspire change and to guide this change in constructive directions. There are likely to be elements in a country that will resist change, for the real or imagined injury which they visualize such change will cause to their positions, influence, or way of life. Change grows out of constructive discontent. An adviser cannot be equally effective with all officials with whom he must deal; he will inevitably influence some more than others.

A fiscal adviser must often recommend unpopular policies such as heavier taxation, tighter expenditure control, or, in extreme cases, devaluation. He will sometimes be accused of harboring motives other than the welfare of the country he is serving—of being imperialist, too conservative, or merely unsympathetic to the regime in power. In the face of this kind of reaction the adviser must remain calm and must retain both his objectivity and his impartiality. He must have a high threshold of frustration.

An adviser's function is not to make policy but to insure that the officials who do form policy have full knowledge of alternatives and consequences. Theirs is the political responsibility; they accept the credit or blame if the policies work well or badly. An adviser must constantly resist being drawn into operating responsibilities, even when local officials are poorly prepared. He should train and advise them but not do their continuing work.

THE GROUP APPROACH

Advisers can usually operate more efficiently when they are members of a team blending various special qualifications; but the team should often be put into a country *seriatim* rather than all at once. The general adviser on policy should normally go first, followed perhaps by an expert on drafting legislation, if legislation is required, then by an organizer of administrative operations, or a budget analyst, or whatever specialty the situation calls for. More than one adviser may serve in a country at the same time, but in all probability not all members of a team will be required at the same time, nor for the same fixed period. By the same token, a particularly useful adviser should perhaps serve more than one tour in a given country, though not necessarily consecutively.

Timing of Advisory Service

It is bad psychology for the supplying agency to terminate an advisory service all at once; it should normally be phased down systematically, with the expert on follow-up activities the last to leave. On the other hand, host government officials should be encouraged to dispense with foreign advisers as soon as possible, and not to become over-dependent on them. This will be easier to accomplish if advisers are careful to avoid operating responsibility.

In many countries fiscal advice should be intermittent rather than continuous. The first step may be to convince top officials to take certain policy measures. Once they are convinced, it may take new legislation to implement these policies. Advisers may not need to be on hand for this stage; indeed, they should ordinarily not be too closely identified with the legislative process— lest it appear they are participating too much in internal political affairs within the host country. Once the enabling legislation has been secured, the next step may be to organize its administration. This may perhaps best be handled by a different adviser, with experience in administration and management. It may be necessary for certain advisers to go back several times to a country they are assisting before a program of extensive change is complete.

The pattern, in brief, is one of complementary advisers—some on relatively short tours, some for longer periods—assisting and replacing one another as the nature of the problems changes.

Defects in Existing Advisory Services

Most of the agencies currently providing technical assistance are not organized to provide it according to the desirable pattern. The United Nations has some flexibility in the terms of its tours but has tended to send either group missions or individual technicians for fixed periods determined in advance. The United States Agency for International Development is required by law to assign direct-hire technicians for fixed periods, and flexibility of assignment is possible only by using contractors or government employees on temporary duty. Moreover, AID has not built permanent teams of advisers capable of supplementing one another's services so that team advice could be continuous even though individual technicians rotated. Part of the problem may lie in the geographic, rather than in the functional, basis of the Agency's operational organization.

The International Monetary Fund, in building its Fiscal Affairs Department, has had the opportunity to profit from the shortcomings of other suppliers of technical assistance and to build a unique team advisory service, using nationals of different countries with supplementary skills and language equipment, employing variable tours, and giving intermittent advice when indicated. Although the IMF is plainly aware of these principles, its new department has not yet functioned long enough to demonstrate whether it will actually operate in this flexible way.

In the opinion of some observers, one trouble with technical assistance offered by the United States government is that it has often been started at the grass roots and has endeavored to work up to policy, instead of beginning with broad policy and working down to the details of implementation. The grass roots or "upside down" approach has resulted from United States AID objectives' being tactically political rather than stemming from a consistent philosophy of economic development.[4]

The United Nations, in its technical assistance activity, has played the fairly passive role of waiting for member countries to ask for help and then of responding to these requests. Often the help requested has not been that most badly needed. Countries in difficulty do not always see their own problems clearly, nor do they always know precisely what help they can most profitably employ. Requests for technical assistance are apt to depend on the receptivity of particular officials within a developing country or on incomplete knowledge on the part of these officials of the range of services the United Nations is in a position to provide.

To be blunt, requests for technical assistance should frequently be inspired by the suppliers, since they should have an objective view of policy. Needless to say, inspiration of this sort requires great delicacy and finesse. Here again the IMF is in a strong position, because it maintains a continuing surveillance over the general economic position and major financial problems of its member countries, and, presumably, finesse is one of its institutional attributes. It therefore can inspire requests for help in dealing with these major problems beginning at a

---

[4]In an appraisal of United States foreign aid policy, E. S. Mason writes: "I, for one, admit the sovereignty of politics in questions of foreign aid and ask only what are the political interests we should attempt to attain. . . . There is, in fact, continuous pressure to use foreign aid for tactical political purposes. Much of the aid thus used is, in my opinion wasted. . . . The principal purpose of foreign aid in my view is to promote the security of the United States and, insofar as our security is dependent on others, foreign aid is an essential part of a mutual security policy. In certain underdeveloped countries this requires assistance in the form of military hardware plus enough economic assistance to permit these countries to mobilize their own resources for military use. In others the essential objective of U.S. foreign aid is the support of governments able and willing to maintain their independence of Communist control." See *Foreign Aid and Foreign Policy* (New York: Harper & Row [for the Council on Foreign Relations] 1964), pp. 32–34.

policy level and working downward as necessary. How the IMF will use this unique opportunity has not yet been thoroughly demonstrated.

VARIETIES OF FISCAL ADVICE

The range of subjects which fiscal advice may cover is considerable, but budget reform, tax policy, and tax administration are among the most common.[5] Countries aspiring to develop will almost invariably face the problem of properly coordinating their budgets with their development planning processes, and usually of modernizing their budgets at the same time.

Budget Improvement

The situation in Iran is a good example of the need for strengthening the budget process. Until very recently the budget of the Iranian government was incomplete; it excluded the numerous government corporations and agencies that have their own sources of revenue. Some of these agencies are engaged in business activities, such as the manufacture and marketing of cigarettes. Others do not sell goods or services but have access to earmarked tax revenues which do not go into general government funds.

As a result of technical advice extending over several years, the Government of Iran for the fiscal year 1343 (1964) finally prepared and presented to the Parliament a comprehensive budget of all activities. For the first time the Iranian Parliament got a complete view of all government receipts and expenditures.

The Iranian budget for 1964 was not presented on a program basis, but instead simply listed agencies for which appropriations were requested, and the proposed objects of expenditure under each agency. All ministries and agencies submitted their estimates at the same time, which was so late in the budget year that no proper examination of the substance of their requests for funds could be made.

For 1965 each agency was given a program structure, required to prepare its budget request according to that structure, given a definite time for a budget hearing, and subjected during that hearing to a searching examination concerning the substance and justification of programs and actual performance in furtherance of those programs. Following these hearings, final estimates for submission to Parliament

---

[5]The IMF has organized its new Fiscal Affairs Department along these three functional lines.

were prepared. In brief, a regular budget cycle for each agency has been established.

A program budget is not the only step in budget reform that needs to be taken by the developing countries; but it is a logical early step and one which makes possible a more intelligent appraisal of the continuing activities of government. Often such an appraisal will reveal many activities that can be discontinued, and others that need strengthening if development is to be accelerated. The latter activities may lie in agencies relatively untouched by the development planning process.

Execution of the budget in many less developed countries will be found to be cumbersome and encrusted with excessive detail. Many countries have elaborate verification of accounts and preexpenditure audit procedures which delay and sometimes thwart the substance of approved programs. Sometimes appropriations are excessively detailed, so that if a small object of expenditure is overrun, an entire program is halted. This result can be avoided if limited flexibility among objects of expenditure is provided for in the appropriations legislation.

Coordination of the budget and development planning processes is nearly always a difficult organizational problem in a developing country.[6] Typically, the development plan and the budget are prepared by different agencies. The development plan may also not be precisely timed from year to year. It is necessary to make the budget exercise the occasion for an annual review and revision of the multi-year development plan. The budget, if complete, should also be the vehicle for financial scheduling of the government's part of the development plan. A good system of progress reporting on development projects is essential to success in this activity.

Many countries with medium-range development plans have adopted the split budget, in which capital outlays are separated from current expenditures. It is my personal view that the split budget, though a useful tool for showing the nature of government expenditure, both encourages fiscal irresponsibility and retards budget and development plan coordination. It is all too easy to depend heavily on borrowing to cover the capital budget, and to tolerate a different and less intensive sort of review (for budget purposes) of capital projects than of continuing outlays. On practical grounds, therefore, it seems

---

[6]For a view of the necessity for this coordination and some of its difficulties, see K. R. Hansen, "Planning as a Continuous Process," *U.S. Papers Prepared for the U.N. Conference on The Application of Science and Technology for the Benefit of the Less Developed Areas*, 8:128–29.

questionable whether fiscal advisers should recommend a double budget to a country that does not already have one unless there are some obvious advantages to be gained.

Budget reform in a less developed country may be less a matter of altering policies than of establishing proper structures for a modern budget and of training people in the proper use of the budget as a management tool.[7] A fiscal adviser is necessarily also a training officer; he should expect to spend a large share of his time training host government officials to use newer techniques and to discard old procedures.

Some of this training can take place in formal courses or seminars; much of it is bound to be informal, on-the-job training, in which the adviser first convinces local officials that there is a better way to operate and then takes them step-by-step through the more efficient procedure. The effectiveness of such training is measured by the ability of local officials to carry on by themselves, and to innovate, after the adviser has departed.

Problems of Tax Policy and Administration

In the tax field the usual problem faced by an adviser is finding sources of additional tax revenue and improving the administrative process of tax collection at the same time. Many less developed countries have complex revenue structures that have grown piecemeal and lack both cohesiveness and the required yield flexibility. Normally, more effective taxation of agriculture will have a high priority among the immediate problems, as was noted in an earlier chapter.[8]

Many countries earmark certain taxes for particular uses—in principle a bad fiscal practice that, over time, usually provides either too much or too little revenue for the activity in question. To establish good fiscal control it will usually be necessary to cease earmarking revenues

---

[7]As one recent writer puts it, "The budget tends nowadays to be the focal point in the presentation and implementation of the Government's economic policy. . . . It has proved to be a convenient occasion on which to embark on a wide ranging review of the general economic situation, an opportunity on the one hand to justify the Government's past action and to persuade people of the appropriateness of any measures that may be proposed for the future, or, on the other hand, to attack and criticize the Government's handling of the situation."—Alan Williams, *Public Finance and Budgetary Policy* (New York: Praeger, 1963), p. 272.

[8]H. Wald makes the same point when he writes that "the very size of the agricultural sector in most countries creates a strong presumption that a substantial portion of the required revenue should be raised in that sector. Exactly how large that portion should be depends on the level and distribution of agricultural income and upon agriculture's place in the over-all development plan." *Taxation of Agricultural Land in Underdeveloped Economies*, pp. 181–82.

and to force all government programs to compete on an equal basis for appropriations. Earmarking merely circumvents the program review normally present in appropriation proceedings.

In many countries the tax problem that may require first consideration is collecting the revenue that is legally due. That such taxes are not collected may be the fault of the revenue legislation, which is unworkable, or of the administration, which is inefficient or corrupt, or both. Unworkable legislation must be replaced by other statues that are administratively feasible. A bad revenue administration must be cleaned up if the government is to have any financial integrity. Usually the laws of the country provide ample punishment for corrupt tax collectors, if these laws are enforced with vigor.

Assuming that the revenue administration is reasonably honest, and competent to deal with the existing tax system, the problem of obtaining additional revenue may still present considerable difficulty. It will be necessary to obtain new legislation, inform taxpayers of their new obligations, and equip the revenue administration with new tools to deal with its new responsibilities. Suppose the new revenue is to be raised by death taxes, where none have been imposed before. The needed educational process may be extensive, and some time will be required before the new tax can be expected to work properly. Spectacular results should not be expected, but the adviser should satisfy himself that progress is both appreciable and steady. The standard of enforcement for new taxes ought to be brought up as rapidly as possible to that prevailing for old taxes.

PERSONAL QUALITIES OF AN EFFECTIVE ADVISER

Perhaps the most valuable quality in a fiscal adviser is a feeling for the degree of readiness for change—an instinct for timing and for what will and will not work in a given situation. This quality encompasses a sense of history, a feeling for politics, discernment about the relation of social change to cultural environment, sensitivity to people, and, of course, his technical equipment. He will not propose policies that are incongruous with the environment, but at the same time he will not be content with inaction or with only minimal progress toward vital objectives, even in a relatively static environment. His function is to goad, cajole, and encourage host government officials to take the right steps, to take them in time, and to avoid moves that are clearly inconsistent with their growth objectives.

There are evolutionary stages in fiscal arrangements even as there are analagous stages of economic development; although occasionally a stage in either sequence may be skipped or its duration shortened, the normal evolutionary process cannot be inverted or scrambled without confusion and loss of efficiency; wise policy does not employ the complex instruments of a late stage of development in dealing with the problems of an emergent country, when these problems can be handled almost as well by simpler means.

Seeing Problems in Perspective

A tax adviser, arriving for the first time in a given country, will undoubtedly find many things about the host country's tax system he would like to change. He must be content, however, to concentrate on the most important problems and to obtain constructive action on these, rather than dispersing his energies over too many fronts. If the problem is obtaining more revenue to restrict consumption and to conserve foreign exchange, he must advise looking for this revenue where it can be obtained most quickly and practically; he should not endeavor to promote reforms that are for the long-range reconstruction of the tax system but which lack immediate revenue significance.

This does not mean that the adviser is compelled always to take a short-range view. On the contrary, he must look forward to the state of development that will prevail ten years hence and to the institutions that will then be in existence. He must visualize the probable growth in tax bases as the economy expands and must anticipate problems of tax compliance and administration that will undoubtedly occur at some later date. Above all he must gear his recommendations to the pace at which progress can reasonably be expected to take place, but at the same time must keep pressing host country officials to do a little better and to move a little more quickly than they think they can. He must generate self-confidence among operating officials, fight apathy and indecisiveness, and see that all necessary changes move in step with one another.

An adviser should look continually for the simplest and most practical solution to a given problem. He should avoid unnecessary complications and refinements, remembering that these can be introduced later if they are actually needed. Too many less developed countries have more complex procedures, regulations, and controls than they need. These red tape activities absorb needless energy that might better be spent on pursuits that would contribute more to economic development.

Substantive Content of Fiscal Advice

The exact subject matter of fiscal advice to a given emerging country cannot be described very readily in general terms. It will depend on the actions the host country has already taken and on the current economic situations it faces. Budget traditions differ, depending on the advanced country which has served as a model. British and French traditions are very different, for example. Tax systems also differ, having evolved in varying circumstances.

Less developed countries do, however, have many common problems. They are all striving to step up their rates of capital formation and are generally expanding public outlays as rapidly as they can to this end. They face common threats of inflation and periodic balance-of-payments crises. They are plagued with structural unemployment and a relatively stagnant technology. Although they may be making progress, this advance is too small for them to keep pace with the more advanced countries; consequently the international per capita income gap grows wider instead of narrower each year.

A properly organized team of fiscal advisers, going from country to country, will find that many of the problems are similar, although each country's problems have their peculiar aspects; but generally the budget structure will be outmoded and an ineffective management tool, and the tax system will be weak, lacking both revenue flexibility and first-rate administration.

A priority job of a fiscal advisory team must almost invariably be to convince host government officials of the need for both budget and tax reforms and to inspire them with the zeal necessary to carry these reforms through once they are initiated. The advisers must outline in detail for their counterparts just what these reforms involve, what people must be trained in what skills, and how the country will benefit once the reforms are effected. Only by being convinced that the benefits are both tangible and realizable can local officials generate the enthusiasm and the drive needed for keeping the process of change moving steadily.

If budget and tax reform actually get underway, a variety of changes will be needed in administrative routines, accounting practices, and government procedures. These can all take place under the guidance and at the urging of other members of the fiscal advisory team, who should gradually withdraw from the scene after training local officials to carry on. These ancillary details of reform are very important, however, since they determine whether the new policies will actually work as they should in practice.

Increasingly, central banks in less developed countries are requesting and receiving technical assistance. Much of this is done among central banks themselves, outside the normal technical assistance channels. The usual terms of reference involve methods of credit control and problems of debt management. Although central bank operations are a field of their own, they are closely intertwined with government fiscal operations. Fiscal advisers should therefore be in close touch with any changes being made in central bank legislation or practice. In some instances the central bank adviser should perhaps be annexed to the fiscal team. The IMF apparently has plans of this nature.

PITFALLS IN ARRANGEMENTS FOR FISCAL ADVICE

The outstanding defect in fiscal advisory services is the patchwork manner in which these services have been provided. Instead of building competent teams to go from one country to another, the aid-providing agencies have tried to recruit specialists for particular duties in individual countries. Although the people recruited have been, in the main, reasonably competent technicians, their work has often lacked the breadth, continuity, and professionalism that a really first-class advisory service requires. Lack of language qualifications and irregular timing of requests for fiscal advice are two elements that have militated against the building of career advisory teams.

As was noted before, terms of reference for fiscal advisory teams have often been either too loosely drawn or too restrictive for the service to be of maximum value. When the advisory team is employed directly by a national or international agency, these terms of reference can sometimes be modified as the work proceeds. When a private group is retained on contract, strict construction of the terms of the contract may limit the effectiveness of the service.

The question of contract personnel versus direct-hire personnel has several components. Generally, contract personnel may be able to establish a closer working relationship with the host government, since they are not regarded by local officials as direct agents of a foreign government. A contractor is also easier to blame if progress does not accord with expectations. On the other hand, contractors are generally more expensive than direct-hire personnel and not necessarily more competent. Few if any contractors have a sufficient volume of business to build a genuine career advisory service. Typically, they get a contract and then search for personnel, offering chiefly financial inducements to attract talent for temporary work. Naturally, the quality of competence they obtain in this way varies considerably.

Many established professional workers in the budget and tax fields are attracted temporarily to foreign service because it offers them the opportunity to travel and to broaden their experience; sometimes they choose it as a retirement occupation. Usually these experts take only one or two foreign assignments. Their experience in an advanced country has not necessarily prepared them properly for the obstacles and frustrations they are likely to meet in a backward country. Their advice may be pitched at the wrong level, either above or below the competence of the recipient officials. Advising foreign governments is a specialty, like any other, that has to be learned through experience.

The Problem of a Proper Viewpoint

Fiscal advisers must be prepared to discard their cultural preconceptions and to look at problems from the standpoint of the host government. This is not easy to do.[9] Commenting on the technical assistance activities of the United Nations, one writer has concluded that

> for the most part the [technical assistance] reports have treated the problem of taxation and the stages of economic development almost exclusively in terms of the potential role of income taxation. This tendency has, from one standpoint, been unfortunate, for the most of the discussion has been inevitably concerned primarily with the criterion of administration. From another point of view, however, this concentration on the role of the income tax is quite understandable, since the technical assistance experts all agree that its functions are unique. A definite concensus exists that only this type of tax offers progression over the complete range of the income size distribution, provides that similar persons will be treated similarly, and ensures a high degree of yield elasticity in the revenue system, particularly under conditions of inflation.[10]

This comment shows clearly that cultural preconceptions have seldom

[9]In a review of United States technical missions to many countries in the 100 years from 1838 to 1938, Merle Curti and Kendall Birr conclude that "Americans based a good many of their plans on middle class assumptions and sought to achieve middle class standards and ends. Yet in most of these countries the middle class and its ideals were either weak or nonexistent. . . . There was little that could be done about the fundamental culture patterns of the country involved. The missions had to work within these patterns as best they could." See their *Prelude to Point Four* (Madison, Wis.: University of Wisconsin Press, 1954), p. 216.

[10]E. R. Schlesinger, "Tax Policy Recommendations of Technical Assistance Missions," OAS/ECLA/IDB Joint Taxation Program, Santiago, Chile, December, 1962. (Mimeographed.)

Chapter 8

been discarded by fiscal advisers. Personal income taxation has often been a preoccupation.

Another comment on the implicit cultural assumptions that often underlie fiscal advice may be cited. According to this author, who is himself an experienced fiscal and economic adviser to foreign governments:

> Foreign experts are often struck by the difference between the overall structure of taxes in underdeveloped countries and in advanced countries. As a general rule, underdeveloped countries rely much more heavily on indirect taxes, such as sales taxes, import duties, and the like, and much less heavily on such direct taxes as income and inheritance taxes, than do advanced countries. At first blush this relatively heavy dependence on indirect taxes strikes the foreign adviser as highly "regressive." Here, however, caution must be exercised. It is often quite impossible to increase the share of tax revenues from income tax merely by increasing tax rates. Indeed, some of the underdeveloped countries already have income tax structures which are heavier and more steeply progressive than those of more highly developed areas. Moreover, the governments of underdeveloped countries have learned how to build into their indirect tax systems a high degree of progressivity. Tunisia, for example, has commodity tax rates which range from nothing on essentials to a high rate on luxuries. Devices such as these may provide a more effective way of relating tax collections to income than an increase in income tax rates; with the institutional framework and administrative system existing in some underdeveloped countries, income taxes are too easily avoided. Finally, with incomes so low and with supply curves of labor and capital turning backward at such low levels of income, unfavorable "incentive effects" may occur at much lower ratios of income tax to income than in advanced countries.[11]

This comment also indicates the problems many fiscal advisers have in putting themselves in the places of the officials they are advising. They must keep their advice practical and yet must lead their counterparts into new territory and inspire them to continue to try modern methods on their own.

The Problem of Absorption

The aid-providing agencies have often overcommitted advisory resources to particular countries, before making certain that the recipient countries would use these resources properly. The result is inevitably frustration for the advisers and a waste of their time and talents so far as the recipient government is concerned. Overcommitment can be avoided by careful preliminary investigation before advisory service is

[11] Benjamin Higgins, "Financing Accelerated Growth," OECD Conference on Problems of Economic Development," Athens, December, 1963. pp. 25–26.

180

furnished, preferably carried out by a single person empowered to make arrangements for others when they are needed and when he is convinced they will be properly employed.[12]

Host countries should ordinarily meet some portion of their advisers' local expenses so that they will realize that advice is not simply gratuitous aid. Willingness to pay for advice may sometimes serve as an index of the need for it and of the value local officials hope to derive from it. This is not invariably the case, however.

In brief, successful technical assistance in any field requires a precise and detailed understanding between the aid-supplying agency and the recipient government about what kind of help will be made available, how far this help will extend, and exactly how it will be utilized by the recipient government. Lacking this precise understanding, and having only vague and contradictory concepts of the mission to be accomplished, fiscal or other advisers are bound to fall short of optimum achievement. Unfortunately, large aid-supplying agencies operating in a great number of fields find it difficult to attain these precise advance understandings.

Some Lessons from Experience

Fiscal advice to less developed countries has not been as effective as it might, because (1) there are too many advisers in the field, and (2) they have operated too much on an *ad hoc* basis, treating each country as a special situation and endeavoring to meet its needs by recruiting individual people or a team for that specific country. There has been too little carryover of principles or of personnel from one country to another. I do not mean that the same substantive advice can be offered to one country after another; merely that the advisory techniques and methods of operation have a degree of transferability. Among the agencies now active in the field, the IMF, perhaps because it is a latecomer, has the best current opportunity to function effectively.[13]

That more less developed countries have not sought fiscal advice is

---

[12]A similar point has been made by L. K. Caldwell, who writes that "realistic and timely appraisal of the expectations and capacities of the host government by the assisting agency and its expert therefore becomes an essential stage in the definition of the role of the expert." See his "The Role of the Technical Expert," *Annals of the American Academy of Political and Social Science*, 323 (May, 1959):98.

[13]The IMF is a latecomer only in the field of fiscal advice; in other areas of advice it has an established tradition.

possibly a result of their not realizing how necessary fiscal changes are in a successful development sequence, and how closely these changes are related to the development planning process. The adoption of a development plan extending over several years necessarily requires updating and restructuring the budgetary process as well as raising additional tax revenues.

In both these areas the services of foreign fiscal advisers can make the transitions easier and the programming of economic growth more effective. The number of less developed countries that have encountered severe fiscal problems soon after embarking on ambitious development programs is eloquent testimony in support of this conclusion.

Even as the developing countries have not yet learned when, where, and how to seek fiscal advice, or in many cases how to use it properly, the aid-supplying agencies have not yet learned how to supply this service most effectively. Building diversified career advisory teams and employing them in a flexible manner appear to offer the best hope for improvement of this service. Many of the principles outlined here for fiscal advice are equally applicable to advisory service in other areas.

9

The Relation of Fiscal Policy to the Stages of Growth

We have seen in the preceding chapters that fiscal policy in a less developed country serves different ends and employs different guiding principles than in a more advanced economy. In the less developed country its objectives (which are primarily long range) include optimizing capital formation and insuring that investment is directed into those fields where the marginal efficiency of capital (in a social sense) is highest. In the advanced country its objectives (primarily short range) are to maintain full employment, to reduce cyclical disturbances, and also to stimulate growth.

Although the growth objective is shared by less and more developed economies alike, the means of moving toward that objective are, or at least should be, quite different in less than in more developed economies. For example, the rule of budget balancing over a complete business cycle, now fairly generally accepted for advanced economies, is much less appropriate for those which are underdeveloped. The role of progressive taxation as a redistributor of personal income is also less clearly applicable in an underdeveloped country.

As we all know, the world is composed of countries in various stages of economic development, ranging from the primitive, nearly self-sufficient, largely barter economies found in parts of Africa and Asia, to highly interrelated and specialized exchange systems. The precepts and techniques of fiscal policy likewise form a heirarchy, ranging from rudimentary to sophisticated.[1]

The purpose of this chapter is to outline briefly how those fiscal

[1] A similar view, not specific to fiscal policy but referring to economic policy generally, has been expressed by J. K. Galbraith, who writes that "economic development is a process, one that extends in range from new nations of Africa, but slightly removed from their tribal structure, to the elaborate economic and social apparatus of Western nations. At each stage along this continuum there is an appropriate policy for further advance. What is appropriate at one stage is wrong at another." See his *Economic Development* (Cambridge, Mass.: Harvard University Press, 1964), pp. 45–46.

policies that are appropriate to different stages of economic development can be selected, adapted, and put to use to serve the development objective in particular emerging countries, and how and when these policies should be modified as development proceeds. My theme is the interaction of policy instruments and the need for congruity between the policy objectives and the policy instruments that are employed and the development sequences that are in progress.

Stages of Growth Constructions

The idea that economic development is a sequence that may be divided into stages is an old analytical concept. Numerous writers, particularly of the nineteenth-century German historical school of economists, have advanced their individual constructions of growth stages. Among these authors were List, Hildebrand, Bücher, Schmoller, and Sombart.[2] More recently, W. Rostow has attempted to redefine these earlier growth stages and to assign countries to various stages in what he calls his growth calendar.[3] In this sense countries at different stages of the development process may be thought of as beads being moved along a string.[4] The difficulty is that all countries obviously do not move along the same string.

Classifications of growth stages are usually based either on the predominant character of economic activity or on the increasing complexity of the exchange process. List, for example, distinguished five stages: (1) savage, (2) pastoral, (3) agricultural, (4) agricultural and manufacturing, and (5) agricultural, manufacturing, and commercial. Disregarding his first two stages, which describe obviously primitive societies, his latter three stages form an early version of the distinction between primary, secondary, and tertiary production, more recently associated with the classifications of A. G. B. Fisher and Colin Clark.[5]

Hildebrand distinguished only three stages: (1) barter, (2) money, and (3) credit. His classification described primarily the nature of the exchange process. Likewise Bücher employed only three stages: (1) the domestic or household economy, (2) the town economy, and (3) the

---

[2]For a discussion of the theories of stages of economic growth, see the essay by B. F. Hoselitz in *Theories of Economic Growth* (Glencoe, Ill.: Free Press, 1960), pp. 193–238.

[3]W. W. Rostow, *The Stages of Economic Growth* (Cambridge: At the University Press, 1960).

[4]The analogy is Galbraith's, *Economic Development*, p. 50.

[5]Fisher, *The Clash of Progress and Security* (London: Macmillan & Co., 1935); and Clark, *The Conditions of Economic Progress* (London: Macmillan & Co., 1940).

national economy. These stages also described primarily the growing complexity and geographic reach of the exchange process.

Schmoller's classification is similar, being composed of five stages: (1) village economy, (2) town economy, (3) territorial economy, (4) national economy, and (5) world economy. These stages appear to have been derived primarily from the economic history of Germany.

More recently, Rostow's classification also distinguishes five stages: (1) the traditional society, (2) the period of preconditions for the take-off, (3) the takeoff into sustained growth, (4) the drive to maturity, and (5) the age of high mass consumption.[6] These stages are, in his words, "not merely descriptive. . . . They have an inner logic and continuity. They have an analytic bone-structure, rooted in a dynamic theory of production."[7] In brief, he believes them to be substantively significant for a theory of economic growth. Whether or not this claim is well founded, Rostow's stages have attracted considerable attention as a classifying mechanism for economic history, but have had relatively little impact on received theories of the development process.

All the authors who have advanced stages of growth classifications have believed that their schemes possessed something more than mere descriptive significance. The test of this belief lies in whether these classifications do, in fact, contribute valuable new insights into our understanding of the process of economic growth, and whether they systematize the theory of this process. Unless they explain the transition from one stage to the next in a particularly apt or useful manner, their significance must remain largely taxonomic.

Value of Stage Growth Concepts

It is the opinion of most students of the growth process, I believe, that stages-of-growth constructions contribute neither very much to our understanding of actual development sequences nor to the theory of the subject. Nevertheless, they remain useful devices for classifying various economic systems and for historical analysis of those economies that have passed into the later stages of whatever classification is employed.[8]

In Rostow's analysis of growth, for example, particular importance

---

[6] Rostow, *Stages of Economic Growth.*
[7] *Ibid.*, pp. 12–13.
[8] See, for example, the review of Rostow's book by H. J. Habakkuk in the *Economic Journal*, September, 1961, pp. 601–4.

attaches to the takeoff stage, which in his view occurs when net investment rises above 10 per cent of national income and remains there; this stage is reached primarily through the operation of a number of propensities, among which are those to develop fundamental science, to apply this science to economic ends, to accept innovations, and to seek material advance.[9] All these inclinations are undoubtedly important in motivating the growth process, but they tell us relatively little that is new or noteworthy about why a particular country experiences a takeoff at a particular time, if indeed there is a definite takeoff period that may be identified in the economic history of that country.

My purpose in this chapter, however, is not to develop a critique of theories of the stages of economic growth, but to discuss the relation of fiscal policies to the stage in a growth sequence that a particular country happens to occupy at the moment. Also involved in this discussion is the relevant question whether an appropriate choice of fiscal policies can accelerate the growth process or can hasten materially the transition from one stage of growth to the next.

FISCAL POLICY IN THE TRADITIONAL SOCIETY

In an economy where growth is very limited and not yet self-sustaining, the scope for fiscal policy is extremely broad. It matters little whether we call such an economy a traditional society, a limited exchange economy, or a primarily agricultural country. Its characteristics are: attachment of a preponderant part of the labor force to agriculture, a substantial sector of productive activity which is not yet market oriented but is carried out primarily for the producers' own consumption; and reliance on traditional techniques which change very slowly and which permit only low productivity per worker. In such an economy the bulk of the population lives fairly close to the margin of subsistence even though natural resources may be abundant. Many of the African countries today fall in this general category, as do certain of the smaller nations of Southeast Asia. A limited class of merchants and traders may have comfortable incomes, however.

The main task of fiscal policy at the early stage of development is to finance an initial expansion of critical size in the program of public investment without either ruinous inflation or frequent balance-of-payments crises, and to insure that this public investment program is

---

[9]See his *The Process of Economic Growth* (New York: Norton, 1952), chap. 1.

actually devoted to areas that will contribute most to getting a cumulative process of expansion started.[10] There is an implicit economic stabilization objective involved here, but the primary objectives of such a fiscal policy are long range.

Institution Building

It is sometimes said that the chief problem at this early stage of development is building institutions that will permit the growth process to go forward. An educated and alert citizenry, a stable structure of government, adequate techniques of policy formulation, and an efficient administrative system for policy execution are all imperative; they must be developed along with the initial expansion of public investment. These institutions can hardly be created *in vacuo* before the expansion of public investment has been undertaken. While these institutions are being built, the development program must of necessity remain small and should be concentrated on those infrastructural areas that are truly vital to the growth process. The danger at this early stage lies in getting too many projects started at once.

Task of Fiscal Policy in First Stage of Growth

The work of fiscal policy in the first stage of growth involves laying out a general plan for public investment, insuring that this plan is properly oriented to the resources and capabilities of the country, securing public acceptance of the plan and of the sacrifices its completion will entail, modernizing the budget process so that it becomes a proper vehicle for plan revision and execution, and strengthening the tax system to support the contemplated development outlay. If the fiscal policy is appropriate it will help expand inputs of effort, skill, and saving, and will also restrain consumption enough to make this saving possible. All this can and ought to be done within a framework of relative financial stability, so that capital flight does not occur and workers do not rebel against the limitation of consumption they must accept.

In the early stages, one very important aspect of fiscal policy will involve rationalization of the budget process to sharpen its use as a

---

[10]A. R. Prest makes a similar point when he writes, "The very minimum that a Government is expected to do nowadays in any country is to remove or cut down the obstacles to economic growth met by the private sector; and much more frequently, it is deemed to have the task of striving for growth in a positive manner both by example and by precept." See his *Public Finance in Underdeveloped Countries*, p. 18.

management tool; it will also involve effective interfacing between the budget and the development planning processes so that a consistent framework for financial scheduling of all government activity can be regularly carried out. In this process all government expenditures must be systematically reviewed and those not essential to development or the maintenance of law and order eliminated. Proposed projects in the development plan must also be reviewed systematically and objectively, so that those with the most favorable ratios of benefits to costs will actually be given priority. Accurate periodic reporting of progress made on development projects and of obstacles encountered must also be built into the budgetary process.

The other prime task of fiscal policy at this early stage of development will be obtaining a substantial increase in tax revenue to finance the transfer of resources to public use. The tax system which exists, and which doubtless consists primarily of indirect levies, must be broadened and the rates increased in a manner that will fall primarily on consumption rather than on investment. Import duties on consumer goods will have to be stepped up and perhaps graduated more than they are. New devices to tax value added in agriculture in some fashion must be developed, and trading profits of the merchant class must somehow be reached. At the same time taxes are being increased, the standard of enforcement must be raised, so that public confidence in the equitable sharing of the heavier tax burden will be maintained. All this can be done within the framework of a tax system consisting for the most part of indirect levies.

Taxation in kind may be a feature of the traditional economy characterized by localized exchange. If so, this taxation should be put on a cash rather than on a barter basis as soon as possible. Eliminating collections in kind at the same time tax rates are raised will tend to force some workers out of the subsistence economy into the exchange system, a desirable concomitant of early-stage economic development efforts.

At this early stage, economic development activities should be concentrated heavily on broadening internal markets by improving transport and encouraging the growth of distribution facilities. Production needs to be oriented more toward the national market and away from purely local sales efforts. Local businessmen should undertake most of the task of broadening internal markets, but they may be assisted by better transport facilities and by government information and government credit.

Agricultural Taxation

In the taxation of agriculture at this earliest stage of development, the choice is often between a tax on farm marketings and a direct tax on land. The latter requires reasonably complete and accurate land ownership and tenure records. If these do not exist, the tax on marketings may be the only feasible one, even though such a tax tends to limit the movement of agricultural produce into trade channels and to limit the geographic expansion of markets—which is an important feature of development at this stage.

If the direct tax on land is feasible it is usually to be preferred, because it is possible to build certain income tax principles into such a tax. The administrative requirements for an equitable land tax are considerably greater, however, than for a roughly equitable tax on gross income from farm marketings. A tax of the latter type will probably, in large part, be shifted forward into food prices and will thus help to restrict consumption.

If exports are exempt from the marketings tax, the flow of agricultural materials into export trade will also be encouraged. This is a necessary change as the imports of goods and services for the public investment program increase, as they certainly will.

Countries just embarking on development efforts often have weak systems of taxing agricultural land or agricultural incomes; a good deal of effort can often be spent profitably on strengthening these systems.[11] Long-range programs of classifying agricultural lands on the basis of productivity may be undertaken, so that property may be assessed more nearly in accordance with its income potential. Relatively heavy taxation of unimproved land has occasionally been recommended, to provide an incentive for investments that will raise agricultural productivity.[12]

[11] R. W. Lindholm writes that "the property tax is a proven revenue raiser under relatively primitive administration conditions, e.g., the United States of the early 19th Century or Japan of the late 19th Century. The tax provides revenues and in doing this applies economic pressure that leads to more efficient use of land. Also the incidence of the tax is very likely to be such that land values will be reduced, the prices of agricultural products will not be increased, but landowners will be stimulated to expand the net income arising from the land they own." See his "Rejoinder" (to D. A. Tichett), *Economic Development and Cultural Change*, 10 (1961–62):215.

[12] The best-known recommendation was made in 1949 by an IBRD mission to Colombia headed by Lauchlin Currie. Australia imposed a progressive tax on the value of unimproved land between 1910 and 1952. The original purpose was to break up large estates. The rates were low, ranging up to only $4\frac{1}{2}$ per cent as a maximum. The tax base

continued overleaf

Because property taxes depend so heavily on local administration, they are apt to be weak in countries where local government is rudimentary. Initiative from the center in improving property tax administration may aid in the development of responsible local government.

Other Revenue Sources

Some students of the fiscal problem of developing economies feel that an income tax is desirable at a very early stage of development, provided it is limited to the top income recipients and no effort is made to generalize it into a mass tax. Having observed this type of income tax at work in certain countries which were not at the lowest level of the income scale, I am inclined to doubt the efficiency of an income tax at this early stage.[13] To be sure, there are certain expanding business profits resulting from economic development efforts that should be tapped; but the attempt to reach these by personal income taxation is often a failure in an economy where good records are not kept and where there is no tradition of cooperation with the revenue service.[14] These profits can be reached after a fashion by business license or gross receipts taxes.

Evan a limited income tax makes heavy demands on the necessarily restricted capacity of a country at an early stage of tax administration; such a tax may also reach, to an extent greater than desirable, those

---

[12] *continued*

was defined by deducting the value of improvements from the assessments. These were frozen at 1939-40 levels for the remaining twelve years the tax remained in force. According to one analyst who has studied this tax in detail, the experience shows that "a progressive rate tax on land is probably not as fiscally suitable for a poor country as a flat rate tax would be."—Richard M. Bird, "A National Tax on the Unimproved Value of Land: the Australian Experience, 1910-1952," *National Tax Journal*, 13 (1960): 386-92.

[13] A similar view has been expressed even more strongly by D. E. Shirley who writes that "extensive reliance on income taxes or other ability to pay measures is a social and economic luxury which the lesser developed nations of the world cannot yet afford." Cf. his article "Income Taxes for Lesser Developed Nations." *National Tax Journal*, 12 (1959), p. 269.

[14] In a well-known article, Richard Goode has given six necessary conditions for successful use of a progressive income tax. These conditions are (1) a predominantly money economy, (2) a high standard of literacy among taxpayers, (3) prevalence of accurate accounting records, (4) a large degree of voluntary compliance on the part of taxpayers, (5) free political democracy, and (6) a higher standard of administration than for other taxes. See his article "Reconstruction of Foreign Tax Systems," *National Tax Association Proceedings*, 1951, pp. 212-22. Also reprinted in Bird and Oldman's *Readings on Taxation in Developing Countries*, pp. 169-79.

potential savings that would go into private investment.[15]

If an income tax is employed at an early stage of development, it should perhaps include a concession for profits reinvested in business expansion. This feature would further reduce the productivity of an income tax and would also complicate its administration.

If a general rule can be devised, I should suggest that no country rely heavily on a personal income tax until it has reached or is close to the takeoff point in Rostow's classification of growth stages.[16] Corporate income taxation may be employed with good effect somewhat earlier.

Comparative studies of fiscal systems show that countries in a low state of development often have surprisingly weak sales and excise tax systems. For example, Martin and Lewis, who studied sixteen countries with a very broad range of per capita income, found that excise taxes raised less than 2 per cent of GNP in the nine poorest countries, compared with an average of over 6 per cent of GNP in the seven richest.[17] Their findings suggest that there might well be considerable scope for strengthening these indirect taxes within the administrative capacity of a country still in a rudimentary phase of development. Sales and excise taxes could, without undue difficulty, be designed primarily to limit consumption in a progressive manner and also to help force more of total output into the monetized section of the economy.[18]

---

[15]A contrary view has been expressed by M. C. Taylor who, on the basis of a survey of Malayan experience with income taxation, writes, "One can become too pessimistic with respect to the compliance and enforcement difficulties of an income tax in lesser developed nations. Apparently, a workable and respectable income tax can be developed given the will to do so and a conscientious and enlightened administrative effort." See his article "Income Taxation in the Federation of Malaya," *National Tax Journal*, 14 (1961): 198–204.

[16]A similar point of view is implied by S. S. Surrey when he writes, "The income tax may well be the favorite of the twentieth century, but it demands twentieth century administration. This requirements is even more urgent when one turns to the complex variations of that tax such as a tax on excess profits or a tax on increases in individual incomes or a tax on expenditures. There are many who urge these variants without any comprehension of the complex legal and accounting problems which they create, without any recognition of the enormous difficulties being faced in the struggle to impose even the basic income tax, and without any realization that even countries with considerable experience in income tax administration have yet to master these specialized types of income taxation." These remarks are made in the course of a general plea for giving tax administration priority over policy reform in the reconstruction of tax systems of less developed countries. See "Tax Administration in Underdeveloped Countries," in *Readings on Taxation in Developing Countries*, ed. Bird and Oldman, p. 505.

[17]A. Martin and W. A. Lewis, "Patterns of Public Revenue and Expenditure," *Manchester School of Economic and Social Studies*, 24 (September, 1956): 203–32.

[18]Panelists who discussed sales and excise taxes before the Ways and Means
continued overleaf

Chapter 9

Rationalizing Public Expenditures

Perhaps the chief scope for fiscal policy in a country at a low stage of development is to be found in expenditure. The main problem consists, as was already noted, in eliminating all nonessential government expenditures for nondevelopment purposes and in making sure that public investments are actually undertaken in proper priority order. This is commonly considered the realm of development planning rather than of fiscal policy; but I am thinking here of planning as a continuous process that does not end when the first formal development plan is prepared.

The essence of adapting the planning process to the realities of economic development lies in constantly revising and rescheduling development projects as the emerging economic situation unfolds. Only where the budget process has been revitalized and oriented toward providing a proper framework for continual revision can effective development planning be said to be in operation. Many countries do not realize how fundamentally they must restructure their normal pattern of government operations to accommodate development planning as a continuing activity.

The creation of an administrative structure that will be conducive to development is a much larger undertaking than it often appears. Economic policies at the center of the power structure must be considered systematically. This calls for good staff work in which the available alternatives are clearly set forth, with objective consideration given to the pros and cons of each possible course of action. The indispensable condition for successful development planning is the establishment of a top-notch staff structure. Without it a development plan is either a vague statement of aspirations or a meaningless exercise in bureaucratic wheel spinning. Countries that are unwilling or unable to adopt a hard-headed and rational process of scheduling all public expenditures are probably better off not to formulate a development program in the first instance. Too often these plans have been little more than window dressing to obtain foreign loans or other assistance.

---

[18]continued

Committee of the United States Congress in June, 1964 were fairly unanimous in stressing that such taxes fell more heavily on consumption, compared with investment, than (progressive) income taxes. See *Hearings on Federal Excise Tax Structure*, Committee on Ways and Means, June 15 and 16, 1964. Those expressing this view were R. A. Musgrave (p. 8), C. L. Harris (p. 15), and O. Eckstein (p. 25).

THE PERIOD OF INITIAL BUT UNCERTAIN GROWTH

Once a less developed country has broken out of its traditional pattern and has instituted some cumulative growth processes, the scope for fiscal policy narrows somewhat, although the requirements for a successful policy at this stage become even more rigorous. The need at this second stage of development is intensive investment in infrastructure—to permit further broadening of markets and to support the steadily growing diversification of productive activity.

It is in the course of this stage that the country ceases to be a monoculture and gradually extends the pattern of its export trade. Its imports have already, from the first efforts at development, shifted toward capital goods and away from consumer goods; but this pattern is constantly reinforced during this second stage, as public investment grows.

Keeping Public and Private Investment in Step

For a country to advance steadily through the second stage of development, public investments in infrastructure must be accompanied by a steadily expanding and broadening volume of private investment in business activity. Small-scale manufacturing of consumer goods for the home market should get underway, protected to a degree, but not excessively, by relatively high duties on imported consumer goods. Investment by foreign business firms in new industries should be especially encouraged at this stage, by guarantees of stability in economic policy and by adequate foreign exchange for the remission of profits. A local capital market should also begin to develop so that investment funds will have more fluidity. Banks should gradually modify their traditional lending patterns, which have probably been geared mainly to financing trade, and should finance industrial projects more extensively.

Features of the Initial Growth Stage

Progress in this second stage of development is characterized by a steadily rising fraction of capital formation in the national product. This product, in absolute terms, will be rising at a rate in excess of the rate of population increase, and therefore per capita income will grow. Consumption is necessarily strictly limited but may increase slightly in absolute terms, even though declining as a percentage of national product. Fiscal policy must provide strong incentives to saving in all forms and to some redirection of these savings toward the newer investment opportunities. If occasional deficits in the public accounts are experienced, methods of financing these deficits outside of credit expansion by the banking system should be developed. Ownership of the public debt should become more widespread.

In this second stage of development many of the initial resistances to change will have been overcome. Confidence in the desire and ability of the government to act in the national interest will have been established, to the point where growing public outlays for investment will command more general support.

The need at this time is a revenue system that will exhibit enough flexibility of yield that tax collections will keep pace with the growing volume of public outlay. The tax system may still consist primarily of indirect levies, but these will become increasingly progressive so that some redistribution of income from the combined effect of taxes and government expenditures is apparent.[19]

Government expenditures for social services other than education will still be minimal because outlay continues to be heavily concentrated on investment projects. If foreign aid is being received, this is the period when it can be put to most effective use in overcoming the acute shortage of capital and in building the new institutions necessary to an expanding economy.

Results of past investments in development will be increasingly apparent as the economy moves through this stage. Per capita income should be expanding steadily, if unspectacularly. Threats of inflation and of balance-of-payments crises will be recurrent, but they must be met by resolute action on the part of the government to maintain relative financial stability.

Increasingly accurate appraisals will be made of the priority of various public investment projects as lessons are learned from past experience. The discipline of the budget process will be increasingly strict as competition for appropriations becomes keener. Understanding will spread that the necessarily severe curtailing of consumption on

---

[19]The exact nature of the relationship between income inequality and economic growth is controversial. According to Kuznets, as development proceeds, inequality first increases and then later diminishes. Inequality is statistically lower, even before direct taxes and public expenditures, in advanced rather than in less advanced countries. These relations are believed by Kuznets, however, to be more results than causes of economic growth. See his article "Economic Growth and Income Inequality," *American Economic Review*, 45 (1955):1–28.

a sustained basis—to finance capital formation—is actually paying off in growing productivity. There will be increasing concern over the equity of the tax structure as the burden of taxation becomes heavier.

I do not mean to imply that all these changes will occur smoothly and without resistance. There will always be dissident elements that do not accept the discipline of economic development or the costs which it inevitably involves. Old class lines will nevertheless become blurred as the new entrepreneurs gain power and influence. An emergent middle class of business managers, professional people, and technicians will be increasingly in evidence.

Other Changes Critical to the Growth Process

It is during this second stage of development that the sharp rise in agricultural productivity which is a precondition for successful industrialization should take place. Fiscal policy can assist this process both in expenditure and receipts. Among the public outlays for development will be outlays for farm-to-market roads; demonstrations of the value of better seeding, fertilizing, and pest control practices; irrigation of arid areas; and the like. Agricultural credit will also be made available more broadly so that individual farmers can take advantage of new techniques. On the receipts side agricultural taxes will be rising and taking new forms—so that farmers are kept under continuing pressure to expand their incomes by better practice.

As employment opportunities outside of agriculture develop, there will be a movement of the labor force toward urban areas. This will also force some changes in agricultural practice, as well as moderate the large volume of seasonal agricultural underemployment. Agricultural productivity seems to rise fastest when the supply of agricultural labor is diminishing and the demand for agricultural materials is expanding rapidly. Growing export trade and expansion of the nonagricultural sectors of the economy are most likely to produce this condition.

Although economic development requires accelerated capital formation, the building of new institutions, and positive economic policies, the fundamental changes to make this progress practical must take place in the attitudes and motivation of people. In this process of modernization, leadership has come in different countries from the military services, the Western-trained professional people, and the new local entrepreneurs. As these groups have moved into political prominence, the objectives of government policy have changed; but the orientation of the people at large has not necessarily kept pace. Only as concern for adopting new methods to raise productivity becomes general are the preconditions for self-perpetuating growth fulfilled.

The need to generate broad concern often causes the transit of this second stage of economic development to take a long time; it depends heavily upon fundamental education and on increasing contact with the values and thought patterns of a growing society. Fiscal policy has a comparatively limited contribution to make to this reconstruction of personal viewpoint. In the main its role is limited to creating the kind of stable economic situation in which this modernization of viewpoint can take place—without being diverted into other, less constructive channels, such as political adventure or revolutionary changes in economic organization.

Evolution of the Tax System

As progress is made toward self-sustaining economic growth, the character of the tax system should gradually change, with more emphasis placed on direct levies. In Wald's analysis of the land tax in less developed countries, for example, his recommendations all point toward remaking these taxes in the image of income taxes. As he puts it:

> The design of the recommendations envisages continuous progress toward bringing much of agricultural income under a country-wide income tax. Starting with corporate enterprises, where they exist in agriculture, and then with the managers of plantations and the wealthier landlords, a country should seek gradually to supplement the land tax with an income tax based on ascertained net income and supported by the necessary taxpayers' accounting records. The combined yield from the income and land taxes should grow in this process, partly because of the expected expansion of agricultural production and continuous improvement of tax collection methods. With the extended coverage of the income tax, the land tax will tend to recede in importance. It may eventually apply primarily to agriculturists earning more than a bare subsistence but not enough to warrant direct assessment of income by the taxing authorities, or it may be turned over to the local or provincial governments and continued as a general tax to finance the growing need for services at these jurisdictional levels.[20]

Whether other indirect taxes can experience this kind of withering away in favor of the personal income tax is a more difficult question. In my opinion this is not to be expected; instead, and in most cases, direct taxation will merely be superimposed upon the indirect taxes already present, although the latter will inevitably become relatively less important in the process.

[20]Wald, *Taxation of Agricultural Land*, pp. 208–9.

Some general and quite productive taxes on business should be implemented during this second phase of economic development. A general sales tax of the value added type might be valuable. This tax makes no distinction among various forms of business organization; is at least partly shiftable; and requires a return form which, although simpler than a net income return form, can subsequently be adapted to that purpose. Both taxpayers and tax administrators may gain valuable experience in the preparation and auditing of these returns. A value added tax at a low flat rate would seem to be preferable to one which graduates rates on the basis of the essentiality of the product or service, as the French tax does.

Central Control and Decentralized Execution

The governmental structure of less developed countries is apt to be highly centralized. Indeed, the establishment of a strong central government is a necessary precondition for rational development planning. One of the problems many countries have experienced as they have moved into the execution of development plans is how to decentralize the continuing planning process so that it will be more responsive to local needs and local capabilities. Decision making in development planning cannot proceed entirely from the top down if the planning process is to be successful. Even the countries that practice authoritarian planning have discovered that there is a practical necessity for some decentralization.

Just as decentralization of the planning process is a necessary but difficult and time-consuming process, so the decentralization of revenue administration is difficult but equally essential. Until decentralization has advanced to a critical point, the capacity of the developing country to employ direct taxation must remain strictly limited. Building an honest and efficient revenue service to cover an entire country and to cope successfully with direct taxes is a large order. In my view direct taxes on business should be attempted before any effort is made to reach individuals in their capacity as income recipients.

In the process of decentralizing both the planning and the collection of revenue, there is much to be said for sharing revenues from particular taxes between the central and the local governments. Countries that are now advanced have not often done this, because revenue needs have not always grown simultaneously at the national and local levels, to mention only one reason. For a developing country, however, sharing offers some distinct advantages, in obtaining uniform tax bases and in strengthening local government as well as in improving both national and local tax administration. Property taxes, general sales or excise taxes, and business taxes seem all to be amenable to some type of revenue sharing, which would also be based on shared administration.

Dynamic Factors in Growth

The key to tax policy during the second stage of economic development is that, although the burden of taxation is steadily increasing, it bears comparatively lightly on business profits so long as these are reinvested in further expansion. Therefore this stage will be characterized by a steadily rising and constantly diversifying volume of private investment. In the course of this investment, new techniques and methods of production are continually being introduced, and so productivity of resources, both human and material, is advancing steadily. Some new industries are being established, but it is the rising productivity in existing industries that is the main feature.

For most countries this means a near revolution in agricultural practice. The more unfavorable the ratio of arable land to population, the more explosive this technological revolution in agriculture must be. Heavily overpopulated countries such as India and Egypt, although more advanced in many respects than other less developed countries, therefore must expect to take longer to reach the period of self-sustaining growth, whether this is called the takeoff period or given some other designation.

An important aspect of government policy during the second stage of development is publicizing the fact that the economy is growing and that this very dynamism of growth is constantly opening up new avenues for private investment at attractive returns. This publicity should consist, not merely of exhortation, but also of detailed facts about when particular public investments in infrastructure will be completed and what these investments will mean in lowering operating costs. The successful private business firms will be those that capitalize on cost-reducing opportunities to expand their sales and to locate new facilities in strategic areas.

Information of this kind is perhaps best disseminated by broad public participation in the continuing planning process. In this process the dialog should encompass not only the investments to be undertaken in the public sector but also the means to be used to finance these investments. Businessmen need to know something about future tax policy as well as about future budgets.

I am assuming in this rough sketch of the second stage of development that, although public investment is increasing, the increase is mainly in the areas which are noncontroversial so far as the scope for public and private business, respectively, is concerned. In other words the development plan does not contemplate a progressive socialization of business by reserving certain areas for public investment only. Road-building, port development, and increased supply of electric power are what I should call noncontroversial investments in infrastructure; nationalization of existing industries or building of new factories entirely for government ownership and control are not. The best check on this tendency toward creeping involvement of government in business is also broad public participation in the planning process, plus political action to keep the scope of public investment rigidly confined.

As the economy advances through the second stage, the dynamic quality in total investment should increasingly be concentrated in the private sector. Government, through its investment program, may have provided the initial momentum to get the growth process started, but the leadership in adapting technology and in creating new combinations of resources should come increasingly from private entrepreneurs. They will realize some of the external economies from a more complete infrastructure, will overcome their old traditions of limited sales at high margins of profit, and will translate lower costs into lower prices for market expansion.

When this dynamic quality in private investment has become generalized and self-reinforcing, the stage will be set for movement into the next stage of development—characterized by self-perpetuating growth and by a decline in the relative share of total investment emanating from the public sector. The chief contribution of fiscal policy during this second stage has been in permitting dynamism in private investment to develop, under conditions of reasonable financial stability, and in directing this dynamism along lines laid out in the total plan. Unless the plan itself is sound, this kind of response in private investment cannot be expected.

FISCAL POLICY DURING THE TAKEOFF

The third, or takeoff, period is characterized by a spurt in investment, primarily in the private sector, by the rapid spread of improved techniques and the rapid growth of new industries that enjoy some comparative advantage. In more advanced economies this stage has sometimes corresponded with the opening up of new territories, such as the American West after the Civil War, or the western provinces of Canada at a later date. In countries without geographic frontier regions, the process has taken the form of rapid spread of factory methods, as in the United Kingdom or Japan. For most less developed countries today, intensive reform in productive methods rather than extensive settlement of new areas is the chief possibility.

Fiscal policy during this stage should concentrate on minimizing the deterrents to private investment. There will undoubtedly still be large-scale public investments in infrastructure, but these will be in fields where a beginning has already been made. There will undoubtedly also be a growing demand for welfare projects and for social services that depend on public financing; but these expenditures should not be permitted to grow too rapidly.

The Revenue Side

Taxable capacity will be growing steadily as past investments generate new incomes and new employment opportunities. Public revenues will also rise if the tax system, although still consisting primarily of indirect levies, possesses yield flexibility that is at least proportional to, if not progressive with, the rise in national product.

If the administrative structure for tax collection has been perfected to a reasonable degree and the public is ready for the change, a start can now be made on making personal income taxation a major revenue source. Initially the provisions of an income tax law should be simple, with relatively high personal or family exemptions and only a limited rate progression. Complications such as special tax rates for capital gains or averaging provisions should be kept out of the law until taxpayers have had sufficient time to become well acquainted with the general requirements of the new tax. Current payment by means of withholding provisions should be employed whenever possible. The income tax should be generous, however, in such matters as depreciation allowances and business loss carryovers.

When an income tax is adopted, a good case exists for taxing income from work at a lower rate than income from property. There is a case in equity for this course since income from personal effort is generally less permanent than income from property and since, generally speaking, income taxes allow no deduction for depreciation of human capital and for training, although these do actually wear out quite as much as machines do. There is also a case for favorable treatment of earned income on incentive grounds since more input of effort, particularly skilled effort, is to be encouraged for the sake of economic growth. If an income tax can be administered with tolerable fairness, it can be administered as effectively with an earned income credit as without it.

Since the number of taxpayers will be limited by the relatively high exemptions, a high standard of enforcement should prevail from the beginning of income taxation. Arbitrary assessments should be avoided, but severe penalties should be imposed in cases of fraud so that a tradition of good voluntary compliance can gradually be built up.

Direct taxation of wealth transfers at death or by gift can be started well before a personal income tax can be managed. The transfer tax is easier to administer than an income tax and has fewer disincentive effects to be concerned about; the main problem is to get self-sustaining growth sequences started.

The Expenditure Side

In the takeoff period the rule of annual budget balancing should continue to be followed as closely as possible. This does not mean that some deficits and surpluses will not occur. International events will from time to time throw the budget out of balance, but progress in the public investment program should not be geared to these external events. The rule is, rather, that deficits and surpluses should not be planned for internal reasons such as temporary variations in employment. The goals of fiscal policy should continue to be essentially long range.

The development planning process needs to be continually strengthened and made more detailed throughout this stage. Planning for the private sector, which should become increasingly important as growth proceeds, should not emphasize control and direction, but information to and cooperation with private business interests. Such controls as the government imposes should be of a general nature, over access to credit and social value of contemplated investment, rather than over particular projects, locations, or procedural plans. Planning for the private sector, in a word, must strengthen incentives to invest instead of weakening those incentives.

As growth proceeds, the role of fiscal policy should gradually contract. From being an initiator of change, this policy should gradually restrict itself to maintaining the kind of financial stability and climate in which private investment can flourish. The real work of economic development must be done in the private sector. Government can create the preconditions and the necessary overhead but should not undertake the whole job of building a business structure.

Historically the countries that have moved through the takeoff phase have usually done so before they had personal income taxes, or at least before those taxes were important revenue producers. Less developed countries today should not expect their own institutional patterns to be markedly different, even though they may reach this stage of development at a much later date.

CONCLUDING REMARKS

It would be possible to continue at some length the discussion of how the goals and the techniques of fiscal policy continue to change in stages of economic growth beyond the takeoff. This would, however, be of only limited concern to countries that have not yet reached the takeoff. In any case the direction of development is clear. The farther a country progresses, the more its fiscal policies become concerned with short-range, anticyclical objectives. It relies more heavily on direct taxation as it advances, and the fraction of its budget that is concerned with social services and welfare activities of various sorts becomes larger.

Welfare activities are not unimportant to continued economic growth; but for poor countries they represent luxuries that either delay more fundamental investment or cause the budget to be overly large. To achieve rapid economic development a country must be willing to give this objective absolute top priority and to sacrifice many other aspirations to it. The price of development is hard work, willingness to postpone increases in consumption, and eagerness to accept change. There is no easy, painless road.

This study of fiscal policy for the developing countries has necessarily concerned itself primarily with general principles. The differences among individual countries are great, and any general principle must be modified to meet an individual country's prevailing situation.

In recent years, as the problems of less developed countries have been subjected to increasing study, an impression has been created that there is a special brand of economic analysis to be applied to the less developed countries. I consider this impression unfortunate. The techniques of analysis and the precepts of policy are the same for countries in all stages of development.

There is, however, a time dimension in all economic policy applications. The policies best calculated to foster additional growth of the United States economy in 1968 are not the same as those that would have had this effect in 1865. India today may resemble the United States of 1865 in certain respects more than it does the United States of 1968.

I am not suggesting that the less developed countries should deliberately court obsolete policy objectives or employ discredited policy techniques. Far from it. My plea is for constructive adaptation of the body of accumulated knowledge to current problems. In writing about fiscal policies and how they are interrelated to the different stages of economic development, my aim has been to make this constructive adaptation a little easier.

Index

Accelerating investment, 20
Active fiscal policy, 56–57
Administrative budget, 8; arrangement of, 8; exclusions from, 8
Advisory services, 166–75; defects in, 170; overcommitment of, 180; timing of, 169–70
Agency for International Development, 171; Annual Report to Congress for fiscal 1963, 78 n.
Aggregate demand, 21–22; effect of public expenditure on, 21
Aggregate revenue and expenditure, 52–60; meaning of, 52
Agricultural methods, 36; difficulty of changing, 118
Agricultural productivity, 35–36, 86–88, 118, 127; and aid, 86–88; barriers to, 87; how fiscal policy can help raise, 189; and industrialization, 36; means of raising, 127
Agricultural taxation, 22, 145; in the first stage of growth, 189–90
Aid, 26; and fiscal policy, 89–95; and industrialization, 88–89
Aid programs, 84–92; content of, 85–86
Allen, G. C., 105 n.
Annual Report of the Secretary General for UNCTAD, 1964, 37 n.
Appropriate tax system, 14, 18
Asher, Robert, 83 n.

Baer, W., 163 n.
Balanced growth, 38–39

Balance of payments discipline, 62–64; and contracyclical fiscal policy, 62–63
Baldwin, R. E., 48 n.
Balogh, T., 39 n.
Bauer, P. T., 33, 65, 84 n.
Beckerman, W., 167 n.
Benefit-cost analysis, 97; techniques of, 40
Benham, Frederic, 83 n.
Bernstein, E. M., 73 n.
Bird, Richard M., 190 n.
Birr, Kendall, 179 n.
Black, Eugene, 100 n.
Bodin, Jean, 86 n.
Broadening markets, 188; in early stage of growth, 198
Buchanan, N. S., 88 n.
Budget authority, 45
Budget Bureau, U.S., 44
Budget concepts, 7–9, 44
Budget, 28–51; coordination with development planning, 44–45, 173; effect of changes in foreign trade on, 60–63; to balance or not, 53–54; training in use of, 42, 53
Budget deficit, 7, 24, 61
Budget execution, 45, 173
Budget imbalance, 58–62; uncontrollable factors in, 58–64
Budgeting, 44–47; as a field for intellectual aid, 53, 93
Budget rules, 4, 74; conclusion concerning, 73–75; is one desirable, 55–56
Budgets, 7–12; as forecasts of the fu-

ture, 7; net and gross measures in, 9–10

Burma, 54 n., 59–60, 98, 132; barter agreement with U.S.S.R., 157; Central Bank of, 153; defects in development planning during 1950's, 60; economic position following Korean war, 152; extrabudgetary transactions in, 11; import tax policy in, 124; joint ventures in, 38; liquor taxes in, 10 n.; public investment program in, 59; revenue expansion during Korean war, 152; rice exports from, 59, 132

Cairncross, A. K., 156 n.
Caldwell, L. K., 181 n.
Capital outlays, 167
Capital-output ratios, 154–55; ex-ante and ex-post, 154; in Indian planning, 155; intercountry comparisons of, 155
Cash budget, 8; uses of, 8
Central banks, 5, 149; as recipients of technical assistance, 178; role in monetary policy, 148–49
Central control, 45; and decentralized execution, 197–98
Checchi, Vincent, 41 n.
Chelliah, R. J., 64 n.
Chenery, H. B., 32 n., 154 n., 155 n.
Christenson, J. B., 115 n.
Chronic inflation, 68–71
Clark, Colin, 184
Clay Committee, 147
Clerk, P. G., 40 n.
Colm, Gerhard, 34
Committee for Economic Development, 5 n.
Comprehensive budget, 51, 53; data needed to prepare, 53; need for, 11–12
Contracyclical fiscal policy, 7, 63, 75; conflict with balance of payments discipline, 62
Costa Rica, 150; alcoholic beverages in, 9–10; credit ceilings, 150; dual exchange rate, 125; excess burden

on monetary policy in 1961, 57, 150
Cost estimates, 40; outdated by inflation, 26
Credit policy, 151; abundant, 5
Creditworthiness, 27; of specific projects and broad plans, 27
Current and capital budgets, 11; as a pretext for fiscal irresponsibility, 68
Currency overvaluation, 163
Currie, Lauchlin, 189 n.
Curti, Merle, 179 n.
Customs duties, 121–26; advantages of, 122; in U.S., 125

Dam, K. W., 115 n.
Death taxes, 141–43; alternative forms of, 141–42; and Anglo Saxon tradition, 142; as a revenue source, 142; pros and cons of, 142–43
Decentralization, 45; need for, 197; of planning and budgeting, 45; of revenue administration, 197
Decision making, 28; decentralized, 197
Denison, E. F., 19 n.
Devaluation, 164
Development, 28–34, 80, 107, 153, 185–91; appropriate technology for, 48–50; banks, 88; business talent for, 49; capital requirements for, 80; price of, 137; skills for, 107–8
Development Assistance Committee, 79
Development planning, 35, 192; and annual budget, 45–46, 50; and export expansion, 32–33, 35; authoritarian, 28–29, 45; coordination with budget process, 44–45; Indian, 155; inflationary gaps in, 26–27; international consultation in, 37; judging the results of, 47; mistakes in, 33–34; need for conservatism, 47; need for continuous testing, 35; need for flexibility in, 50; in Pakistan, 29; personnel requirements for, 46–47; process, 46; role of foreign advisers in, 30–31; structures for, 29–30; underlying orientation of,

35–36; use of consultants in, 30

Development plans, 28–48; feasibility of, 46–47; intercountry variations in, 26; subschedules for, 46–47

Development policy, 29, 33, 188; relation of organization mix to, 101

Development projects, 54; costing of, 54

Diamond, William, 41 n.

Direct controls, 26, 72; effects of, 72

Direct taxation, 12, 196; as a long-run goal, 144; requirements for, 16; when to emphasize, 200

Disaggregation, 43; of development plan, 43

Disequilibrium, 68–70; strategy of, 71–72

Diversification, 67; in agriculture, 195

Dosser, D., 43 n.

Due, John, 119, 127 n., 140 n.

Eagly, R. A., 20 n.

Echaus, R. S., 48 n.

Economic development, 1–2, 18–27; administrative structure for, 29–30; as a process guided by the state, 2; takeoff stage in, 199–203

Economic growth, 1–2, 18–27, 183–203; alternative paths to, 19; changes necessary for, 2; as a goal of national policy, 1–2; defined, 3 n.; Malthusian, 19; measurement of, 3 n.; nature of, 1–2; relation to fiscal policy, 18–23, 145; resistance to, 2; Ricardian, 19

Economic Report of the President, Jan. 1963, 18

Education, 39, 196; films for, 106

Effective Demand, 20–21; Keynsian theory of, 20–21

Egyptian steel industry, 158–59; political motivation for, 159

Ellis, H. S., 88 n.

Estate taxes; *see* death taxes

Excess profits taxes, 143

Exchange rates, 160; and fiscal policy, 160–62; consequences of outdated parities, 162–64

Excise taxes, 133–35, 191; and consumer choice, 133–34; at early stage of development, 191; products and services taxed, 133; and subsistence sector, 134; temporary exemptions from, 113

Expenditure and tax policies, 54–55; needed reforms in, 92–93

Exports, 156–60; adding value to, 36–37; barriers to, 163; expansion, 160, 195; *vs.* import substitution, 38–39

Export taxes, 60, 130–33; benefits and costs of, 131–33; as fiscal expedients, 130

Extrabudgetary items of revenue and expense, 10–11

Fiscal advice, 165–82; amenability of host government officials to, 167–68; arrangements for, 165–66; and cultural preconceptions, 179–80; defects in past practice, 170; definition of, 165; initial missions, 166; intermittent, 170; need for simplicity in, 176; need for strict objectivity in, 168–69; payment for, 181; pitfalls in arrangements for, 178–82; response of host government to, 168; substantive content of, 177–78; suppliers of, 165; terms of reference for, 166; timing of, 169–70

Fiscal adviser, 167–69; popularity of, 169, 176; qualities for effectiveness, 175–77

Fiscal and monetary policies, 148–54; obstacles to harmony, 153–54; relative ease or tightness, 151

Fiscal and trade policies, 155–59

Fiscal arrangements, 175; evolutionary stages in, 176

Fiscal policy, 3–7, 56–72, 89–95, 147–64, 183–203; active or neutral, 56; alternative objectives of, 64–68; balance with other economic policies, 57–58; and cyclical disturbances, 3; definition, 3; and exchange rate policy, 160–64; formula *vs.* discretionary flexibility, 63; implementation of, 28; Keynesian assumptions of, 4–5; meaning and scope of, 3; present-day view of, 4; relation to economic growth, 18–19; relation to monetary policy, 5–6, 148–54; risk of poor timing, 63; strength dependent on other controls, 57; structural effects of, 6; task in first stage of growth, 187–89; in the traditional society, 186–92; unifying nature of, 27

Fiscal policy goals, 57, 64–67, 183; diversification, 67; lessening inequality, 65–66; multiple ones, 64–65; promoting saving, 64

Fisher, A. G. B., 184

Flexible tax system, 61

Floating exchange rate, 161–62

Foreign advisers, 90; diminishing effectiveness of, 167

Foreign aid, 76–96; as catalyst for growth, 26; effect on economic growth, 83; how to limit dependence on, 89; lack of settled philosophy toward, 85, 90; multiplier, 95; per capita volume of, 82–83; political basis of, 76–77, 95; provided by France and Germany, 78; unequal distribution among recipients, 82–83, 95

Foreign exchange control, 152

Foreign exchange reserves, 54

Foreign source income, 110; U.S. tax treatment of, 113–14

Foreign tax credit, 113

Friedman, Milton, 88 n.

Friedman, W. G., 110 n.

Functional finance, 61

Furnivall, J. S., 102 n.

Galbraith, J. K., 183 n., 184 n.

Geiger, Theodore, 34

General sales taxes, 135–37

Geographic concentration of investment, 39–40

Gift taxes, 143

Goode, Richard, 123 n., 190 n.

Government, 41, 103–4; budgets, factors in size of, 10; and business, 99–101; employment, 93; monopolies, 103–4

Groves, Harold M., 18 n.

Growth, 23–24, 25; balanced or unbalanced, 70–71; dynamic factors in, 198–99; factors favorable to, 19; publicizing of, 198; stages of, 184–85

Gumpel, H. J., 115 n.

Habakkuk, H. J., 185 n.

Haberler, G., 31 n., 157 n.

Hagen, E. E., 40 n., 49

Hall, C. A., 58 n.

Hansen, Bent, 56 n.

Hansen, K. R., 173 n.

Hansen, N. M., 43 n.

Harberger, A., 149 n.

Hawtrey, R. G., 148 n.

Heckscher, E. F., 2 n.

Helleiner, G. K., 60 n.

Heller, Walter, 64

Herve, M. E. A., 163 n.

Hicks, J. R., 158 n.

Higgins, Benjamin, 143 n., 180

Hindu undivided family, 142

Hirschmann, A. O., 70 n.

Hoselitz, B. F., 184 n.

Human capital, 101

Huneer, Guy, 167 n.

Import, 38; expansion during economic development, 157; methods of replacement, 37

Import taxes, 121–26; means of improvement, 122–23; need for simplifying, 122, 126; varying rates, 122

Income inequality, 16

Income taxes, 138–41; annual audits, 139, 168; complications of, 140; at early stage of development, 140, 190; general features of, 138–39; progressive rates, 140; record keeping for, 138; relative bearing on work and property, 200; schedular,

139; source collection of, 200; varying effectiveness, 17; voluntary assessment of, 168; when appropriate, 141, 191

India, 16 n., 33

Industrilization, 24, 33, 41, 88–89

Infant industries, 158

Inflation, 23–27; and the balance of payments, 24; conflicting consequences of, 25–26, 69–70; conflicting effects on growth, 25; cost push and demand pull elements, 70; and direct controls, 71; gap, 26, 72–73; and growth, 23–24; less developed countries more prone to, 74; mechanism of, 69; as a route development, 72–73; and saving, 24–25; and wage restraint, 73

Infrastructure, 68; noncontroversial investments in, 199

Initial growth stage, 193–99; features of, 193–94

Input-output, 43; as an investment planning technique, 42–43

Institution building, 109, 187

Intellectual aid, 89; scope for, 93–94

International Chamber of Commerce, 110 n.

International commodity agreements, 156

International Monetary Fund, 94, 95 160, 170

International tax treaties, 114

Investment, 31–33; climate, 99–100, 108; geographic dispersion of, 41–42; need for pioneering quality in, 42; shift to inventories during inflation, 69

Investment incentives, 98–117; design of, 109–10; limited effectiveness of, 116; nature of, 102–3; preconditions for, 99, 105–6; as special privileges, 109; varied purposes of, 102, 110

Investment planning, 32, 97, 193; for private sector, 148; France, 43; methods of, 43–47

Investment priorities, 31–32

Investment projects, 27

Investment tax concessions, 112

Iran, 91; budget improvement in, 172; fiscal and monetary policies in, 151; import tax policy in, 124; redistribution of income in, 152

Japan, 105, 127 n.; agricultural productivity before 1960, 36; as a model for industrialization, 105; rapid development after 1878, 35

Jewkes, John, 29, 47 n.

Johnson, H. G., 161–62

Joint ventures, 38, 110

Kahn, A. R., 34 n.

Kaldor, N., 22, 143 n.

Kalmanoff, G., 110 n.

Kauffman, K. M., 111 n.

Keynes, Lord, 4 n., 20–21, 74

Kilby, Peter, 107 n.

Kozyzaniak, M., 13 n.

Krause, L. B., 115 n.

Kuznets, Simon, 33, 67, 194 n.

Labor force, 195

Land reform, 66; as an alternative to development, 66

Land taxes, 126–30, 189; African, 127; areas of resistance, 128; as a brake on consumption, 128; means of improving, 128–30

Land tenure, 66; and methods of taxation, 127

Latin countries, 92; deficient budget systems, 93

Legislative process, 61; and development planning, 50–51

Lent, George E., 23 n., 111 n.

Less developed countries, 98, 141, 157, 181, 186, 193; overpopulated or not, 86

Lessening inequality, 16, 65–66; as an object of fiscal policy, 65–66; uncertain effects on development, 66

Levin, J. V., 132 n.

Lewis, J. P., 35 n.

Lewis, W. A., 66 n., 191 n.

Licensing, 104–5; and the public interest, 104 n.

Limited domestic market, 37–38
Lindholm, R. W., 189 n.
Liska, George, 77 n.
List, F., 184
Lombardini, Gino, 34 n.
Lotteries, 16

Marginal product, 34–35; rule, 31–32; social *vs.* private, 31
Martin, A., 191 n.
Mason, E. S., 171 n.
Mature economies, 21
Meir, G. M., 48 n.
Mexico, 15, 143
Mills, L., 115 n.
Minority groups, 49–50; as a source of business talent, 49
Mobilization, of private savings, 109
Monetary policy, 145, 148–54
Monopoly, 117
Moore, F. T., 154 n.
Montgomery, J. D., 85 n.
Morgan, T., 156 n.
Moussa, Pierre, 80
Multiple exchange rates, 163–64
Musgrave, R. A., 13 n., 58 n., 192 n.

National accounts budget, 8–9; timing of expenditures in, 9
Net worth taxes, 143; in India, 143
New industries, 38
Nigerian marketing boards, 60 n.
Note issue, 10; franchise tax on, 10
Nurkse, Ragnar, 70 n., 94

O.E.C.D., 78–79; disbursements to less developed countries by members of, 79
Open Market Committee of the Federal Reserve System, 5
Organization mix, 98–103; relation to development policy, 101–2
Owen, Elizabeth, 113 n.

Pakistan, 29, 162 n.; Planning Commission, 119
Panama, 15; Fiscal Survey of, 112 n., 140 n.

Papanek, G. S., 49 n.
Parkinson, J. R., 162 n.
Parkinson's first law, 93
Patel, I. G., 73 n.
Peacock, A. T., 43 n.
Period of initial but uncertain growth, 193–99
Persmazoglu, J., 150 n.
Personal taxes, 140; in Africa, 140; non-income forms, 140
Pigou's paradox, 101
Planning, 47; adapting to economic development, 197; coordination with budget process, 44–45; and the legislative process, 50–51; models for, 34–35; for the private sector, 88; and progress reporting, 43
Plasschaert, S., 120 n.
Policy questions, 123–25
Poole, K. E., 119
Portfolio investment, 82
Prest, A. R., 133 n., 187 n.
Private investment, 80–82, 153; dynamic quality in, 193; in extractive industries, 81; minimizing deterrents to, 109
Program budget, 44
Progressive taxation, 17; and inequality, 16–17
Property tax, 128–29; assessments as investment incentives, 113
Public Administration Service, 44 n.
Public expenditure, 6, 68, 192
Public finance, 93
Public investment, 20, 194
Puerto Rico, 115
Purchasing power parity, 161

Ranis, Gustav, 36 n., 89 n.
Rationalizing public expenditure, 192
Restrictive monetary policy, 5
Retaliation in trade, 159–60
Revenue, 52–53, 119–46; Act of 1962, 114; earmarking, 53; steps in obtaining additional, 175
Richman, P. B., 111 n.
Robinson, Joan, 1 n.
Roseman, Alvin, 78 n.

Rosenstein-Rodan, P. N., 34 n.
Ross, S. G., 115 n.
Rostow, W., 184–85
Rothwell, K. L., 130 n.
Rubin, Seymour J., 79

Sales tax, 135–36, 191; administration of, 137; and excise taxes, 133–37, 191
Samuelson, P. A., 75 n.
Saving, 64, 101–2, 109
Say, M. L., 52 n.
Schlesinger, E. R., 179 n.
Schmoller, G., 184
Schultz, T. W., 105 n.
Second stage of development, 193–99
Seers, Dudley, 69 n., 166 n.
Shirley, D. E., 190 n.
Smith, Adam, 119
Smith, D. T., 119
Smithies, Arthur, 19 n., 68 n.
Social accounting, 101
Social overhead, 39; case for concentration in, 39–40; how much, 39–42
Split budget, 68, 173
Stages of economic growth, 183–86; usefulness of, 185
Steuart, Sir James, 20
Stourm, Rene, 52 n.
Streeten, Paul, 70 n.
Structural unemployment, 18
Subsidies, 116
Surrey, S. S., 114 n., 191 n.

Takeoff stage, 199–202; expenditure policy during, 201–2; revenue policy during, 200–201
Tawney, R. H., 104 n.
Taxable capacity, 120
Taxation, 12–18, 121–44; as a consequence of development strategy, 16; of farm marketings, 189; in kind, 188; of land and agricultural production, 126–30; special burden on agriculture, 22–23; structural effects of, 144–46
Tax concessions, 110–17

Taxes, 12–18, 121–44; defined, 12; direct and indirect, 12; earmarking of, 151; progressive and regressive, 12; relative shiftability of different, 12–14; yield flexibility of, 73, 194
Tax holidays, 111
Tax incidence, 13
Tax policy, 119–20
Tax ratios, 14–17; in developing countries, 15; as an index of development, 15–16
Tax shifting, 12–14; forward and backward, 12–13
Tax sparing, 114–15; treaties, 115
Tax structures, 14; diversity in, 14; need for periodic review, 145–46
Tax system, 14, 120, 144; building of, 144; defined, 14; equity in, 144; evaluation of, 119–20; intercountry differences in, 14
Tax yields, 55, 188; appropriate flexibility in, 55; dependence on foreign trade, 55
Taylor, M. C., 115 n., 191 n.
Teaching skills, 107–8
Technical assistance, 53, 89; contract vs. direct-hire personnel, 178; requests for, 171; requirements for success of, 181–82
Technology, 48–49; from abroad, 49–50; as an offset to profit remission, 49
Tehran, 124
Trade, 155–64; conservative policy, 160; and fiscal policies, 156–58; policy and industrialization, 38; restrictions, 117
Traditional society, 186–92

Underdeveloped countries, 86; limited fiscal capacity, 120
United Nations, 79, 92, 165, 170; 1951 committee of experts, 61 n.; technical assistance activities, 92, 171
U Nu, 60, 105 n.
U.S. Aid program, 76–86; and agricultural productivity, 85–88; failure to influence budget or tax policies,

90–91; geographic distribution of, 82–83; reward and penalty aspects, 90

U.S. Department of Commerce, 81, 106

U.S.I.A. libraries, 107

U.S. private foreign investment, 80–82

Urbanization, 195

Urquidi, Victor, 3 n., 30–31

Value added taxes, 136–37, 197; French use of, 136; shifting of, 136

Veblen, T., 102

Vernon, Raymond, 32 n.

Wald, Haskell, 126 n., 174 n., 196

Walinsky, L. J., 59 n., 132 n.

Ward, Barbara, 118 n.

Waterston, A., 29 n.

Welfare activities, 202

Williams, Alan, 174 n.

Wit, Daniel, 84 n.

World Bank, *see* I.B.R.D.

Wu, Yuan Li, 34 n.

Yamey, B. S., 33, 66 n.

Yield flexibility, 73, 194

Zuntz, Michael, 149 n.